# THE TOLKIEN AND MII

Also by Colin Duriez:
*The C.S. Lewis Handbook*

# COLIN DURIEZ

MONARCH
Tunbridge Wells

*Cover illustration and title lettering
by Rodney Matthews*

ISBN 1 85424 118 4

Printed in Great Britain for
MONARCH PUBLICATIONS
Owl Lodge, Langton Road, Speldhurst, Kent TN3 0NP
Clays Ltd, St. Ives plc
Typeset by J&L Composition Ltd, Filey, North Yorkshire

To my mother

*Anar kaluva tielyanna*

# Contents

# Foreword

## The Reality of the Fantastic

If you've paid good money for this book, then the chances are you'll be fairly keen on the writings of J.R.R. Tolkien. Therefore, it may come as something of a shock to you to know that there are those who are left absolutely cold by *The Lord of the Rings* and the other tales of Middle-earth.

Some people simply can't get to grips with an author who goes to such elaborate lengths in creating an entire history, geography, literature and language as background to a work of fiction.

Ironically, it is just this feature of *The Lord of the Rings* that others find most appealing. For them—and, I might as well own up and say, for me as well—the real strength of Tolkien's writing doesn't rest on such conventional elements of good fiction as story and character, excellent though he is at both, but on a skilfully created sense of fantastic realism.

Few other writers, before or since, have attempted anything on quite so grand a scale, and even fewer have created other worlds that—whether in those insouciant tales of *The Hobbit* or *Farmer Giles of Ham*, or in that complex fantasy epic, *The Silmarillion*—are so beguilingly convincing.

Why then did Tolkien labour so intently and take such meticulous care over something which isn't, in the literal sense of the word, 'true'? Essentially, he saw no conflict between the fantastic and those things which could be verified by reason, logic or science; indeed, he firmly believed that if the fantasy writer approached his subject with the same degree of reason as would be expected of the non-fiction writer, the better the resulting fantasy would be.

It was a belief that stemmed from Tolkien's Christian view of the creative artist. Man, he said, had a natural desire to create because he was himself a created being 'made in the image and likeness of a Maker'.

Tolkien went so far—some may say too far and too fancifully—as to suggest that a writer's creations might actually become, in some sense, part of God's greater Creation. 'All tales may come true,' he hazarded, 'and yet, at the last, redeemed, they may be as like and as unlike the forms that we give them as Man, finally redeemed, will be like and unlike the fallen that we know.'

For a great many readers, Tolkien's worlds don't have to come true—they *seem* true already. It doesn't matter to them why this should be; it is enough that it is. So what then is Tolkien saying in his stories? Unlike his friend C.S. Lewis, he was not fond of allegory (and only once wrote in that genre, with his short story *Leaf by Niggle*); but he did passionately believe in what he referred to as the 'applicability' of fantasy.

Tolkien knew that the most fantastical adventure remains a hollow artifice if it fails to engage its readers on an emotional level. Though we and Tolkien's characters are worlds apart, we identify with their feelings, share their dreams and fears. Which is why, heart in mouth, we follow Frodo and Sam on their struggle through the ash-pits of Mordor towards Mount Doom; or why real tears start in our eyes when we read of the ill-starred romance of Beren and Lúthien.

And the presiding virtue in so many of Tolkien's tales is hope. Always, even in the longest and darkest night of

Middle-earth, there glimmers a light—however small and flickering—of humanity, compassion and courage.

These and many other aspects of the fantasy realms of J.R.R. Tolkien are discussed by Colin Duriez in this book. Here you will find a listing of all the people, places and things of importance in Tolkien's writings. This, of course, is extremely useful if, for example, you can't quite remember who Amras was; what you would do with lembas; where in Middle-earth you would find Caras Galadon; or what you might expect to see in the Halls of Mandos.

The book also contains details of Tolkien's life, his friends and colleagues and the writers and thinkers who influenced his work; and—most importantly—summarises his beliefs and the way in which they are revealed in his books.

This volume will prove a welcome addition to any Tolkien reader's bookshelf, since wherever you dip into its pages you can reckon on gaining some new understanding of Middle-earth or the man of extraordinary vision who created it. Apart from which, it is impossible to read Mr Duriez's book without wanting to read—or reread—Professor Tolkien's books, which is an undoubted compliment to both authors.

*Brian Sibley*

# *Preface*

J.R.R. Tolkien is such a widely-read author that it is difficult to believe that, once upon a time, his publishers were convinced that *The Lord of the Rings* might well make a financial loss for them. In those unenlightened days, the learned Professor could mutter the word 'Orc' at uncouth behaviour, or exclaim 'Mordor in our midst' at an ugly example of modern life, without his meaning being known to the general public.

Even readers who have ventured into Middle-earth through reading *The Hobbit* or *The Lord of the Rings* may not realise the full treasures to be found in Tolkien's other writings, and in his thinking. The relationship between his life, his work as an Oxford scholar, and his fiction is itself fascinating.

Other readers may have travelled in *The Silmarillion*, published after Tolkien's death. Many find this book strangely different from the other, more popular works. Some are overwhelmed by the proliferation of new names and places, yet attracted by a sense of depth and richness—and of even more of a world to explore.

*The Tolkien and Middle-earth Handbook* is intended to introduce, or remind readers of, the abundance that exists in Tolkien's thought and imagination. It makes no claim to be exhaustive (a veritable encyclopedia would be required), but to be helpfully selective. Selection was the most difficult of my tasks. By interweaving Tolkien's life, thought and writings in this dictionary format new discoveries can be made. To allow readers to follow through themes and subjects that capture their interest I have used asterisks within articles to show other references. If this omits a significant cross-reference I give it at the article's end. Where appropriate, I have added further reading. At the end of the book is a list of J.R.R. Tolkien's works (most of which are described within the handbook). There is also a simple reference guide which groups together many of the related articles.

A central problem for readers of Tolkien is the sheer quantity of his unfinished writing, most of which has now been published, it seems. Reading this unfinished material is the only way we can receive the stories from the ages of Middle-earth preceding *The Lord of the Rings*. For example, the tale of Beren and Lúthien in *The Silmarillion* is essentially a summary. In reading the unfinished *Lay of Leithian*, published in another volume, rich detail and dimension are given to the story. Unexpectedly, a fragment elsewhere might yield further detail. Similarly, our knowledge of the story of Túrin would be impoverished without the long telling of it in *Unfinished Tales*. Once we have got to know the stories thoroughly by reading through incomplete material left by Tolkien they become a permanent part of our imaginations.

These stories are important too in order to become familiar with Tolkien's mythology. It is difficult to get to know say the First Age of Middle-earth by reading Tolkien's historical or chronological summaries. *The Silmarillion* alone introduced many hundreds of new names, making comprehension difficult and sometimes frustrating. Tolkien, in his *Letters*, isolated four stories in particular which stand independently, with the history of the First Age as background. Two of these four stories are given a fair space in *The Tolkien and Middle-earth Handbook*, because they provide such a helpful way in to Tolkien's mythology. The two are the tales of Beren and Lúthien, and of Túrin Turambar, each of which could have been written by Tolkien on a scale approaching that of *The Lord of the Rings*.

12

Significant works of art and literature—like Tolkien's *The Lord of the Rings*, and the background of its invented mythology, set in 'Tolkien's world'—challenge the human understanding and imagination. The challenge is just as real, I believe, as when a new philosophy or scientific theory is thought out. Human beings are always in the process of being shaped. Without challenge, we specialise and stagnate. (Tolkien was particularly antagonistic to mechanisation.)

We are all on a journey—for which the quest to destroy the Ring in *The Lord of the Rings* is an image, with applicability to us. Tolkien, by challenging us, helps us to go in a right direction, and arrive at a certain destination. One of the songs of Middle-earth characteristically says:

> The Road goes ever on and on
> Down from the door where it began.
> Now far ahead the Road has gone,
> And I must follow, if I can . . .

As Bilbo said to Frodo, 'It's a dangerous business . . . going out of your door.'

Tolkien's portrayal of new possibilities helps us to have the refreshment and moral strength to persevere over what is true, noble, right, pure, lovely and admirable. Tolkien challenges the spirit of our age, which says that there is no meaningful journey—either because there is no road, or because all roads lead to the same destination. The fact that Tolkien is so popular with readers in numerous countries shows that many people are attracted by the hope that shines through his work.

My thanks are due, in writing this book, to Steve and Heather Burrage, and to Brian Sibley, for their encouragement; to Tony Collins, whose idea the book was; to Paul Cavill, and to Christina Scull of The Tolkien Society, for their helpful comments on the first draft; to Leicester University Library for its facilities; and to The Marion E. Wade Collection for help with the bibliography. I must acknowledge my debt to Robert Foster's indispensable *The Complete*

*Guide to Middle-earth*, and thank Leland Ryken for kindly giving permission to reproduce the excellent chart on pages 243–246 from his *Triumphs of the Imagination* (IVP, 1979).

*Colin Duriez*

# The Tolkien and Middle-earth Handbook

# A

**Adûnaic**  On the great island of Númenor,★ Adûnaic was the common language of the Dúnedain,★ the men of the West. It was the ancestor of Westron,★ or Common Speech, represented by English in Tolkien's writings about Middle-earth.★

The name derives from adûn, 'west'.

**Adûnakhôr, Ar–**  In the Second Age★ (born 2899), he was nineteenth king of Númenor.★ Symbolically, he broke with tradition and took his name in Adûnaic★ rather than in Elvish.★ It blasphemously means 'Lord of the West'. He forbade the use of Elven languages and persecuted those faithful to the true West and the rule of Ilúvatar.★

***Adventures of Tom Bombadil* (1961)**  A collection of light verses from *The Red Book of Westmarch,*★ supposedly written by Bilbo Baggins,★ Sam Gamgee★ and other hobbits,★ and rendered into English from Westron★ by J.R.R. Tolkien, who adds an explanatory note. They are mainly concerned with legends and jests of the Shire★ at the end of the Third Age.★ Tolkien's talent for songs, ballads and witty riddles fits well into a hobbitish setting. The collection is named after a major piece in it. The contents include two poems about Tom Bombadil.★ He and Gandalf are regarded by the hobbits, says Tolkien, as 'benevolent persons, mysterious maybe and unpredictable but nonetheless comic'. The first poem beautifully reveals Bombadil's affinity with nature.★

**A Elbereth Gilthoniel**  An Elven chant attributed to the Elves★ of Rivendell★ in honour of Elbereth Gilthoniel, or Varda,★ the greatest of the seven Queens of the Valar★ (the angelic guardians of Middle-earth★), and most approachable by Elves, humans and hobbits.★ Only the first verse is recorded, written in Sindarin★ Elvish. The chant of praise and intercession was sung in the house of Elrond,★ as recounted in *The Fellowship of the Ring*.★ Sam Gamgee's★ invocation of Elbereth in *The Two Towers*, in Shelob's Lair on the fringes of Mordor,★ echoes this chant. Tolkien translates both prayers in *The Road Goes Ever On*.★

He translates the recorded stanza of the chant as: 'O! Elbereth who lit the stars, from glittering crystal slanting falls with light like jewels from heaven on high the glory of the starry host. To lands remote I have looked afar, and now to thee, Fanuilos, bright spirit clothed in ever-white, I here will sing beyond the Sea, beyond the wide and sundering Sea.'

**Aelfwine**  Originally called Eriol in the early form of Tolkien's mythology, *The Silmarillion*.★ Aelfwine was a mariner to whom the tales of the First Age★ were told. He provided a narrative framework for the tales. His name means 'Elf-friend'. There are several versions of the Aelf-wine story, but the basic idea is that a British mariner by chance finds the Lost Road that leads to the Uttermost West and arrives at Tol Eressëa,★ where he hears the tales of the Elves.★

*See also* COTTAGE OF LOST PLAY; *THE LOST ROAD*.

**Afterlithe**  The hobbit★ name for July, from Old English *aefterlith*. Hobbit month-names reinforce the link between their language and that of the Rohirrim,★ who, like hobbits, originally dwelled in the North, east of the Misty Mountains.★ Tolkien uses Old English sources for words and names of the Rohirrim.

*See also* WESTRON.

**Afteryule**  The hobbit★ name corresponding to January, from Old English *aefter Geola* ('after Winter-Solstice'). Hobbit month-names reinforce the link between their language and that of the Rohirrim,★ who, like hobbits, originally dwelled in the North, east of the Misty Mountains.★ Tolkien uses Old English sources for words and names of the Rohirrim.

*See also* WESTRON.

**Ages of Middle-earth**  There were several Ages of Middle-earth. Prior to the Ages Ilúvatar★ created the world, first in conception in Music (*see AINULINDALË*) and then in giving it actual being.

Before the beginning of the First Age (taken as the rising of the sun) the Valar★ and later also many of the Elves★ are established in the Uttermost West, or Valinor.★ Fëanor makes the great gems, the Silmarils,★ which provide the underlying motif for *The Silmarillion*.★ Morgoth★ darkens Middle-earth★ by destroying the Two Lamps and brings shadow to Valinor by extinguishing the Two Trees.★ He hides in the cold North of Middle-earth, north of Beleriand.★

Beleriand in the First Age is the setting for the tales of *Beren and Lúthien the Elf-maiden,*★ *Túrin Turambar*★ (or, the Children of Húrin) and *The Fall of Gondolin*.★ Eärendil★ the mariner sails to Valinor to intercede on behalf of the free peoples of Beleriand. The First Age is chronicled in *The Silmarillion*. In the Second Age the star-shaped island of Númenor★ (Atlantis) is given to the Dúnedain, the Men of the West, for their faithfulness in resisting Morgoth. Sauron,★ Morgoth's lieutenant, secretly forges the great Ring★ in Middle-earth. He succeeds in aiding the corruption of Númenor, resulting in its destruction (*see THE AKALLABÊTH*). The very shape of the world is changed into a globe, and Valinor is no longer accessible, except by the Straight Road.★ There is a great and successful western alliance against Mordor.★

In the Third Age the Ring remains lost for many centuries. Gondor★ is a great power. Hobbits★ migrate to the Shire.★ The events of *The Hobbit*★ and *The Lord of the Rings*★ take place. The Fourth Age opens our present era of the domination of mankind, and the fading of the Elves, where the Christian era unfolds (*see* CHRISTIANITY, TOLKIEN AND). The original geography★ of Middle-earth changes into its present shape, though some parts, such as turn-of-the-century Warwickshire★ and Worcestershire, resemble that original world (in this case, the Shire). In unfinished stories of Tolkien, Aelfwine★ voyages to Tol Eressëa,★ and, in our own time, Alboin finds the Lost Road,★ travelling back in time to Númenor. According to Tolkien's *Letters* (Letter 211) we may now be in a Sixth or even Seventh Age.

**Aglarond**    In *The Two Towers*,★ the caverns of Helm's Deep (Sindarin Elvish,★ 'glittering caves, place of glory'). Gimli★ the Dwarf was astonished and enraptured at the beauty of these caves originally worked by the men of Númenor,★ and used by the Rohirrim★ as a refuge and storage place. After the War of the Ring★ Gimli settled there with other Dwarves and became Lord of the Glittering Caves.

***Ainulindalë***    This is 'the Music of the Ainur' (the Ainur★ are the angelic beings, Valar★ and Maiar★). It is also called 'the Great Music' or 'the Great Song'. It is also the name of the narrative of creation attributed to Rúmil★ of Tirion★ in the First Age★ (*see THE SILMARILLION*). The music expressed the blueprint of creation, the providence and design of Ilúvatar. The music parallels the personification of wisdom in one of the most beautiful passages of the Bible, Proverbs chapter 8. There wisdom represents the standard by which God works as he envisages the creation he is to make.

The Music develops three themes of Ilúvatar the Creator. The first theme, in which the Ainur, the angelic powers, were allowed to participate, presented the form of the yet-to-be-created world. Into this theme Morgoth★ (then called Melkor) introduced discord as a result of his rebellion. The second theme, in which the development of the world was revealed, overcame the discord, using it to enhance the Music. This theme is prophetic of divine providence★ in creation. The third theme, in which the Ainur or powers played no part, had as its subject the creation of 'the Children of Ilúvatar', that is, the Elves★ and mankind.

The Great Music was thus synonymous with the conception and creation of the world out of nothing, as well as its subsequent development. The rebellion of Morgoth works out throughout the  invented history of Middle-earth, a central theme in Tolkien's work.

The Valar first take on the role of preparing the world for the arrival of Elves and, later, mankind. They steward the world and provide its light,★ first the Two Lamps, then the Two Trees,★ and finally the sun and moon. The stars also play an important function in revealing the care and design of Ilúvatar. In the Third Age,★ several lesser Valar, or Maiar, take on human form in order to serve as guardians against the reviving power of Sauron,★ originally Morgoth's lieutenant. One of these is Gandalf.★

C.S. Lewis may have been inspired by the *Ainulindalë* in the creation of Narnia by the song of Aslan in his *The Magician's Nephew*, and in the Great Dance at the climax of his science-fiction story, *Perelandra*. Song is an important theme throughout Tolkien's fiction, for instance in the tale of Beren and Lúthien the Elf-maiden.★ Several of his poems were set to music by Donald Swann, and by Stephen Oliver for the BBC Radio production of *The Lord of the Rings* in 1981.

**Further reading**

J.R.R. Tolkien, *The Silmarillion* (1977); 'The Music of the

Ainur' in *The Book of Lost Tales, I* (1983); 'The Ambarkanta' or 'The Shape of the World' in *The Shaping of Middle-earth* (1986); '*Ainulindalë*' in *The Lost Road* (1987).

**Ainur** Angelic powers, 'the Holy Ones', created before the making of the world by Ilúvatar.★ Their order of being includes the Valar,★ and the lesser powers, the Maiar.★ Some of their number, both of the good and those turned to evil, entered the realm of the world and participate in its events. The Ainur are male and female and, though spiritual beings, can take on real physical bodies.
  *See also* ANGELS; EVIL.

**Akallabêth** An Adûnaic★ (or Númenórean) name given to Númenor★ after its destruction, meaning 'the downfallen'. A section of *The Silmarillion*★ is called this name. It concerns the history of Númenor from its foundation to its destruction.

**Aldarion, or Tar-Aldarion** The Mariner King of Númenor,★ the sixth king of the island. His story is told in 'Aldarion and Erendis', in *Unfinished Tales*.★ His only child was a daughter, Ancalimë. The king altered the law of succession so that a female could reign, and she became queen.

**Allegory** An extended metaphor, or sustained personification. In literature, a figurative narrative or description which conveys a hidden meaning, often moral. Key examples in English literature are John Bunyan's *The Pilgrim's Progress* and Edmund Spenser's *Faerie Queene*. Tolkien's short story, *Leaf by Niggle*★ is an allegory.

  When *The Lord of the Rings*★ first appeared some interpreted the One Ring★ as meaning the atomic bomb. Apart from the fact that the Ring was conceived before the bomb existed or was known about as a possibility, such an interpretation is wrong in treating the work as an allegory. Tolkien pointed out that such an interpretation confused meaning with applicability. In his Foreword, he writes: 'I much prefer history, true or feigned, with its varied applicability to the thought and experience of readers. I think that many confuse "applicability" with "allegory"; but the one resides in the freedom of the reader, and the other in the purposed domination of the author.'

*See also* IMAGINATION.

**Almaren** An island in the middle of a great lake deep inland in Middle-earth,★ the original dwelling place of the Valar.★ It was ruined when Morgoth★ destroyed the Two Lamps which illuminated the world.

**Alqualondë** Harbour city of Telerin★ Elves★ in Valinor,★ the 'Haven of the Swans'. As they entered the harbour, ships passed through a large natural arch. The Elven ships originally reached this haven from Middle-earth★ with the aid of great swans.

**Aman** The specific name of the vast western continent in which Valinor★ lay.

*See* GEOGRAPHY OF MIDDLE-EARTH.

**Amandil** The last lord of Andúnië in Numénor,★ leader of the faithful remnant and father of Elendil.★

**Amon Obel** A prominent hill in the Forest of Brethil.★ Túrin★ dwelt here at the time when the woodmen made their stronghold at Amon Obel. He married Nienor★ here, unaware that she was his sister.

**Amon Rûdh** One of the oldest of the early settlements of Dwarves★ in Beleriand★ in the First Age.★ It was a hill rising steeply, with sheer rocky cliffs in places. A Dwarf, Mîm, dwelt in its caverns, and Túrin's★ outlaws made their hideout here.

**Amras** Elf★ and son of Fëanor,★ twin brother of Amrod.★ The brothers were killed attacking the people of Eärendil★ at the Mouths of Sirion,★ in an attempt to recover one of the Silmarils from Elwing.★

**Amrod** Elf★ and son of Fëanor,★ twin brother of Amras.★ The brothers were killed attacking the people of Eärendil★ at the Mouths of Sirion,★ in an attempt to recover one of the Silmarils from Elwing.★

**Anárion**   At the end of the Second Age★ he escaped, with his father Elendil★ and brother Isildur,★ from the destruction of Númenor.★ With them he founded the Númenórean realms in exile in Middle-earth.★ He was Lord of Minas Anor and died in the siege of Barad-dûr, during the great alliance against Sauron.★

**Anarríma**   A constellation formed by Elbereth★ before the creation of the Elves★ by Ilúvatar.★

**Ancalagon**   Greatest of the winged dragons★ of Morgoth,★ destroyed by Eärendil★ at the end of the First Age.★ His falling body broke Thangorodrim.★

**Andram**   In Sindarin Elvish★ this means 'the Long Wall'. It is a distinctive feature of the landscape of Beleriand,★ an escarpment cutting right across the region.
   *See* GEOGRAPHY OF MIDDLE-EARTH.

**Anduin**   The 'great river' of north-western Middle-earth, important during the Second and Third Ages.★ It flowed from North to South around 1,500 miles, running between the Misty Mountains★ and Mirkwood,★ and further south between Gondor★ and Mordor.★ The hobbits★ originated from the Anduin region, and the river plays an important part in the events of *The Lord of the Rings*.★ The ruling Ring★ of Power was lost in the river at the death of Isildur★ and discovered there by Sméagol (Gollum★).

**Anfauglith**   An area north of Beleriand.★ It was given this name (literally 'great-thirst-ash') after it was scorched in battle by Morgoth.★ Before its desolation, the area was called Ard-galen.★ By mistake, Túrin killed his friend Beleg★ in this region.
   *See also* BATTLES OF BELERIAND.

**Angband**   The stronghold of Morgoth★ in the icy North of Middle-earth,★ north of Beleriand,★ and originally destroyed by the Valar.★ After Morgoth returned to Middle-earth★ with the stolen Silmarils he rebuilt Angband, and made Thangorodrim.★ Here Morgoth used slaves and bred monsters and Orcs.★

**Angels**  As an orthodox Christian like C.S. Lewis★ or John Bunyan, J.R.R. Tolkien believed in the literal existence of angels. They appear historically, for example, in the Gospels, at the annunciation of Christ. For imaginative force and freshness, he, like Bunyan and Lewis, avoids the term 'angel'. Whereas Bunyan uses 'Shining Ones' in *The Pilgrim's Progress*, and Lewis employs the terms 'Oyarsa' and 'eldila' in his *The Cosmic Trilogy*, Tolkien writes of the Valar★ and Maiar.★ He wished to capture the imaginative vitality of the Old Norse or Olympian gods, yet to portray beings acceptable to someone who believes in 'The Blessed Trinity'. The Valar and Maiar represent the activity of God (Ilúvatar★). Tolkien's is not a deistic world (*see* NATURAL THEOLOGY, TOLKIEN AND).

The Valar and Maiar are partly modelled on biblical angels. The biblical angels are witnesses of creation, whereas the Valar participate in making the world (even though they are distinct creations of God themselves). The nearest biblical equivalent to the Valar is the personification of wisdom in Proverbs 8. Like biblical angels (e.g. Abraham's visitors) the Maiar can take on human (or human-like) form, as with Gandalf,★ Melian,★ Sauron★ in Númenor,★ and possibly Tom Bombadil.★ The intermarriage of Melian and the Elvish King Thingol echoes the marriages of 'Sons of God' and daughters of men in early Genesis. The Valar also take on appearances at will (as Ulmo,★ for example, appears to Tuor★).

As in the Bible, there are fallen angels: Sauron, Morgoth★ or Melkor (equivalent to Lucifer), and the Balrogs.★ There seems to be no equivalent of ordinary demons. The Orcs don't seem to be capable of moral choice (being bred into evil by Morgoth, originally from captured Elves★). Also like biblical angels, the Valar can be militant, as at the end of the First Age,★ when Morgoth and his forces are overcome by their intervention.

Unlike in the Bible, in Tolkien, the Valar are more like

intermediaries between God (Ilúvatar*) and the beings of Middle-earth. They also have a demiurgic role in creation (like God in Plato's myth of *Timaeus*). It is interesting that C.S. Lewis, and the puritan, John Bunyan, do not have an intermediary role for angelic beings. God directly and personally communicates (as in Christ and Aslan, the creator-lion of Narnia) as well as using messengers and angelic interpreters. In Tolkien, angels have a subtle and pervasive role in providence,* working in and behind events. One of the functions of Gandalf the Maia is that of interpreting providential events.

Elves, who symbolically represent an aspect of mankind, have some angelic qualities. Their Elven quality* enters human life and history through example and intermarriage (such as the marriage of Beren* and the Elf-maiden Lúthien*). Angels have made a number of appearances in contemporary fiction, as in C.S. Lewis' *The Screwtape Letters* and *The Cosmic Trilogy*, Harry Blamires' *Highway to Heaven*, and Frank Peretti's colourful *This Present Darkness*. Tolkien's famous forerunners include John Milton (*Paradise Lost*) and Dante (*The Divine Comedy*). They also include the unjustly neglected John Macgowan, and his *Dialogues of the Devil*.

Tolkien seems to be inspired by momentous sections of the Bible that portray the unseen world behind human history, for instance, the scene in the heavenly court at the beginning of the Book of Job, or the portrayal of Wisdom in Proverbs. In total, though *The Lord of the Rings* is an heroic romance, and the tales are the main interest of *The Silmarillion* and accounts of the Second Age,* Tolkien's work on the Three Ages of Middle-earth may perhaps be seen as a modern apocalypse. Biblical apocalyptic is grounded in the Hebrew imagination. Tolkien, however, based his fictional overview of time and history on a northern European imagination.

*See also* APOCALYPTIC, TOLKIEN AND.

**Anglachel**   A sword forged by Eöl from meteoritic iron. (*See* TÚRIN TURAMBAR, THE TALE OF.)

**Angmar**   In the Third Age,★ the Witch-kingdom ruled by the Lord of the Nazgûl,★ the Witch-king.

**Annúminas**   The first capital of Arnor,★ built by Elendil,★ who kept a palantír★ here. The name means 'tower of the west', or 'sunset-tower'. The city became deserted during Arnor's decline, but was re-established by Aragorn★ as the northern capital of the Reunited Kingdom at the beginning of the Fourth Age.★ It was located on the shore of Lake Evendim, not far from the Shire.★

**Apocalyptic, Tolkien and**   The purpose of sub-creation,★ according to Tolkien, is to 'survey the depths of space and time'. Whereas his friend C.S. Lewis explored space in his science fiction, *The Cosmic Trilogy*, Tolkien surveyed time in his invented mythology of Middle-earth.

Tolkien's history of the Three Ages of Middle-earth might be seen as a modern apocalypse—an unveiling of hidden realities. The biblical apocalyptic books and passages are grounded on a Hebrew imagination in a near-eastern setting. Tolkien is grounded in a northern European imagination. His purpose is fictional, rather than historical and prophetic.

Apocalyptic in the Bible provides hope and consolation★ in hard times (a glimpse, for Tolkien, of the *evangelium*). 'Apocalyptics flourished in times of national crisis,' according to a Bible dictionary. Tolkien, like his fellow Inklings,★ saw the modern world as in crisis. This sense of crisis is vividly portrayed in C.S. Lewis' book, *The Abolition of Man*.

The purpose of apocalyptic is to reveal the hand of God in history. It can also be cosmological, revealing mysteries of the cosmos. Both these elements are true of Tolkien's writings (*see* PROVIDENCE; *AINULINDALË*). Biblical apocalyptic is concerned with the problem of evil★ and suffering. Tolkien, too, in his writings, is intensely aware of evil.

25

In *Tolkien and The Silmarillion*, Clyde S. Kilby points out:

There is evidence that had his story continued to its full and concluding end the ubiquitous evil of such as Morgoth and Sauron would have ceased. He intended a final glorious eventuality similar to the one described in the Book of Revelation with the true Telperion reappearing, the earth remade, the lands lying under the waves lifted up, the Silmarils recovered, Eärendil returned to earth, the Two Trees rekindled in their original light and life-giving power, and the mountains of the Pelóri levelled so that the light should go out over all the earth—yes, and the dead be raised and the original purposes of Eru executed (pp. 64–65).

Tolkien's apocalyptic element may be one of the reasons for his popularity, and why he seems so contemporary. There is strong evidence that western culture is now in deep crisis, and Tolkien has rediscovered or refreshed symbols that point to hope in this present darkness.

*See also* DEATH; ANGELS.

**Aragorn**  In *The Lord of the Rings*★ Aragorn was a member of the Company of the Ring,★ the true heir of Isildur★ in disguise. Frodo★ and the other hobbits★ encountered him in the inn at Bree as a Ranger known as Strider. In fact, Aragorn was the last Chieftain of the Dúnedain.★ After the War of the Ring★ he was crowned, and restored the old northern and southern kingdoms. He was the Beren★ of his day, like Beren marrying an Elf-maiden, Arwen,★ who resembled Lúthien★ in beauty.

Aragorn had the characteristics of a Christian king, with his healing★ hands, humility, the sacrifice of years as a Ranger, and power over evil.★ In him, the wisdom of Númenor★ was restored.

The Company of the Ring found him a wise companion, and a leader after the loss of Gandalf.★ His strategy of passing through the Paths of the Dead helped to bring victory in the War of the Ring.

**Arda** The world, or earth.

*See also* GEOGRAPHY OF MIDDLE-EARTH.

**Ard-galen** A large plain lying north of Dorthonion,★ and between it and Thangorodrim.★ It was wasted by Morgoth★ during one war (*see* BATTLES OF BELERIAND), an example of the effect of evil on the natural world. The resulting desolation was named Anfauglith.★

**Argonath** In *The Lord of the Rings*,★ great carved rocks between which the River Anduin★ flowed. They were statues of Isildur★ and Anárion.★ They were built to mark the northern boundary of Gondor.★

**Arkenstone** In *The Hobbit*,★ a great white jewel found by Bilbo Baggins★ in the hoard of Smaug★ the dragon.★ It had been found originally beneath Erebor★ by the Dwarf, Thráin I, and was the prized treasure of the Kings of Erebor. It had a little of the glory of a Silmaril.

**Army of the West** An alliance of men of Gondor★ and Rohan★ which marched to the Gates of Mordor★ to distract Sauron's attention from the Ring-bearer, Frodo,★ and Sam,★ in *The Lord of the Rings*.★

**Arnor** The northern kingdom of the Númenóreans in Middle-earth.★ Elendil★ established it after escaping the destruction of Númenor.★

**Arwen** The Elven★ daughter of Elrond.★ For most of the Third Age★ of Middle-earth★ she lived in Rivendell★ and Lórien.★ Aragorn★ met her in Rivendell and they fell in love. Their love—the love of a mortal for an immortal Elf—echoed that of Beren★ and Lúthien.★ Like Lúthien, Arwen chose mortality (*see* DEATH) by marrying Aragorn. Her dark beauty resembled that of Lúthien, and for it, and because she chose to leave the Elves, she was called Evenstar. Her presence in *The Lord of the Rings*★ helps to recall the great history of the First Age,★ so represented in the story of Beren and Lúthien.

**Athelas**   In Middle-earth,★ a healing★ plant brought from
Númenor.★ It grew only in the places where Númenóreans
had lived or camped. In the hands of Aragorn,★ or other
heirs of Elendil,★ it had potent powers of restoration.

**Auden, W.H. (1907–1973)**   A major figure in Anglo–
American poetry, and a literary critic, W.H. Auden was
born in Britain and later became a US citizen. Like Tolkien,
his family took him to Birmingham as an infant. He went
up to Oxford in 1925, the year Tolkien moved there from
Leeds to become Professor of Anglo–Saxon. His tutor was
Nevill Coghill.★ As an undergraduate, Auden developed a
particular liking for Old English literature. Like Tolkien, he
had a deep interest in Northern mythology. Like C.S.
Lewis, he was a late convert to Christianity.

Auden referred to the effect that Tolkien had on him
during his Inaugural Lecture delivered as Professor of
Poetry before the University of Oxford on 11th June 1956:

> I remember [a lecture] I attended, delivered by Professor
> Tolkien. I do not remember a single word he said but at a
> certain point he recited, and magnificently, a long pass-
> age of *Beowulf.* I was spellbound. This poetry, I knew
> was going to be my dish. I became willing, therefore, to
> work at Anglo-Saxon because, unless I did, I should
> never be able to read this poetry. I learned enough to read
> it, however sloppily, and Anglo-Saxon and Middle
> English poetry have been one of my strongest, most
> lasting influences.

Tolkien was greatly encouraged by Auden's enthusiasm for
*The Lord of the Rings*. He wrote on the quest★ hero★ in
Tolkien's work, and corresponded and discussed with him
about the meaning of his work (*see LETTERS OF J.R.R.
TOLKIEN*).

His reviews counteracted some of the negative criticism
of the trilogy. In Humphrey Carpenter's biography of

Auden there is reproduced a photograph of him absorbed in reading *The Hobbit*,★ taken in the 1940s. In 1965 Auden intended to collaborate with the writer Peter Salus on a short book on Tolkien in the *Christian Perspectives* series. He failed however to gain Tolkien's approval for such a project so, unfortunately, it was dropped.

## Further reading

Neil D. Isaacs and Rose A. Zimbardo (editors), *Tolkien and the Critics* (1968); W.H. Auden, *Secondary Worlds* (1968); Humphrey Carpenter, *W.H. Auden: A Biography* (1981).

**Aulë**   One of the Valar,★ or angelic powers. He was master of crafts and husband of Yavanna.★ He made the Dwarves.★
**Avallónë**   Harbour and city of the Elves★ on the island of Tol Eressëa.★ Its quays were lit by lamps, and it had a distinctive white tower.

# B

**Baggins, Bilbo**   Hobbits are described elsewhere in this Handbook. Bilbo Baggins is the unlikely hero★ of Tolkien's *The Hobbit*, the title referring to him. He is a creature of paradox, summed up in his role as a bourgois burglar in the story. Hobbits aimed at respectability—not only by being comfortably off, but by not having any adventures or doing anything unexpected. Bilbo's reputation is tarnished for ever when he is suddenly caught up in the quest★ for dragon's★ treasure. He finds this more congenial than he thought. A new world is opened up to him as in later years he becomes somewhat of a scholar, translating and retelling tales from the older days (*see THE SILMARILLION*). The quest also develops his character, though he always retains the quality of homeliness★ associated with hobbits and the Shire.★

Thorin Oakenshield's remark concerning Bilbo is perhaps an apt summary of his many-sided character: 'A hobbit full of courage and resource far exceeding his size, and if I may say so possessed of good luck far exceeding the usual allowance.' The 'good luck' noticed by Thorin is in fact the unusual presence of providence★ working out in events using him as a key agent. Thorin also notices his personal qualities. Freewill is an important theme in Tolkien, particularly the voluntary commitment to the struggle against darkness and evil,★ sometimes against all odds.

In Bilbo's make-up, Tolkien draws attention to unusual blood inherited from his mother. This unhobbitlike quality emerges and develops as Bilbo partakes in the adventure. Most important for him, however, is not the finding of the treasure (which leads to Smaug★ the dragon's death), but his discovery of the One Ring.★

In Tolkien's Middle-earth★ tales there is not a novelistic delineation of character. Essentially, people or beings are in character as Dwarves, Elves, Men, Ents, Maiar, Orcs and so on. This is how we know them. Often, however, there is surprising individuality in this role. For example, Queen Melian★ and Gandalf★ are Maiar, yet dazzlingly distinct. Similarly, hobbits like Bilbo, Frodo,★ Sam or Merry have their own marked traits.

We are told of Bilbo's love of maps; his liking for runes and letters and cunning hand-writing—although his own was 'a bit thin and spidery'; his passion for riddles—an asset which saves his life; his sudden burst of pity for Gollum,★ and his kind-heartedness in returning the sleeping jailor's keys; his 'sharp inquisitive eyes'; his skill at stealth, shooting stones, blowing smoke-rings, and cooking; and his constant lament about not being back in his comfortable hobbit-hole. These traits reveal something of his character.

The effect of the Ring on his character is complex. In developing *The Lord of the Rings* from seeds in *The Hobbit*, Tolkien was forced to change the account of Bilbo's finding of the Ring. The change however is convincing in terms of the Ring's power over an individual. Bilbo was never mastered by it, and voluntarily (with prompting from Gandalf) passed it on to Frodo, the new Ring-bearer.

**Brief chronology**

(Dates are in Third Age★ years.)
2846   Birth of Bungo Baggins, Bilbo's father.

2852    Birth of Belladonna Took, Bilbo's mother. Her brother Hildifons went off on a journey and never returned.

2880    Marriage of Bungo Baggins and Belladonna Took.

2890    Bilbo Baggins born in the Shire, son of Bungo Baggins and Belladonna Took.

2926    Death of Bilbo's father.

2934    Death of Bilbo's mother.

2941    Bilbo is persuaded to join Thorin's company of Dwarves as burglar.

2942    Return to Hobbiton.

2980    On the death of Frodo's parents, Bilbo makes him his heir.

3001    Bilbo's huge farewell birthday party. He takes up residence in Rivendell.

3021    Bilbo leaves Middle-earth.

**Baggins, Frodo**    Frodo is a hobbit* of the Shire, and a hero* of *The Lord of the Rings*,* which is the source of information about him and his deeds.

Frodo grew up in Buckland,* the only child of Drogo Baggins and Primula Brandybuck. After his parents' death, Frodo was adopted by his distant relation Bilbo Baggins,* hero of *The Hobbit*,* joining him in Bag End. Frodo was highly intelligent, with a gift for languages (he eventually learned Sindarin* Elvish). When Bilbo left the Shire, he passed on to him the One Ring,* not knowing its real nature. When Gandalf* discovered what the Ring was he advised Frodo to leave the Shire for Rivendell,* to escape the Nazgûl.* At Rivendell, the Company of the Ring* was formed. With the help of Sam Gamgee,* Frodo bore the Ring to Mount Doom, where it was destroyed, and the power of Sauron* broken. Never fully recovering from his suffering, Frodo passed over the Sea to the Undying Lands of Aman* for healing.* Frodo supplemented the writing of Bilbo in the Red Book of Westmarch* with his account of the War of the Ring★ and the quest★ that took him to Mount Doom.

## Brief chronology

(Dates are in Third Age★ years.)

2908 Birth of Drogo Baggins, father of Frodo.
2920 Birth of Primula Brandybuck, mother of Frodo.
2968 Birth of Frodo Baggins.
2980 Death of Frodo's parents in a drowning accident.
3001 Bilbo leaves the Shire, and Frodo inherits his poss-
     essions.
3018 On Gandalf's advice, Frodo flees from the Shire with
     the Ring.
3019 Frodo is briefly Mayor of Michel Delving.★

**Balar, Isle of**  A large island in the Bay of Balar, to the south-west of Beleriand,★ into which the River Sirion flowed. The Elves who chose to go to Valinor★ were transported there on a floating island, Tol Eressëa.★ Part of this broke off, forming the Isle of Balar.

**Balrogs**  Demons of fire that served Morgoth. The name is Sindarin Elvish, meaning 'Demon of Might'. In being, Balrogs were Maiar,★ and carried whips of flame. The Balrog killed by Gandalf★ in *The Lord of the Rings*★ survived the destruction of Morgoth's stronghold in the First Age.★
*See also* EVIL.

**Barfield, Owen (*b* 1898)**  A core member of The Inklings,★ Owen Barfield was a child of 'free-thinking' parents, one a London solicitor. After serving in World War I, he studied at Wadham College, Oxford,★ reading English. At Oxford he formed a life-long friendship with C.S. Lewis,★ and also became an anthroposophist, an advocate of the religious school of thought developed by Rudolph Steiner. For several years he was a freelance writer, before joining his

33

father's legal firm. His first book deeply influenced C.S. Lewis and Tolkien. The influence on Tolkien has been cogently argued by Verlyn Flieger in her study, *Splintered Light*.

**Barrow-downs**   In *The Lord of the Rings*, the downs east of the Old Forest get their name from the Great Barrows, or stone-chambered burial mounds. They dated back to ancient days, before men had crossed to Ered Luin—the Blue Mountains—into Beleriand. Earlier in the Third Age★ evil spirits from Angmar★—the 'barrow-wights'—had possessed the burial mounds, making the region an area of dread.

**Battles of Beleriand**   In *The Silmarillion* are recorded the troubled centuries during the First Age★ in which Morgoth★ occupied Angband.★ The five major battles and the final Great Battle provide a backdrop to the tales set in Beleriand★ and are not described in as much detail as the major stories, such as that of Beren and Lúthien.★

The first battle was Morgoth's initial attempt to gain mastery of Beleriand. Those Elves then living there, led by King Thingol★ of Doriath,★ resisted a two-pronged attack in the East and West. As a result of the war, Melian★ wove a girdle of magic protection around Doriath.

The second battle was called Dagor-nuin-Giliath, the 'Battle Under Stars'. Morgoth, hearing of the return of Fëanor★ and his Elves to Middle-earth, attacked them in Mithrim before they were established. The battle took place before the first rising of the moon (hence the battle's name). In the conflict Fëanor was mortally wounded, and Maedhros was captured by Balrogs★ and taken to Angband.

The third battle was dubbed Dagor Aglareb, 'the glorious battle'. Fingolfin★ to the west and Maedhros to the east attacked Morgoth's assault forces of Orcs.★ As his army retreated across Ard-galen★ it was slaughtered. The battle was followed by a siege of Angband.★

The fourth battle was graphically called Dagor Bragoll-ach, or 'Battle of Sudden Flame'. In a long period of peace during the siege, the Elvish stronghold of Nargothrond★ was completed, and Gondolin★ established. Morgoth however was busy devising new weapons of horror associ-ated with fire. Rivers of fire scorched Ard-galen, to the north of Beleriand. Armies of Orcs were joined by Bal-rogs★ and Glaurung the dragon.★ Dorthonion★ was taken. Finrod Felagund★ was rescued by Barahir,★ father of Beren.★ Fingolfin★ was so angered by the great loss of Elves and Men that he challenged Morgoth to a duel. Though he was slain, he inflicted seven mighty wounds on Morgoth, bitter to his pride.

The fifth battle was a great defeat, called Nirnaeth Arnoediad, 'Battle of Unnumbered Tears'. A great alliance of Elves, Men and Dwarves led by Maedhros failed in an offensive against Morgoth's stronghold. All of the northern highlands, with the exception of Gondolin, fell under the control of Morgoth. Glaurung the dragon★ and Gothmog the Balrog★ helped to lead Morgoth's forces. Húrin,★ father of Túrin★ Turambar, was captured by Morgoth.

The final battle of Beleriand was called the Great Battle, or War of Wrath. The Valar responded to the intercession of Eärendil and directly intervened against Morgoth's tyranny. During this battle Morgoth released his new evil, winged dragons. Their leader, Ancalagon the Black,★ was slain by Eärendil, and crashed down upon Thangorodrim. Eagles,★ led by Thorondor,★ played an important part in defeating the dragons.

**Belegaer** 'The Great Sea' of the West that in the First Age★ separated Middle-earth from the Undying Lands of Tol Eressëa★ and Valinor★. Also called the Western Sea. In the Second Age★ the great star-shaped island of Númenor★ lay in it. After the reshaping of the earth, following the downfall of Númenor, the Straight Road★ (or Lost Road) passed over it, leading beyond the planet to the Undying

Lands. The Ring-bearers Bilbo Baggins★ and Frodo Baggins,★ and later Sam Gamgee,★ took this road, leaving Middle-earth from Grey Havens.★

**Belegost**  In *The Silmarillion*,★ a city of the Dwarves in the Blue Mountains (Ered Luin★). They were friendly with King Thingol★ of Doriath.★ After the Great Battle (*see* BATTLES OF BELERIAND) at the end of the First Age,★ many of its inhabitants moved east to Khazad-dûm,★ under the Misty Mountains.★

**Beleriand and its realms**  In later ages all the land that was swallowed up by the sea in the north of Middle-earth★ was described as Beleriand. All the area west of the Ered Luin,★ the Blue Mountains, was engulfed. This vast range of mountains provided a distinctive boundary for Beleriand to the east. In fact Beleriand was only part of this area in the First Age,★ with great areas to the north controlled by Morgoth,★ the source of struggle and many wars (*see* BATTLES OF BELERIAND).

For simplicity, the westlands can be divided into four geographical regions. These are the northern territory of Morgoth, the central highlands, the main area of Beleriand, and the Ered Luin—the Blue Mountains.

The northern territory had two distinctive features, the Iron Mountains and the dusty, cold desert plain of Ard-galen★ (which had been grassy and fertile before scorched by Morgoth's wars). Tolkien describes the Iron Mountains as standing 'upon the regions of everlasting cold, in a great curve from East to West, but falling short of sea upon either side'. Morgoth's stronghold at Thangorodrim,★ was located at the southern escarpment of the Iron Mountains.

The central highlands could be divided into three areas from West to East, forming the natural boundary to the north of Beleriand. Westmost was the region of the mountains of Hithlum.★ To Hithlum's east, divided by the vale of the river Sirion,★ its sheer sides pine-covered, were the highlands of Dorthonion,★ and the Encircling Mountains associated with the secret city of Gondolin.★ Yet further east, separated by the pass of Aglon, were the Hills of Himring.

The central highland region received warmer winds from the south and west, but the winters were cold. *The Atlas of Middle-earth* provides further information about climate, topography and land formation.

Beleriand was bounded to the north by the central highlands, to the east by Ered Luin, the Blue Mountains, to the west by the great sea of Belegaer (over which lay Valinor★), and to the south by the Bay of Balar★ and by the largely impenetrable forest of Taur-im-Duinath. Strictly, its southern boundary was the River Gelion as it curved westward to the sea, but few Elves or men visited the coastal region between the estuaries of the rivers Sirion★ and Gelion.

The distinctive features of Beleriand were the great uplift or 'Long Wall' of Andram,★ running from east to west, and its rivers, notably the southward flowing River Sirion and its tributaries, including the River Narog. Its central area was dominated by the forested realm of Doriath.★ Westwards and south, the River Narog flowed through the hilly region of the High Faroth, the westward extension of the uplift or wall of Andram. Here the centre of the Elven Realm of Nargothrond★ was located. As the Sirion encountered the wall of Andram further east it flowed underground for many miles before emerging below the wall at the Gates of Sirion. Between Nargothrond and Doriath, Amon Rûdh★ rose above the plain.

The Blue Mountains, the Ered Luin, were one of the chief ranges of the world of the First Age, forming a natural boundary to Beleriand in the east. The mountains were the source of the tributaries of the River Gelion, flowing through Ossiriand,★ Land of Seven Rivers, 'filled with green woods wide and fair'. In the mountains only the Dwarves★ lived. They carved out the cities of

Nogrod* and Belegost,* and mined copper, iron and other ores.
*See also* GEOGRAPHY OF MIDDLE-EARTH.


**Further reading**

J.R.R. Tolkien, 'Quenta Silmarillion' (sections 105–121), in *The Lost Road* (1987); Karen Wynn Fonstad, *The Atlas of Middle-earth* (1981).

**Beleriand, The Lays of** See THE LAYS OF BELERIAND.

**Beorn** In *The Hobbit** he gives succour to Bilbo Baggins* and Thorin* and his company of Dwarves.* He is Chieftain of the Beornings (men of the Vales of Anduin), but is not typical, in being a skin-changer, able to shift shape (a quality shared by Lúthien* in the tale of Beren and Lúthien*). As well as a shape-changer Beorn is also a beserker, a figure plucked by Tolkien from the northern imagination. Beorn helped to win the Battle of the Five Armies, killing Bolg, leader of the Orcs.*

**'Beowulf: The Monsters and the Critics' (1936)** Like J.R.R. Tolkien's essay, 'On Fairy-Stories',* this lecture provides an important key to his work both as a scholar and a writer of fiction. *Beowulf* is one of the earliest works of English literature, and one of the greatest.

In his lecture, the Professor expresses dissatisfaction with existing *Beowulf* criticism. In fact, it had not been criticism proper, he complained, as it had not been directed to an understanding of the poem as a poem, as a unified work of art. Rather, it had been seen as a quarry for historical data about its period. In particular, the two monsters which dominate it—Grendel, and the dragon*—had not been sufficiently considered as the centre and focus of the poem. Tolkien argued that what he called the 'structure and conduct' of the poem arose from this central theme of monsters.

Tolkien's approach to literature here resembles that of his friend, C.S. Lewis,* who argued for an intrinsic rather than extrinsic concern with works of poetry and fiction, notably in his book, *The Personal Heresy* (1939), co-written with E.M.W. Tillyard, who took a somewhat contrary position.

It was clear to Tolkien that the *Beowulf* poet created, by art, an illusion of historical truth and perspective. (C.S. Lewis called such illusion 'realism of presentation'.) The poet had an instinctive historical sense which he used for artistic, poetic ends. Tolkien:

> So far from being a poem so poor that only its accidental historical interest can still recommend it, *Beowulf* is in fact so interesting as poetry, in places poetry so powerful, that this quite overshadows the historical content, and is largely independent even of the most important facts . . . that research has discovered.

In a literary study of *Beowulf,* Tolkien argued, we must deal with a native English poem that is using in a fresh way ancient and mostly traditional material. The important question is not the poet's sources, but what he did with them.

In considering the monsters, which are so pivotal to *Beowulf,* Tolkien points out what he believes is the rareness and esteem of dragons in northern literature. Only two he finds significant, one of which is Beowulf's 'bane', and the other Fafnir, the dragon of the Volsungs, is alluded to in the poem. The author of *Beowulf,* for all his greatness and nobility of mind, had not made a mistake in his artistic choice of theme.

The choice of theme actually accounts for the greatness of the poem, argues Tolkien. Other contemporary writers were capable of similar literary style, yet those which have survived are in his opinion lesser works. There is in fact no incongruity between style and theme in *Beowulf*. The power comes from 'the mythical mode of imagination'. Tolkien was to take this idea further in his lecture, 'On Fairy-Stories',★ delivered several years later.

What Tolkien then goes on to say is strikingly true of his own stories: 'The significance of myth is not easily to be pinned on paper by analytical reasoning. It is at its best when it is presented by a poet who feels rather than makes explicit what his theme portends; who presents it incarnate in the world of history and geography, as our [*Beowulf*] poet has done.'

Tolkien points out the danger and difficulty of accounting for the mythical mode of imagination in a work like *Beowulf*.

> Its defender is thus at a disadvantage: unless he is careful, and speaks in parables, he will kill what he is studying by vivisection, and he will be left with a formal or mechanical allegory, and, what is more, probably one that will not work. For myth is alive at once and in all its parts, and dies before it can be dissected. It is possible, I think, to be moved by the power of myth and yet to misunderstand the sensation, to ascribe it wholly to something else that is also present: to metrical art, style, or verbal skill.

Myth is extra-literary, as was argued by C.S. Lewis in *An Experient in Criticism* over twenty years later.

The prince of the heroes of the North was a dragon★ slayer, as was Beowulf. Tolkien sees the dragon as a potent symbol. 'Something more significant than the standard hero, a man faced with a foe more evil than any human enemy of house or realm, is before us, and yet incarnate in time, walking in heroic history, and treading the named lands of the North.' The *Beowulf* author not only uses the old legends in a fresh and original fashion, but provides 'a measure and interpretation of them all'. In the poem we see 'man at war with the hostile world, and his inevitable overthrow in time'. The question of the power of evil,★ the question of Job, is central. Beowulf 'moves in a northern heroic age imagined by a Christian, and therefore has a noble and gentle quality, though conceived to be a pagan'.

In *Beowulf* there is a fusion of the Christian and the ancient North, the old and the new. Yet the imagination of the *Beowulf* author had not developed into an allegorical one. Allegory★ was a later development. His dragon, as a symbol of evil, retains the ancient force of the pagan northern imagination; it is not an allegory of evil in reference to the individual soul's redemption or damnation. He is concerned with 'man on earth' rather than the journey to the Celestial City. 'Each man and all men, and all their works shall die . . . The shadow of its despair, if only as a mood, as an intense emotion of regret, is still there. The worth of defeated valour in this world is deeply felt.' The poet feels this theme imaginatively or poetically rather than literally, yet with a sense of the ultimate defeat of darkness.

The *Beowulf* poet indicates the good that may be found in the pagan imagination, a theme powerfully explored by C.S. Lewis in *Till We Have Faces*. In holding such a view, Lewis was heavily influenced by Tolkien.

Tolkien's conclusion is that

In *Beowulf* we have, then, an historical poem about the pagan past, or an attempt at one . . . It is a poem by a learned man writing of old times, who looking back on the heroism and sorrow feels in them something permanent and something symbolical. So far from being a confused semi-pagan—historically unlikely for a man of this sort in the period—he brought probably *first* to his task a knowledge of Christian poetry . . .

There are a number of parallels between the author of *Beowulf*, as understood by Tolkien, and Tolkien himself. Tolkien is a Christian scholar looking back to an imagined

Northern European past. The *Beowulf* author was a Christian looking to the imaginative resources of a pagan past. Both made use of dragons and other potent symbols; symbols which unified their work. Both are concerned more with symbolism than allegory. As with the *Beowulf* author, what is important is not so much the sources but what Tolkien did with them. Like the ancient author, also, Tolkien at his most successful created an illusion of history and a sense of depths of the past.

**Beren**  In *The Silmarillion*,★ the son of Barahir who cut a Silmaril from the Iron Crown of Morgoth★ to gain the Elf-maiden Lúthien★ as wife, as told in the story of Beren and Lúthien.★ After being killed by Carcharoth★ the wolf he was allowed to return from the dead after Lúthien's intercession and choice of mortality.★ The two then lived in Tol Galen in Ossiriand, to the east of Beleriand,★ where their son Dior was born. Beren avenged the murder of Thingol★ his father-in-law by Dwarves, and recovered the Silmaril, now set in the Nauglamír.★ The Númenórean kings descended from him. His grand-daughter, Elwing,★ married Eärendil★ the mariner.

**Beren and Lúthien the Elf-maiden, The tale of**  This is one of the greatest stories of *The Silmarillion*,★ like *The Lord of the Rings*,★ a heroic romance, though on a smaller scale. Tolkien himself, in a long letter (Letter 131), reveals that it is 'the chief of the stories of *The Silmarillion*, and the one most fully treated'. There are both poetic and prose versions, though none of the poetic versions is complete. The story has great beauty in itself, but much of the unfinished poetry is outstanding, found in *The Lays of Beleriand*.★ The story had a personal meaning for Tolkien, also, as Beren and Lúthien were pet names for himself and his wife, Edith. The conception of the story was tied up with an incident where the two of them had wandered in a small wood in Roos, north of the Humber estuary. There, among hemlock, she danced and sang to him. Beren, in the story, encounters Lúthien dancing among hemlock in the woods of Neldoreth. For both Beren and Tolkien it was a time of memories of danger: Tolkien was on leave from the battles of World War I. When Edith died in 1971 he included 'Lúthien' on her gravestone.

The tale of Beren and Lúthien belongs to the history of Beleriand,★ during the First Age★ of Middle-earth.★ Lúthien was an Elven princess, the daughter of King Thingol,★ ruler of Doriath,★ and Queen Melian,★ and thus immortal. Beren was a mortal man, the son of the heroic Barahir.★ The period is that of the fourth battle,★ the Battle of Sudden Flame.

Many of Tolkien's characteristic themes emerge in this story, including healing★ and sacrifice,★ evil,★ death★ and immortality, and romantic love. The motif of the Silmarils is a unifying thread of the stories of the First Age, part of the greater motif of light★ and darkness. Another unifying feature is the shadow of Morgoth,★ and his lieutenant Sauron.★ Through the marriage of Beren and Lúthien, the Elvish quality was preserved in mankind in future generations—even into the Fourth Age★ when mankind became ascendant, and the Elves waned. In the tales of sorrow and of ruin of that period, when Morgoth and Sauron achieved such wickedness, the story of Beren and Lúthien brought hope and consolation both to Elves and to those of mankind who were faithful against the darkness.

Barahir,★ the father of Beren, resisted Morgoth and remained in the north of Beleriand, in Dorthonion.★ Eventually, Barahir had only twelve companions remaining, and made his hideout near a beautiful lake, Tarn Aeluin, to the east. By treachery, Sauron discovered his lair and ambushed the outlaws. Providentially,★ Beren had been sent away on a perilous spying mission, and was the sole survivor. Sauron's Orcs★ had hacked off the hand of Barahir upon which was the ring of Felagund, a gift for rescuing him in battle. Pursuing the Orcs, Beren retrieved the hand with great daring and 'defended by fate', and thereafter wore the ring.

Aided by the birds and beasts Beren remained a solitary outlaw against Morgoth in Dorthonion for four more years. His fame spread throughout Beleriand, and even into the magically fenced realm of Doriath,★ to the south of Dorthonion, beyond the mountain range of Gorgoroth, the Mountains of Terror. Finally forced to flee Dorthonion, Beren climbed the high regions of Gorgoroth. From here he saw, far off, the Hidden Kingdom of Doriath. It was 'put into his heart' to go there, where as yet no mortal man had gone.

The journey there alone was considered to be one of Beren's great deeds. He had to pass through the dangerous precipices and their preternaturally dark shadows. Beyond these, he crossed the wilderness of Dungortheb, where the good and evil powers of Queen Melian★ and Sauron★ contested each other, and where spiders and nameless monsters prowled. Finally, he had to pass through the protective mazes that Melian had woven around Doriath.

Beren was grey and bowed by his journey. It was summertime when he wandered into the Forest of Neldoreth, through which flowed the river of Esgalduin. One evening, at moonrise, he came upon Lúthien. In the forest glades beside the river he saw her dancing upon the unfading grass. Seeing this most beautiful of all the Children of Ilúvatar, Elves and Men, healed all memory of pain in Beren. Tolkien writes, in 'The Lay of Leithian':

> Such lissom limbs no more shall run
> on the green earth beneath the sun;
> so fair a maid no more shall be
> from dawn to dusk, from sun to sea.
> Her robe was blue as summer skies,
> but grey as evening were her eyes;
> 'twas sewn with golden lilies fair,
> but dark as shadow was her hair.

44

> Her feet were light as bird on wing,
> her laughter lighter than the spring;
> the slender willow, the bowing reed,
> the fragrance of a flowering mead,
> the light upon the leaves of trees,
> the voice of water, more than these
> her beauty was and blissfulness,
> her glory and her loveliness . . .

When she vanished from his sight he was as a person enchanted. Knowing no name for her, he called her Tinúviel, which is Nightingale, daughter of twilight, in Elvish.★ He sought for her all winter, and then, on the eve of spring, Lúthien sang again, and danced, and her song awoke the spring. The spell of silence also broke from Beren, and he called aloud the name Tinúviel. The trees echoed the name, and Lúthien did not flee. As she looked on Beren, she fell in love with him. Tolkien writes: 'In his fate Lúthien was caught, and being immortal she shared in his mortality, and being free received his chain.'

Beyond Beren's hope she returned to him, and secretly they passed the spring and summer together through the forest. Daeron the renowned minstrel, whose compositions were inspired by the beauty of Lúthien, and who loved her, betrayed Beren and Lúthien to her father, King Thingol. The king sent his servants to drag Beren to the splendid Menegroth,★ the Thousand Caves. Lúthien forstalled them by leading her lover to the throne of Thingol, treating him as she would a guest of honour. In scorn and anger the king demanded to know why Beren had entered his forbidden realm. Beren, awed both by the splendour of Menegroth and the king, was silent, but Lúthien introduced him as foe of Morgoth and a man whose deeds were sung even among the Elves. As he looked at Lúthien, and glanced to Melian, it seemed to Beren as if words were given him. His quest, he said, was the greatest treasure of all, Lúthien, daughter of Thingol. Her worth was above all gold, silver or jewels.

To secure, as he thought, the death of Beren, Thingol told him that he too desired a treasure that was withheld. If Beren could bring to him, in his hand, a Silmaril from the Iron Crown of Morgoth, then, if she wished, Lúthien could set her hand in his. With these words, he brought about the eventual end of the protected realm of Doriath, for he was caught within the curse or doom of Mandos.* This doom had been brought on by the disobedience of the Elves to the Valar,* a disobedience especially associated with Fëanor.*

Beren declared that next time he came before the king, his hand would hold a Silmaril from the Iron Crown.

Leaving Doriath unhindered, Beren passed westward and south to Nargothrond,* the realm of the Elvish King Felagund. It was Felagund who had given the ring to Beren's father, Barahir. When King Finrod Felagund heard Beren's tale, and discovered who he was, and found out Thingol's desire for the Silmaril, his heart was heavy. His oath to Barahir had to be fulfilled, but in so doing he would be drawn into the curse associated with the Silmarils.

Celegorm* and Curufin,* sons of Fëanor,* dwelled in Felagund's halls. Their vow was to possess the jewels, which contained light* from the Two Trees* which had originally lit the Uttermost West, or Valinor.* They would not support Felagund in his wish to help Beren in his quest. Realising his isolation, Felagund cast down his silver crown. Ten warriors however stood with him, and he left his brother, Orodreth to rule in his place. On an autumn evening Beren, Felagund and the band of men set off towards Angband,* stronghold of Morgoth in the Uttermost North. As they neared the western pass in which Sauron's tower was located they surprised and killed a company of Orcs, and disguised themselves as them. They fell nevertheless into Sauron's hands, and a contest of power ensued between Felagund and Sauron. Sauron's song of power was of treachery and darkness; Felagund's of resistance and endurance. Felagund at last fell down, and the company were cast into a deep pit, the secret of their quest still unknown to Sauron. One by one, a werewolf started to devour the companions.

Far away in Doriath, Lúthien sensed the horror of these happenings, and discovered Beren's whereabouts from Melian, her mother. Her attempt to leave the realm secretly was betrayed by Daeron, and she was kept a prisoner in a great beech tree. By enchantment she escaped, only to fall into the hands of Celegorm and Curufin, who were hunting with their hounds away from Nargothrond. One hound, Huan,* had come long ago from Valinor, and could understand speech. He befriended Lúthien, and helped her escape the two sons of Fëanor, who schemed to have her marry Celegorm. For speed, Huan allowed her to ride on his back as they went together northward towards Sauron's tower. Only Beren and Felagund remained alive in the pits of Sauron. As the werewolf crept up to devour Beren Felagund made a great effort. Bursting his bonds he struggled with the wolf, slaying it with his teeth and hands, yet was mortally wounded. Bidding farewell to Beren, the fair and beloved Elf fulfilled his oath in death.

As Beren mourned his friend in black despair, Lúthien stood on the bridge leading to Sauron's island tower. She sang a song that the mightiest of walls could not stop. Thinking he dreamed, Beren heard it, and himself sang a song challenging Sauron. It was a song he had composed in reverence to Elbereth,* praising the Seven Stars, the Sickle of the Valar placed in the heavens by her as a sign of the ultimate defeat of Morgoth.

Hearing Beren's song, Lúthien sang a greater song. Sauron recognised the singer, and, smiling, thought to capture her for Morgoth. As he sent wolves, one by one, to capture her the hound Huan silently destroyed them. Even Sauron's greatest werewolf, the dreaded Draugluin, was no match for Huan. Then Sauron himself took on the form of a werewolf (for, as a Maia,★ he could take on any earthly form) and challenged the hound of Valinor. Though Sauron shifted shape again and again during the battle, he failed to free himself from Huan's grip. At last, Sauron yielded, and, taking the form of a vampire, fled eastwards to Taur-nu-Fuin,★ and possessed it.

Beren and Lúthien were now free for themselves again. Huan, as well as many Elves freed from Sauron's isle, returned to Nargothrond. Their return, with the story of Lúthien's bravery, stirred the people of the realm against Celegorm and Curufin. The unpopular brothers set off northwards, heading for Himring, where another brother, Maedhros★ dwelt. The faithful Huan was with them. The party encountered Beren and Lúthien on the borders of Doriath. They tried to kill Beren and capture Lúthien. Huan however protected the couple, but even so Beren was badly wounded. By her arts and her love she healed him. Beren was torn between his oath to Thingol to gain the Silmaril and his love for Lúthien. While she slept he left her in the care of Huan and slipped away.

Lúthien bade Huan follow Beren's northward trail towards Morgoth's stronghold at Thangorodrim.★ Passing the ruins of Sauron's isle, Huan took the skins of the werewolf Draugluin, and Sauron's messenger vampire. Wearing these fearful shapes, Huan and Lúthien sped northwards, overtaking Beren at last. Then, by the advice of Huan and the skill of Lúthien, Beren took on the shape of the werewolf, and Lúthien the bat-form, with its great fingered wings, barbed with iron claws. Howling, Beren rushed towards Angband, with the bat that was Lúthien wheeling and flittering above him.

As they approached the gate of Angband, they were seen by Carcharoth,★ the tormented and specially bred werewolf of Morgoth. Throwing off her disguise, Lúthien challenged the wolf, commanding him to sleep. The pair then passed through the gate, and down twisting stairs to the very throne of Morgoth. As Morgoth saw her beauty he lusted for her, leaving her free for a time as he gloated over his thought of possession. This was his downfall, for she sang a song of enchantment that caused him and his court to fall into a deep sleep. As Morgoth slipped forward his crown fell off his head, allowing Beren to cut a Silmaril from it. Its radiance shone through the flesh of Beren's hand as he held it.

Morgoth stirred in his sleep, and, in sudden terror, Beren and Lúthien fled towards daylight. Carcharoth was waiting for them. Lúthien was exhausted by her efforts, but Beren held up the Silmaril to dispel the wolf. Suddenly the wolf bit off Beren's hand holding the jewel. The fire from the Silmaril tormented his innards, maddening him, and causing him to rush away howling. Beren lay dying from the poisoned wound, while, with what strength she had, Lúthien tended to him. Just as the quest for the Silmaril seemed doomed, three mighty eagles came to their rescue. They were watchful in that region to help the victims of Morgoth. They flew far south, over the hidden and beautiful city of Gondolin,* and eventually to the borders of Doriath. After a long time, Beren revived to hear Lúthien singing soft and slow beside him. Her love had drawn him back from death. She and Beren came before the throne of Thingol, where the one-handed man claimed Lúthien for his wife. The Silmaril, he said, was in his hand, holding up his empty arm.

News came that Carcharoth, still maddened by the Silmaril burning inside him, had burst into Doriath. Beren, Thingol, Huan and others set off to chase him. As Huan attempted to dislodge the wolf, he sprang at Thingol. Beren leapt in front of the king and was mortally wounded. Huan fought Carcharoth to the death, and then himself died, in fulfilment of an ancient prophecy. The Silmaril, cut from Carcharoth, was put in Beren's remaining hand, and he held it up and gave it to Thingol, saying the quest was achieved. Lúthien reached Beren before he died, and bade his spirit await her beyond the Western Sea.

Beren's spirit tarried until Lúthien came to the dim shores of the Outer Sea. Leaving her body, like a cut flower, Lúthien entered the Halls of Mandos, where Beren's spirit was. Kneeling before Mandos,★ the Vala, Lúthien sang. Her song mingled the themes of the sorrow of the Elves and the grief of mankind, the two kindred races made by Ilúvatar★ to inhabit earth. Mandos was moved to pity, and he sought the advice of Manwë,★ who governed the world under Ilúvatar's hand.

Lúthien was given the choice of going to Valinor★ or becoming mortal like Beren, taking him back to Middle-earth, to live there without certainty of either life or joy.

She chose mortality,★ and Beren and she lived in mortal form in Ossiriand. Lúthien herself was the product of a marriage between an Elf and one of the Maiar,★ so she already had angelic blood in her veins. This angelic inheritance was added to the Elvish inheritance she gave to Beren. For about forty years the two lived in Tol Galen, and their only child, Dior,★ was the father of Elwing,★ who married the great mariner Eärendil.★ After the deaths of Beren and Lúthien, Dior inherited the Nauglamír,★ the necklace in which the Silmaril was set.

The writer of *The Silmarillion* observes of Lúthien, who had beauty of both spirit and form: 'In her choice the Two Kindreds have been joined; and she is the forerunner of many in whom the Eldar see yet, though all the world is changed, the likeness of Lúthien the beloved, whom they have lost.'

Tolkien, in the same letter mentioned above, points to the tale's theme of apparent foolishness (*see* THE HERO). He comments:

Here we meet . . . the first example of the motive (to

50

become dominant in Hobbits) that the great policies of world history, 'the wheels of the world', are often turned not by the Lords and Governors, even gods, but by the seemingly unknown and weak—owing to the secret life in creation, and the part unknowable to all wisdom but One, that resides in the intrusions of the Children of God into the Drama. It is Beren the outlawed mortal who succeeds (with the help of Lúthien, a mere maiden even if an Elf of royalty) where all the armies and warriors have failed: he penetrates the stronghold of the Enemy and wrests one of the Silmarilli from the Iron Crown. Thus he wins the hand of Lúthien and the first marriage of mortal and immortal is achieved. As such the story is (I think a beautiful and powerful) heroic-fairy-romance, receivable in itself with only a very vague general knowledge of the background (Letter 131).

**Bilbo Baggins**   *See* BAGGINS, BILBO.

**Birmingham**   A major city in England which, along with the West Midlands, Tolkien regarded as home. When his father, Arthur Tolkien,★ died in 1896, the family settled at Sarehole Mill,★ then outside of the city boundary. Tolkien attended King Edward's School, then located near the city centre. The T.C.B.S.,★ which started life as a schoolboy club, would meet at the tea room in Barrow's Stores in Corporation Street.

Birmingham had gained city status in 1889. It is the largest manufacturing city in England, and the chief hardware city in the world. The Industrial Revolution began in nearby Ironbridge. Birmingham's metal industries have been important since the last half of the seventeenth century.

Birmingham was an Anglo-Saxon settlement, mentioned in the Domesday Book. After the Norman Conquest it became the property of the Bermingham family. By the end of the thirteenth century a market town had grown up

51

at the Bull Ring where several routes intersected. The Bull Ring remains the name of the modern city centre, rebuilt after wartime bombing.

**Black Riders**   *See* NAZGÛL.

**Black Speech**   Devised by Sauron★ in the Second Age★ and revived by him in the Third Age,★ it may have been a perverted form of Quenya Elvish. The Orcs of Mordor★ used a debased form of Black Speech. The only example of pure Black Speech given in Tolkien's writings is the inscription on the One Ring★ in *The Lord of the Rings.*★

*See also* ELVISH.

**Bombadil, Tom**   Possibly one of the Maiar★ (Tolkien was uncertain of his status), but certainly 'Master of wood, water and hill'. He was a nature spirit, mastered by none and refusing possession★ himself. Like the biblical Adam, he was a name-giver. In *The Lord of the Rings,*★ he gave to the ponies of the hobbits names that they 'answered to for the rest of their lives'. There is a comic, hobbitish description of him in the collection of verse, *Adventures of Tom Bombadil.*★ Like the wizards,★ he appeared like a man, though unlike them he had been in Middle-earth from earliest days. As Bombadil told the hobbits: 'Eldest, that's what I am . . . Tom was here before the river and the trees; Tom remembers the first raindrop and the first acorn. He made paths before the Big People, and saw the Little People arriving . . . When the Elves passed westwards, Tom was here already, before the seas were bent.' The bending of the seas refers to the sundering of Valinor★ from Middle-earth after the destruction of Númenor.★

Tom Bombadil was the name given to him by hobbits (he was known in Buckland★); he was known by other names to Elves, Dwarves and Men.

He was also well known to Tolkien's children. Tom Bombadil was a Dutch doll belonging to Michael Tolkien. It had a splendid feather in its hat. He became the hero of the poem 'The Adventures of Tom Bombadil', published in

1934. Barrows referred to here were familiar on the Berkshire Downs not far from Oxford. Tom Bombadil eventually re-emerged in *The Lord of the Rings*.

**The Book of Lost Tales, 1 & 2 (1983, 1984)** These make up the first two volumes of *The History of Middle-earth*,★ a collection of early or unfinished pieces edited by Tolkien's son, Christopher Tolkien.★ Explanatory commentaries are added. *The Book of Lost Tales* represents Tolkien's first major imaginative work. He began it during World War I, and abandoned it several years afterwards.

The first volume contains narratives relating to Valinor,★ the Undying Lands to the Uttermost West of Middle-earth. The second is made up of stories set in Beleriand★ in the First Age.★ *The Book of Lost Tales* is the first form of the 'Quenta Silmarillion', The Silmarillion proper which only constitutes part of the published book, *The Silmarillion*.★

A striking feature of *The Book of Lost Tales* is Tolkien's attempt to put The Silmarillion into an accessible narrative framework. It concerns Aelfwine★ (or Eriol) who, by chance, sails to Tol Eressëa,★ an Elvish island close by the coast of Valinor. There, in a Warwickshire-like setting, he discovers the Cottage of Lost Play. Here is narrated to him the tales of the creation of the world, Morgoth's destruction of the light of the Two Trees★ of Valinor, and other stories of The Silmarillion. There are significant differences of detail from the final form of the stories, but they are clearly recognisable. In *The Book of Lost Tales* are the only full narratives of the Necklace of the Dwarves (Nauglamír★) and the Fall of Gondolin.★ The second volume contains the history of Aelfwine, a narrative picked up in *The Lost Road*.★

**Boromir** One of several tragic figures in Middle-earth,★ another being Túrin Turambar.★ He appears in *The Lord of the Rings*,★ and his 'fatal flaw' is pride. He disdained the idea of the hobbit,★ Frodo Baggins,★ bearing the One Ring★ to Mordor.★ Instead, he believed that its power should be used against the Dark Lord, Sauron.★ Because of his pride, he was unable to overcome his lust for the Ring, and, in madness, tried to kill Frodo. This act proved providential★ in driving Frodo to leave the Company of the Ring★ just before an Orc★ attack. Repentant, Boromir bravely sacrificed★ his life defending the hobbits Merry Brandybuck★ and Pippin Took.★

Boromir was the son of the proud Denethor,★ Steward of Gondor,★ and brother of the wise Faramir.★ Had he lived he would himself have become Steward. Boromir had gone to Rivendell★ to seek the answer to a dream he and his brother had had, and thus became chosen to join the Company of the Ring.

**Brandybuck, Meriadoc 'Merry'**   Merry and Pippin Took were the closest friends of Frodo Baggins★ in the Shire,★ and were allowed to join the Company of the Ring★ in *The Lord of the Rings*.★ After the death of Boromir, Merry, with Pippin, was taken captive by Orcs★ of Saruman.★ After escaping into Fangorn★ Forest, they travelled with the Ent★ attack on Isengard. Merry pledged service to King Théoden★ of Rohan.★ He secretly rode with Éowyn,★ Théoden's niece, to Gondor★ where they killed the Lord of the Nazgûl.★

After the War of the Ring Merry returned to the Shire where he helped to clean up the forces of Saruman. He eventually became Master of Buckland.★ In later life he became somewhat of a scholar, writing such works as *Herblore of the Shire, The Reckoning of Years* and *Old Words and Names in the Shire*.

**Bree**   In *The Lord of the Rings*,★ the main settlement of the Breeland; a town of both Men and hobbits.★ It was located at the crossing of the Great East Road and the North Road. Frodo★ and his friends stayed here at the ancient Prancing Pony Inn.★ In *The Return of the Shadow*★ is reproduced Tolkien's sketch, showing the plan of Bree.

**Brethil, Forest of**   In *The Silmarillion*,★ this is a forested part of Beleriand★ associated with the story of Túrin,★ who lived with the people of Brethil before he slew the dragon, Glaurung. Though originally the possession of the Elven king, Thingol,★ Brethil was given to the Haladin★ in return for guarding the strategic Crossings of Teiglin.

**Buckland**  A region of the Shire★ in *The Lord of the Rings*★ located to the east, before the Old Forest. It was the family territory of the Brandybucks, nominally ruled by the Master of Buckland. Frodo's mother was a Brandybuck, and he grew up here, until adopted by Bilbo.★

# C

**Cair Andros**   In *The Lord of the Rings*, an island in the River
  Anduin.★ It lies about fifty miles north of Minas Tirith.★
  The island is shaped like a ship, hence its name, Sindarin★
  Elvish★ meaning 'ship long-foam'. Another significant river
  island in Middle-earth is Tol Sirion.★ There is a small river
  island on the Avon at Warwick,★ beside the castle, which
  Tolkien would have known.

**Calaquendi**   In *The Silmarillion*,★ these are 'Elves of the
  Light': Elves★ who lived, or at one time had lived, in
  Valinor.★ They were the High Elves.

**Caras Galadon**   In *The Lord of the Rings*,★ the 'City of the
  Trees' in Lórien.★

**Carcharoth**   In *The Silmarillion*,★ Morgoth's great wolf of
  Angband,★ especially bred for evil★ deeds. He bit off the
  hand of Beren★ which clutched a Silmaril stolen back from
  Morgoth. In agony he ran from Angband and eventually
  entered Doriath,★ where he was killed by Huan,★ the
  hound of Valinor,★ after mortally wounding Beren. His
  name can be translated as 'the red maw'.

**Celeborn**   An Elf of Doriath★ in the First Age★ and relation
  of King Thingol★ who married Galadriel.★ He remained
  with her in Middle-earth after the destruction of Beleriand.★ In *The Lord of the Rings*★ he dwells in Lórien.★

Galadriel tells the Company of the Ring:* 'Together through ages of the world we have fought the long defeat.' Part of their story is found in *Unfinished Tales*.*

**Celeborn**  A white tree which grew in Tol Eressëa,* a seedling of Galathilion. In a later age Nimloth* grew from its seed.

**Celebrimbor**  Noldorin* Elf whose name means 'Hand of Silver', son of Curufin* of the House of Fëanor.* After the death of Finrod Felagund he remained in Nargothrond,* though his father was expelled. In the Second Age* he was the most notable of the smiths of Eregion.* He made the Three Rings of the Elves.* When Sauron* made the One Ring* to rule the others Celebrimbor realised his evil* intent. He was slain by Sauron when Eregion was occupied.

**Celegorm**  The third son of Fëanor* in *The Silmarillion*.* He was a Noldorin* Elf.* With his brother Curufin* he was lord of the region of Himlad, north-east of Doriath.* They fled to Nargothrond* when Morgoth's* forces overwhelmed the region. He was master of Huan,* the hound of Valinor,* given him by the Valar* Oromë, who had taught him much about animals and hunting. In the tale of Beren and Lúthien the Elf-maiden* he falls in love with Lúthien* and plots to marry her. He and his brother try to murder Beren.* He was eventually killed by Dior* at Menegroth* when he and his brothers tried to regain the Silmaril recovered by Beren.

**Chieftains of the Dúnedain**  The two kingdoms of the ancient Númenóreans in the North and South were Arnor* and Gondor.* Whereas Gondor was tended by Stewards when the line of kings failed, the more devastated northern kingdom never lost its royal line. The heirs of Isildur* took on the disguise of Rangers* in the wild, though they retained the long life span (*see* DEATH). The Aragorn of the Company of the Ring* in *The Lord of the Rings** was the sixteenth and last Chieftain. The Chieftains were brought up in Rivendell,★ educated in the rich history of Middle-earth.★ Here, in Elrond's★ house, were kept the heirlooms of the Line of Isildur, including the Ring of Barahir and the broken sword which figured in prophecies of the returning king.

The Chieftains along with other Rangers acted as guardians, protecting Eriador★ from Orcs★ and other evil creatures. Their protection of the Shire made a peaceful hobbit★ existence possible; a fact not often appreciated until first Bilbo,★ then other hobbits, became involved in events in the wider world.

**Children of Ilúvatar**   This was the name given to Elves★ and mankind, as both peoples were directly created by Ilúvatar,★ rather than being the work of the Valar,★ his demiurgic agents of creation. The Dwarves★ didn't have this title, as they were made by the Valar, Aulë,★ though it was necessary for Ilúvatar to breathe life into them to make them personal beings.

**Christianity, Tolkien and**   According to Paul H. Kocher, Tolkien was inspired and guided on his way by the mythology of Denmark, Germany, Norway and especially Iceland (see MYTH; IMAGINATION). The Norse pantheon of gods was headed by Odin. This is particularly clear as embodied in the Icelandic *Elder Edda* and *Younger Edda*, and the Icelandic sagas. As a Christian, Tolkien rejected much of the Norse world outlook, but admired its imaginative power. Those elements that he could transform into Christian meaning, he kept. Of course, he rejected the idea of a polytheistic assembly of gods. Also, he rejected its concept of fate, which conditioned not only mankind, but the gods. Instead, he attempted to portray a biblical vision of providence.★ This was a central theme of his fiction. Equally central was a passionate portrayal of freewill, which also rejected fate.

Although Norse–Icelandic mythology has a void or chaos at the beginning of creation, this is not the biblical creation out of nothing, *ex nihilo*, to which Tolkien was committed. So there is a sharp distinction here between Tolkien's invented mythology and that of the old Norse peoples.

Paul Kocher points out that Tolkien also rejected the Norse idea of the ending of the world in the Twilight of the gods (Ragnarok). Yet, imaginatively, he retains the northern atmosphere of heroic endurance, as in the Elves enduring the Doom of Mandos,★ or in the stoicism of the great army of the West advancing to the gates of Mordor.★ Tolkien has, in place of the Twilight of the gods, suggestions of a Last Battle at the end of the ages after the Fourth Age★ of Middle-earth★ that is full of the Christian hope of the end of the world.

Tolkien sets *The Silmarillion*★ in a pre-Christian age (like the author of *Beowulf*) so it can't express the full hope of Christianity, only prefigure it. According to Kocher, its theme is 'Morgoth's implanting of the seeds of evil in the hearts of Elves and Men, which will bear evil fruit until the last days'. In this outworking of the theme of evil,★ Sauron★ plays a crucial role in the first Three Ages of the world of Middle-earth.★

An important element in the embodiment of Christian meaning in Tolkien's fiction comes from his theory of sub-creation.★ *The Silmarillion, The Lord of the Rings*★ and even *The Hobbit*★ are attempts at sub-creation, and as such try to 'survey the depths of space and time'. Tolkien is particularly concerned with time, and Christian apocalyptic.★ That is, his theme is to reveal the essential meaning behind human history. Pre-eminently like the biblical Book of Revelation, he is concerned to bring hope and consolation in dark and difficult days.

To appreciate the freshness and depth of Christian

meaning in Tolkien's work, he can be compared with John Milton, the author of the epic poem, *Paradise Lost*. It could be argued that the legacy of Milton's work is with us still, in science fiction and fantasy. There are important parallels between Tolkien's fiction and Milton's great work—both are a study of evil,★ and a defence of God's ways to mankind. In Tolkien, Morgoth★ and his servant Sauron★ are of central importance, as Satan is in *Paradise Lost*. The very title of Tolkien's popular trilogy refers to Sauron, the dark Lord of the Rings. As also in Milton's work, the theme of fall from grace (disgrace) and into sin or chosen wickedness predominates.

Clyde S. Kilby was able to spend much of the summer of 1966 working with Tolkien on the unfinished *The Silmarillion*, and asked him many questions concerning the underlying meanings of his work. In his little book, *Tolkien and The Silmarillion*, he discusses Tolkien as a Christian writer. Kilby describes him as a Tridentine Roman Catholic, a convinced supernaturalist. He believed in a personal yet infinite God who could answer prayer. He and his wife believed that one of their sons had been healed of a heart complaint. Talking to Tolkien had been a major factor in the conversion of C.S. Lewis to Christianity. Tolkien had a high view of Mary the mother of Jesus. His own faith was tied up with that of his mother, who had been ostracised for her faith. He believed that this was a factor in her death. He lost her before his teens. Kilby also mentions Tolkien's work on *The Jerusalem Bible*.

Although the name of God doesn't appear in Tolkien's fiction (there he is called Ilúvatar★), it is full of Christian meaning. Tolkien spoke to Clyde Kilby, for instance, of the invocations to Elbereth★ Gilthoniel. The Professor characteristically wrote in *The Road Goes Ever On*: 'These and other references to religion in *The Lord of the Rings* are frequently overlooked.' The meaning, in fact, is implicit rather than explicit. It is incarnate in the whole world of the story. Tolkien deliberately avoided cultic or other explicit references to religion. His interest was in theology, philosophy and cosmology—the elements which make Christianity a world outlook rather than merely a matter of private and public religious experience. It was part of Tolkien's view of mankind as sub-creator, in God's image, that human sub-creations would be like all possible worlds created by God in having a moral and religious character or 'nature'.★

Before and since Tolkien's death there have been numerous articles and books on the meaning of his fiction. Kilby records Tolkien's favourable reaction to an essay sent him from Australia, concerned with the themes of kingship, priesthood and prophecy in *The Lord of the Rings*. He endorsed the spirit of the essay in finding Christian meaning in his work, even though, as he remarked, it displayed the tendency of such scholarly analysis to suggest that it was a conscious schema for him as he wrote. He didn't deliberately try to insert Christian meaning into his work—a point over which he disagreed with C.S. Lewis, in whose fantasy he felt the Christianity was too explicit.

A fruitful way of considering Christian meaning in Tolkien is in terms of his commitment to a natural theology.★ C.S. Lewis, in his book, *Miracles*, emphasised the importance of presuppositions or our preunderstanding in approaching historical and natural events. Tolkien, on the contrary, finds real history and natural events a reliable guide to truth in themselves. Whereas traditional natural theology concentrates on the revelation of God in nature and cosmology, Tolkien particularly finds inevitable theology revealed in language and story, or myth.★

Clyde Kilby points out that Tolkien believed in the *anima naturaliter christiana*, 'the sense of God and responsibility to Him inborn in mankind'. This sense is both reflected in language and story and reinforced by them.

61

Tolkien's thinking about this inevitable structure of the language of story is most clearly found in his essay, 'On Fairy-Stories'.★ Here he finds the attributes of escape,★ recovery★ and consolation.★ Consolation, particularly, is loaded with Christian meaning, focused on the *evangelium*. This structure of story is vindicated by the greatest story of all, told in the biblical gospels. This has the story qualities of escape, recovery and consolation, yet is, astoundingly, true in the real world, in actual human history.

The inspiration for Tolkien's fiction came from such Christian works of medieval English literature as *Beowulf* and *Crist*. One sentence in the latter in particular inspired the tale of Eärendil★ the mariner. The line was *Ëalä Eärendel engla beorhtast ofer middengeard monnum sended*. Commenting on this sentence in a letter to Clyde Kilby, Tolkien declared that these are 'Cynewulf's words from which ultimately sprang the whole of my mythology'. Tolkien gave a literal translation of the line to Kilby: 'Here Eärendel, brightest of angels, sent from God to men.'

As well as his natural theology, Tolkien was deeply inspired by, or at least found himself using parallels with, biblical imagery. Kilby is useful in pointing out some of these biblical associations. A study of them would take a whole book. These associations include biblical imagery of trees,★ the fall★ of mankind and some angels, the personification of Wisdom in Proverbs 8, and the biblical portrayal of heroism (*see* HERO).

In a letter to W.H. Auden★ (in 1965), Tolkien commented on *The Lord of the Rings* in relation to Christian theology: 'I don't feel under any obligation to make my story fit with formalized Christian theology, though I actually intended it to be consonant with Christian thought and belief.'

*See also* STORY, THEOLOGY OF.

**Further reading**

Paul H. Kocher, *A Reader's Guide to the Silmarillion* (1980); Clyde S. Kilby, *Tolkien and The Silmarillion* (1976).

**Círdan**  A mariner and shipbuilder (his name means 'ship-maker'), Círdan was among the wisest of the Elves★ in Middle-earth.★ In the First Age★ he was associated with the harbours of The Falas, to the west of Beleriand.★ He was forced to withdraw to Arvernien, at the mouths of the River Sirion,★ where he provided a haven for fleeing Elves and Men, including Elwing.★ After the destruction of Beleriand he became Lord of the Grey Havens. Círdan possessed one of the Elven Rings, Narya,★ which he humbly passed on to Gandalf.★

**Cirith Gorgor**  The haunted pass into Mordor★ in *The Lord of the Rings.*★

**Cirith Ungol**  The high pass into Mordor★ used by Sam and Frodo★ in *The Lord of the Rings.*★ Shelob's★ Lair effectively protected the pass.

**Coghill, Nevill (1899–1980)**  Professor of English Literature at Oxford★ from 1957 to 1966, and a member of The Inklings.★ After serving in World War I, he read English at Exeter College, Oxford, and in 1924 was elected a fellow there. As an undergraduate attending the Essay Club at Exeter College, he heard Tolkien read aloud 'The Fall of Gondolin',★ from The Silmarillion.★ He was also a member of The Kolbitar★ club. Coghill was admired for his theatrical productions, and for his translation of Chaucer's *Canterbury Tales* into modern English couplets.

**Company of the Ring**  In *The Lord of the Rings,*★ the fellowship which accompanied the Ring-bearer, Frodo,★ on his perilous quest★ to destroy it. The Company represented all the free peoples: Elves,★ Dwarves,★ hobbits★ and Men.

Gandalf★ also accompanied Frodo. The Company consisted of the hobbits Frodo, Sam, Merry and Pippin; the wood Elf Legolas;★ the Dwarf Gimli; and the Men Aragorn★ and Boromir.★ The Company first lost Gandalf in Moria,★ and then later was divided at the death of Boromir,★ Sam and Frodo going on alone to Mordor. They were reunited after the destruction of the Ring.★

**Consolation**    Tolkien believed that consolation was a central quality of good fantasy or fairy-tale—the kind of story he wrote in *The Lord of the Rings*★ or 'The tale of Beren and Lúthien the Elf-maiden'. The quality is related to that of escape★ (but not escapism). There are things 'grim and terrible to fly from', says Tolkien. 'These are hunger, thirst, poverty, pain, sorrow, injustice, death.' But even when people are fortunate enough not to face such extremes 'there are ancient limitations from which fairy-stories offer a sort of escape, and old ambitions and desires (touching the very root of fantasy) to which they offer a kind of satisfaction and consolation'. Some include the desire 'to visit, free as a fish, the deep sea' or to fly among the clouds. There are also primordial desires to survey the depths of space and time (*see* SUB-CREATION) and to converse with animals.

The desire for talking animals comes from a sense of separation from nature,★ from the fall.★ C.S. Lewis tried to define such a desire like this:

We do not want merely to *see* beauty . . . We want something else which can hardly be put into words—to be united with the beauty we see, to pass into it, to receive it into ourselves, to bathe in it, to become part of it. That is why we have peopled air and earth and water with gods and goddesses and nymphs and elves.

The oldest desire of course, Tolkien points out, is to escape death.★ This desire is a common characteristic of the fairy-stories of human beings. Elves would be concerned to escape deathlessness.

Tolkien feels however that the consolation of fairy-stories has a more important aspect than 'the imaginative satisfaction of ancient desires'. This is the consolation of the Happy Ending. He coins the term *eucatastrophe* for this ending. Just as tragedy★ is the true form of drama, its highest function, *eucatastrophe* is the true form of the fairy-tale. Such *eucatastrophe*, the sudden 'turn' in the story, 'is not essentially "escapist" or "fugitive". In its fairy-tale—or otherworld—setting, it is a sudden and miraculous grace: never to be counted on to return.' This is not to deny or make light of sorrow and failure, for their possibility 'is necessary to the joy of deliverance'. What is denied, says Tolkien, is 'universal final defeat'. This denial is '*evangelium*, giving a fleeting glimpse of Joy, Joy beyond the walls of the world, poignant as grief'. This joy★ 'rends indeed the very web of story, and lets a gleam come through'.

The source of joy and consolation is objective (as it was for Tolkien's friend C.S. Lewis). Reality itself is the grounding of the meaning of such stories. In his essay on fairy-stories, Tolkien explicitly links consolation with the Christian gospel (*see* CHRISTIANITY, TOLKIEN AND).

*See also* 'ON FAIRY-STORIES'; APOCALYPTIC, TOLKIEN AND.

**Cottage of Lost Play** *See THE BOOK OF LOST TALES, 1 & 2.*

**Cuiviénen** In *The Silmarillion*,★ a bay in the far east of Middle-earth★ by the shores of which the Elves★ awoke, after being created by Ilúvatar.★ The name means 'awakening-water' in Quenya.★ From here the Elves were called to their long journey to the West.

**Curufin**  In *The Silmarillion*,★ an Elf,★ and son of Fëanor,★ who took the Oath★ of Fëanor and thus came under the Doom of Mandos.★

# D

**Dale**  This city-kingdom of Men related to the Edain★ was situated on the southern slopes of Erebor,★ the Lonely Mountain. At the time of the events of *The Hobbit*★ it was deserted, having been destroyed by Smaug★ the dragon,★ its inhabitants fled to Esgaroth★ (Lake Town). Bard the bowman, a descendant of the old Kings of Dale, rebuilt it after slaying the dragon. Relations thereafter with the Dwarves★ of Erebor were re-established. In the War of the Ring★ Dale was besieged by Sauron's★ forces, by which time it had grown in size and prosperity.

**d'Ardenne, Simonne**  A philologist who was a student of Tolkien's in the 1930s, studying for an Oxford B.Litt. She was a Belgian graduate who eventually taught at the University of Liege. She and Tolkien collaborated on several projects, including her edition of *The Life and Passion of St Julienne*. The advent of World War II interrupted their association, and they did little work together after the war, though their friendship continued.

*See also* PHILOLOGY, J.R.R. TOLKIEN AND.

**Dark Elves**  This sometimes refers to Elves★ in the First Age★ who did not cross Belegaer, The Great Sea, to Valinor,★ and thus did not see the light★ of the Two Trees.★ Sometimes it refers more specifically to the Elves at the very beginning who refused to join the westward march from Cuiviénen.★

67

**Dead Marshes**  In *The Lord of the Rings*,★ an extensive area of marshland east of Emyn Muil, encountered by Frodo★ and Sam. They are west of the battle plain of Dagorlad, and get their name from the fact that the marshes had encroached upon the graves of those slain in ancient battles. The faces of putrifying warriors can be glimpsed deep in its pools. The uncanny atmosphere is enhanced by peculiar, candle-like flames called 'candles of corpses'.

**Dead men of Dunharrow**  Men of the White Mountains of Gondor★ at its founding swore allegiance to Isildur.★ Influenced by Sauron★ they refused a call to battle against Mordor.★ As a result, they were cursed to remain as spirits in or near the White Mountains until Isildur's heir (revealed in *The Lord of the Rings*★ as Aragorn★) called upon them to fulfil their oath. Under Aragorn's authority they overwhelmed the Corsairs of Umbar★ on the River Anduin★ at Pelargir, a vital phase of the War of the Ring.★

**Death**  Tolkien commented, in his essay on fairy-stories, that 'death is the theme that most inspired George McDonald'. Though Tolkien was impatient with MacDonald,★ he owes a great deal to him. There are affinities between 'good death' in MacDonald (in, for instance, his *Phantastes, Lilith* and *At the Back of the North Wind*), and Tolkien. Death is also a theme which greatly inspired Tolkien, and is central to his mythology of Middle-earth.★ Much of his thinking about the theme is found in his published *Letters*,★ where he often patiently explained his fiction to those who wrote to him with enquiries.

Centrally, Tolkien saw 'mortality' as a special gift of God to human beings. While this would be 'bad theology' in the primary world, in his invented world the idea helped to elucidate truth, and was, he believed, a legitimate basis for legends.

In biological terms, explained Tolkien, Elves★ and humankind are one race—they are capable of intermarriage. Biologically, however, there would also be some difference accounting for the fact that one was immortal and one was not. Elves have certain aspects of human beings (*see* ELVEN QUALITY), as well as freedoms and powers humans desire. 'The beauty and peril and sorrow of these things is exhibited in them. . .'

Tolkien's invention of a mortality–immortality contrast opens up all kinds of imaginative possibilities; for example, sacrifice★ in Lúthien's★ momentous choice of mortality for the sake of Beren.★ Her choice, and efforts to have that choice, exhibit some of the meaning of her love. Centuries later, long after the death of the once immortal maiden, the most beautiful to walk the earth, Arwen★ makes a similar choice in order to be one with the mortal Aragorn.★

Another variation in the theme of death is the allowance made to the Númenóreans★ of a triple span of mortal life. For the faithful, this served to deepen their sense of identity as created beings who would expect to die eventually, and to pass on to a greater, but still human, fulfilment. A good Númenórean died of freewill, letting his or her life go, as Aragorn did. But for the rebels, seduced by the malice of Sauron,★ there was a deepening fear of death, which led to their ill-fated attempt to occupy the Undying Lands of the West.

Sauron's deceit was that the lands had a magical property of deathlessness. In fact, it was only the beings—the Valar,★ Maiar★ and Elves—who were the immortal of the land, conferring blessing on it.

Time of course is fundamental in relation to mortality. Here other imaginative possibilities are played out by Tolkien. A person such as Galadriel★ has an existence which spans three Ages of Middle-earth. In contrast, Men with a short life-span would be willing to lay down their lives fighting the enemy, Morgoth.★ The Elves of the Third Age in particular were conscious of the increasing burden of immortality, as they experienced the gradual fading and decline of their race in Middle-earth, making way for the domination of mankind.

Yet other imaginative possibilities arise. Though death is a gift to human beings, healing★ and escape★ from death are desirable. Such healing and escape provide a vivid image of the very heart of human life—the timelessness and transcendence of our relationship with God and with other human beings. Escape from death, and healing, are a constant theme in Tolkien's tales of Middle-earth. Frodo★ and Faramir★ are near death, Frodo on several occasions. Gandalf (though a Maia) sacrifices his physical life for his friends, but is sent back to complete his work in a transformed body. The Ring-bearers Bilbo★ and Frodo, and eventually Sam, are allowed to pass over into the Undying Lands of the West for proper healing and rest (though eventually even they would die, or be changed, like the biblical Enoch and Elijah). Such healing and escape from death provide what Tolkien calls consolation.★

**Denethor**   The final Steward of Gondor,★ the southern kingdom of the exiled Númenóreans. As told in *The Lord of the Rings*,★ he was suspicious of Gandalf,★ as he was opposed to the crown of Gondor going to the heir of Isildur,★ revealed as Aragorn. He clung to power instead of displaying the true stewardship exemplified in Gandalf.

He had married the tragic Finduilas of Dol Amroth on the southern coast. She had pined away for the sea, living in Minas Tirith.★ Their children were the very different brothers, Boromir,★ proud and ambitious like his father, and Faramir.★

In his wisdom Denethor perceived that Sauron's★ attack on Gondor would come in his lifetime. He started looking into the palantír★ of Gondor to discern the Dark Lord's plans. He thus came under the influence of Sauron's subtle distortions, leading eventually to despair and madness.

Denethor is one of a number of tragic characters in the history of Middle-earth.★

**Descent into the underworld**  *See* UNDERGROUND PLACES AND JOURNEYS.

**Dior**  In *The Silmarillion*,★ son of Beren★ and Lúthien★ the Elf-maiden. He was father of Elwing★ (mother of Elrond★ and wife of Eärendil★ the mariner). After the murder of the Elf King Thingol★ he attempted to restore Doriath.★ After the second deaths of Beren and Lúthien he received the Silmaril set in the Nauglamír,★ the necklace of the Dwarves.★ The jealous sons of Fëanor★ murdered him in Menegroth.★ Dior had the blood of three races, mankind, Elves★ and Maiar,★ flowing in him.

**Dol Guldur**  In the Third Age,★ a fortress built by Sauron★ in south-western Mirkwood.★ In a background event to *The Hobbit*,★ Gandalf★ travelled to Dol Guldur to ascertain the identity of its ruler. After being driven out by the White Council,★ Sauron fled to Mordor.★ In the War of the Ring, Dol Guldur was used as a stronghold by Sauron's forces.

**Doom of Mandos (Doom of the Noldor)**  The prophecy by one of the Valar,★ Mandos,★ of the tragic events that would overtake the Elves★ who left Valinor★ to return to Middle-earth to recover the Silmarils stolen by Morgoth.★ The prophecy was particularly directed at the House of Fëanor,★ but encompassed Elves and Men who became involved. The Doom followed Fëanor's dreadful oath to recover the gems, the Kinslaying of Elves and defiance of the will of the Valar. The Curse or Doom of Mandos works out in tragic events throughout the history of the First Age★ in Middle-earth,★ in, for example, the tale of Beren and Lúthien the Elf-maiden.★

**Doriath**  A great Elven kingdom in Beleriand,★ associated with many events of the First Age,★ as recorded in *The Silmarillion*.★ It was ruled by King Thingol★ and Queen Melian.★ Their beautiful daughter was Lúthien,★ called the Nightingale. To protect Doriath from the power of Morgoth,★ Melian wove a magic barrier around the mainly wooded kingdom. By demanding of Beren★ that he obtain

71

a Silmaril in order to marry his daughter, Thingol enmeshed Doriath in the Doom of Mandos.★

*The Lord of the Rings*★ describes Lórien,★ which was modelled upon Doriath by Galadriel.★

**Dor-lómin** An area north of Beleriand★ between two mountain ranges running roughly north–south, the Ered Lómin and the mountains of Mithrim, in Hithlum.★ When Elves★ returned from Valinor★ to Middle-earth★ Fingon controlled Dor-lómin. It eventually became the home of the Mannish House of Hador.★ In the battles of Beleriand★ Morgoth★ overran the area. Dor-lómin is associated with the life of the hero★ Túrin Turambar.★

**Dorthonion** A highland region north of Beleriand★ in *The Silmarillion.*★ Its name means 'land of pines' because of its great forests. As Morgoth★ gained in ascendancy, Dorthonion was eventually abandoned by Elves★ and Men. Sauron★ fled here after his encounter with Lúthien★ and Huan.★ Because of its ensuing corruption, the region was renamed Taur-nu-Fuin ('forest-beneath-night'), the Mirkwood★ of the First Age.★

**Dragons** Bred by Morgoth,★ these evil beings brought terror to Beleriand★ and elsewhere, as chronicled in *The Silmarillion.*★ In *The Hobbit,*★ Bilbo★ encounters the winged dragon, Smaug,★ in Erebor.★

In his essay, 'Beowulf: The Monsters and the Critics',★ Tolkien paints a vivid picture of the symbolism of the dragon as an enemy more evil than any human foe. The *Beowulf* poem is something new, 'a measure and interpretation' of all northern legends of dragons. He explains:

> Beowulf's dragon, if one wishes really to criticize, is not to be blamed for being a dragon, but rather for not being dragon enough, plain pure fairy-story dragon. There are in the poem some vivid touches of the right kind . . . in which this dragon is real worm, with a bestial life and thought of his own, but the conception, none the less,

approaches *draconitas* rather than *draco*: a personification of malice, greed, destruction (the evil side of heroic life), and of the undiscriminating cruelty of fortune that distinguishes not good or bad (the evil aspect of all life). But for *Beowulf*, the poem, that is as it should be. In this poem the balance is nice, but it is preserved. The large symbolism is near the surface, but it does not break through, nor become allegory. Something more significant than a standard hero, a man faced with a foe more evil than any human enemy of house or realm, is before us, and yet incarnate in time, walking in heroic history, and treading the named lands of the North.

In the human beings of Middle-earth, like Elves,★ hobbits★ and Men, there can also be a dragon-like quality. It could be presented as a psychological state, the 'dragon-complex' (to invent a name for it). The quality is that of possession,★ possessiveness. A dragon like Smaug embodies possessiveness vividly in his great, but useless, hoard. But possessiveness applies to knowledge, power over others, and many other areas. Fallen creatures like Fëanor, Morgoth and Sauron★ are characterised by the dragon-complex, the lust to possess. The Silmarils (and later, for the Dark Lord, the Ring★) symbolise this lust.

As a foil to this complex are creatures who have no desire to possess, or who are lost in their joy in creating. They include Ilúvatar★ himself, father of all, Aulë the Valar,★ Sam (over whom the Ring has little power), and Tom Bombadil.★

Tolkien could be criticised for attributing such evil to dragons which, like Orcs,★ were bred for wickedness, and hence had no moral choice. Human beings are wrong to be dragon-like, bestial, but a dragon is a dragon. However, as symbolic embodiments of nameless evil dragons have great imaginative power.

*See also* HERO; EVIL.

**Dúnedain** *See* EDAIN; CHIEFTAINS OF THE DÚNEDAIN.

**Dunharrow**  In *The Lord of the Rings*,★ a high fortress and refuge in Rohan.★

**Durin**  In *The Silmarillion*,★ one of the Seven Fathers of the Dwarves,★ who awoke at Ilúvatar's★ command in Khazad-dûm.★ He was the ancestor of Durin's Folk, who were the most significant family of the Dwarves in the Third Age.★

**Dwarves**  In Tolkien's Middle-earth,★ Dwarves are one of the free peoples, especially created by Ilúvatar,★ rather than being brought into existence by his agents, the Valar.★ One of the Valar, Aulë,★ did shape them, but could not give them personal life. Although the Dwarves were not his concept, Ilúvatar had pity on Aulë, and gave his creation life. But the seven figures that Valar had shaped had to sleep until Ilúvatar woke them. Chief among the seven was Durin.★

Designed by Aulë to resist the evils of Morgoth,★ Dwarves were short and hardy. Though proud, Dwarves resisted evil. Like their shaper, Aulë, Dwarves were drawn to the substances of the earth, metals, minerals and precious stones. They were great craftsmen. A great temptation for them was possession.★

Dwarves lived long lives, not marrying as a rule until they were a hundred. They had their own, secret language.

In *The Hobbit*,★ Bilbo★ travelled with a party of Dwarves, Thorin★ and Company, to seek dragon's★ treasure. In *The Lord of the Rings*,★ Gimli the Dwarf is a member of the Company of the Ring.★ His friendship with the Elf, Legolas,★ helps to heal an ancient enmity.

**Dyson, H.V.D. 'Hugo' (1896–1975)**  A member of The Inklings,★ Dyson was seriously wounded at Passchendaele before reading English at Exeter College, Oxford.★ As an undergraduate, he heard Tolkien read 'The Fall of Gondolin'★ (part of *The Silmarillion*) to the Essay Club at Exeter College. On a windy night in 1931, he helped Tolkien to persuade C.S. Lewis★ of the truth of Christianity. After lecturing in English at Reading University he was, in 1945, elected Fellow and Tutor in English Literature at Merton College. He retired in 1963.

# E

**Eä**   The material universe, or the world. In Elvish★ Eä means simply 'it is' or 'let it be', the word used by Ilúvatar★ to bring the world into existence out of nothing. Creation itself is larger than Eä, as the Valar and other angelic orders are created beings, even though they are agents in the shaping of Eä.

**Eagles**   Eagles play an important part in the events of Middle-earth,★ and are associated with the providence★ of Ilúvatar,★ the creator of all. They were brought into being by Manwë★ and Yavanna★ at the very beginning. They were noble, immense creatures (the wing-span of Thorondor was 180 feet), large enough to carry Men and hobbits.★ Their providential acts included the protection of Gondolin,★ the rescue of Beren★ and Lúthien★ after they stole back a Silmaril from Morgoth,★ the protection of Tuor★ and other survivors of the Fall of Gondolin,★ the fight against winged dragons★ at the end of the First Age,★ aiding Bilbo Baggins★ and Thorin's★ Dwarves★ in the events recounted in *The Hobbit*,★ and the rescue of Sam and Frodo★ from the slopes of Mount Doom.★ Eagle-shaped clouds presaged the destruction of Númenor.★ In the story of Aldarion★ and Erendis, in *Unfinished Tales*, there is the sign of an eagle on Aldarion's ship.

**Eärendil the mariner**   In *The Silmarillion*,★ Eärendil is a key

76

figure, with associations of Christ himself. After interceding on behalf of the Elves★ and Men of Middle-earth,★ in distress from the evil★ of Morgoth,★ he 'sailed out of the mists of the world into the seas of heaven with the Silmaril upon his brow'. His star in the sky was a sign of the providence★ of Ilúvatar,★ providing hope. The name 'Eärendel' in the Old English poem *Crist* provided an important seed for the growth of Tolkien's invented mythology. The story of his life and voyage is one of the earliest elements in Tolkien's fiction.

*See also* EÄRENDIL, THE VOYAGE OF.

**Eärendil, The Voyage of**    Tolkien considered this as one of four key stories of *The Silmarillion,*★ standing independently of the history and annals of the First Age.★ In his *Letters* (Letter 131), Tolkien wrote of Eärendil:

> He is important as the person who brings the Silmarillion to its end, and as providing in his offspring the main links to and persons in the tales of later Ages. His function, as a representative of both Kindreds, Elves and Men, is to find a sea-passage back to the Land of the Gods, and as ambassador persuade them to take thought again for the Exiles, to pity them, and rescue them from the Enemy. His wife Elwing descends from Lúthien and still possesses the Silmaril. But the curse still works, and Eärendil's home is destroyed by the sons of Fëanor. But this provides the solution: Elwing casting herself into the Sea to save the Jewel comes to Eärendil, and with the power of the great Gem they pass at last to Valinor, and accomplish their errand—at the cost of never being allowed to return or dwell again with Elves or Men. The gods then move again, and great power comes out of the West, and the Stronghold of the Enemy is destroyed; and he himself thrust out of the World into the Void, never to reappear there in incarnate form again. The remaining two Silmarils are regained from the Iron Crown—only

to be lost . . . The ship of Eärendil adorned with the last Silmaril is set in heaven as the brightest star. So ends *The Silmarillion* and the tales of the First Age.

Unfortunately, the tale, or tales, of Eärendil cannot be reconstructed from Tolkien's unfinished work in as great detail as the tales of Beren★ and Lúthien,★ and Túrin Turambar.★

*See also* ELWING; VALAR.

**Edain** Strictly, this is the plural name for Men in Sindarin★ Elvish.★ In First Age★ Beleriand,★ however, the name was associated with Men of the Three Houses of Elf-friends, rather than mankind in general. This association carried through to the Men of Númenor★ and their descendents in the Third Age★ of Middle-earth,★ such as Aragorn.★ These were called Dúnedain, 'Men of the West'. The Edain were enriched by marriages with Elves,★ as with Beren and Lúthien,★ and Aragorn and Arwen.★

*See also* ELVEN QUALITY.

**Edoras** In *The Lord of the Rings*,★ the capital of Rohan, situated on the River Snowbourn and containing the great feast-hall of Meduseld.

**Elanor** A star-shaped yellow flower of Lórien,★ appearing in the winter. Sam and Rosie Gamgee★ named their first child after the flower. Because of her beauty Elanor Gamgee was called 'the Fair'.

**Elbereth** The popular Sindarin★ name for the Vala★ Varda,★ meaning 'star-queen'.

*See also A ELBERETH GILTHONIEL.*

**Eldar** Originally this term, meaning in Quenya★ 'people of the stars', referred to all Elves.★ Later, it was used to refer to the Three Kindreds (the Vanyar,★ Noldor★ and Teleri★) who were summoned to the Great Journey west from their birthplace in Cuiviénen★ by the Vala★ Oromë.★

**Elendil** Elendil the Tall was the son of Amandil,★ leader of the faithful in Númenor.★ When Númenor was destroyed he escaped with his sons Isildur★ and Anárion★ to Middle-earth,★ where he founded the Númenórean realms Arnor★ and Gondor.★ At the end of the Second Age★ he, with Gil-galad,★ was killed during the overthrow of Sauron.★

**Elrond** An Elf★ whose life spanned the three Ages of Middle-earth★ chronicled in *The Silmarillion*,★ *The Lord of the Rings*★ and other writings. Son of Eärendil★ and Elwing,★ he chose to be an Elf, unlike his brother, and daughter Arwen★ (who married Aragorn★). Tolkien's central theme of death★ and immortality touches his life.

Elrond founded Rivendell★ after the fall of Eregion★ to Sauron.★ He married Celebrían, daughter of Galadriel★ and Celeborn.★ Their children were Elladan, Elrohir and Arwen. Throughout the Third Age★ Elrond helped the Dúnedain of the North. He brought up Aragorn, a Chieftain of the Dúnedain.★

**Elven quality** In his invented mythology of Middle-earth,★ Tolkien intended that his Elves★ were an extended metaphor of a key aspect of human nature. This 'Elven quality' in human life was a central preoccupation of Tolkien's. Elves, like Dwarves, hobbits, and the like, 'partially represent' human beings (Letter 131, in *Letters*★).

The idea of embodying qualities in fiction was one he shared with his friend, C.S. Lewis.★ Lewis for instance wished to embody or make incarnate the quality of joy. Both men were imaginatively struck with the quality of 'northernness' (*see* IMAGINATION). Both incorporated events and situations which had a quality of the numinous.★ In the last century, George MacDonald,★ whom Lewis regarded as his 'master', was also preoccupied with the capture of qualities in fiction, particularly fantasy. The quality of holiness, for example, is so tangible in his *Phantastes* that Lewis described it as baptising his imagination★ long before he became a confessing Christian.

In Tolkien's mythology, and also in other fiction (such as *Smith of Wootton Major*★), Elves represent what is high and

79

noble in human beings. In particular, they represent the arts. In their highest form, Tolkien regarded the arts as sub-creation,★ work done in the image of God and his created world. The Elves may in fact be taken as a metaphor of human culture, highlighting its meaning. They were to teach their arts and crafts to human beings (Letter 131, *Letters*).

Tolkien's depiction of the ideal in human life could well be interpreted as Platonic and élitist. However, in my view, his depiction is ultimately rescued from such an interpretation by two key factors, though there is undoubtedly a Platonic element in Tolkien. The first factor is that Tolkien balances the 'Elven' side of human nature with the homely. Like MacDonald and Lewis, he founds his fantasy on the ordinary and on homeliness (*see* NATURE). The second factor is that Tolkien conscientiously tried to make his invention consonant with Christian belief. In the orthodox Christianity★ of Tolkien, the material world is a real creation of God's, where Christ's incarnation and continued (though glorified) humanity are central.

Though in later life Tolkien disliked MacDonald's fantasy, there is in fact a deep affinity between the two writers below the surface. His reaction to MacDonald was a creative one, as was his reaction to some of Lewis' fiction (for example, *The Chronicles of Narnia*, which he regarded as too allegorical). The recurring figure of the Wise Woman or the Great-Great-Grandmother in MacDonald's fairy-stories for children represents the same kind of 'Elven' or faerie quality as Tolkien's Elves.

How does Tolkien move from inventing a race of Elves in a story to presenting them as an extended metaphor of human life and culture?

In Tolkien's tales of the First Age★ of Middle-earth, the subject of The Silmarillion★ proper, the Elves are dominant. As the Second★ and Third Ages★ progress the Elves decline and fade. In 'The Later Annals of Valinor' (in *The Lost Road*★) it is recorded: 'The Sun was set as a sign of the waning of the Elves, but the Moon cherisheth their memory.' However, key tales (such as that of Beren and Lúthien the Elf-maiden★) record intermarriages between Elves and humans which introduce the Elven quality dramatically into human history. For instance, Eärendil,★ an ideal human being and Christ-figure, is the son of a human, Tuor,★ and an Elf, Idril.★

Tolkien comments (Letter 131, *Letters*):

> The contact of Men and Elves already foreshadows the history of the later Ages, and a recurrent theme is the idea that in Men (as they are now) there is a strand of 'blood' and inheritance, derived from the Elves, and that the art and poetry of Men is largely dependent on it, or modified by it.

By the time of the Fourth Age★—where mythology such as Tolkien's has moved into history—the Elven quality mainly persists in human form. The three Ages recorded in Tolkien's Middle-earth stories and annals are pre-Christian. Our present Fourth Age and beyond is the Christian era, where the Elven quality is perhaps now pre-eminently a spiritual one, associated with Christianity, the grace of the gospel (or *evangelium*), and the presence of the Holy Spirit. Tolkien inclines to a 'spiritual' view of art.

The previous paragraph may make Tolkien's aims seem more ambitious than they were. He was largely concerned with making a 'mythology for England', with his mythology providing an imagined history. He was trying to compensate for what he saw as the destruction of a rich literature in Old English. Surviving texts like *Beowulf* give a hint of what might have existed. Meanwhile words and phrases gave tantalising clues to a missing mythology, such as the word 'Eärendel' in the text of *Crist*. In the unfinished story, *The Lost Road*,★ it is supposed that certain Old English words point back to a forgotten language. This is the language of Tolkien's invention, Elvish,★ which he feigned was more discovery than invention.

81

In a secondary way, Tolkien embodied the same 'Elven quality' in human figures. This embodiment is more complex because humans are subject to the 'gift of Ilúvatar', death,★ whereas Elves are immortal. The Númenórean★ humans, though, were granted a life-span far exceeding the normal. They were however to view death positively (it had no association of punishment for rebellion against God, as in actual history). Death was meant to highlight the eternal quality within themselves, which carried the promise of continuing life in the future in the plan of Ilúvatar.★ The good Númenóreans were in fact enriched by their acceptance of providence.★ In culture, laws and the arts, theirs was a great civilisation, a standard for all human society.

Tolkien, like C.S. Lewis, was persuaded by the view of their mutual friend, Owen Barfield,★ that language and symbolism have become increasingly abstract through history. In Tolkien's beginning, there are real Elves (and a real Númenórean civilisation). Now there is merely an 'Elven quality' to human life, which some can see clearly and others fail to perceive at all. In all the abstraction, there has been a real loss. He sees such a loss restored by the *evangelium*, as he points out in his key essay, 'On Fairy-Stories'. Tolkien concludes: 'God is the Lord, of angels, and of man—and of Elves. Legend and history have met and fused.'

Tolkien saw the 'Elven quality' embodied and made real in the incarnation, death and resurrection of Christ. It may reveal itself at any time in ordinary mortals. Though not so ordinary, Clyde Kilby saw such a quality in Tolkien when he spent some weeks working with him. After Tolkien's death he wrote:

He had the life of a mortal man, a little more than threescore years and ten. Yet he had Elvish immortality too, as thousands know from acquiring a measure of it themselves through his works. Tolkien was 'other-worldly' in the best sense of that term . . .

Whether Tolkien will survive as a significant literary figure is a question no man can presently answer. What many of us know now with great assurance is that he survives deeply and joyously in us.

Aragorn★ expressed the hope that Tolkien was intent in capturing through his 'Elvishness'. As Aragorn lay dying he said to his wife Arwen,★ an Elf who had taken Lúthien's choice of human mortality: 'Behold! we are not bound for ever to the circles of the world, and beyond them is more than memory.'

*See also* 'ON FAIRY-STORIES'.

**Elves** In his *Letters*★ (Letter 181) Tolkien describes the 'mythology' of Middle-earth★ as being 'Elf-centred'. The mythology is embodied in *The Silmarillion,*★ which concerns the First Age.★ The Elvish framework of *The Silmarillion* particularly shows up where it is compared with *The Hobbit* and *The Lord of the Rings,*★ both of which could be said to be hobbit-centred, the narrative being composed by hobbits.★

In his essay, 'On Fairy-Stories',★ Tolkien speaks of the relationship between what he called sub-creation,★ and faerie, which is 'the realm or state where faeries have their being'. As Elves belong to faerie, their conception lies at the very centre of Tolkien's fiction.

In terms of the story, Elves are, like mankind, the Children of Ilúvatar.★ They are not part of the creation fashioned through the agency of the Valar,★ but direct creations of God. They are personal, thinking, speaking and creative beings.

The Elves awoke at Cuiviénen.★ They soon divided into two groups: the Eldar,★ who took part in the Great Journey westwards at the summons of the Valar, and those who refused the call. The First Age★ was the golden age of the

Elves. In the later ages they were a remnant in Middle-earth,★ tending to gather in small Elven-realms, or refuges. As they faded, mankind gradually became ascendant.

Elves resembled mankind (*see* ELVEN QUALITY), and could marry them, as the Elf-maiden Lúthien★ did with Beren.★ They were however immortal; tied, even should they die, to this world. The varieties of Elves resulted from the fundamental early division into two groups. Some varieties were the Vanyar,★ the Noldor,★ the Teleri★ and the Sindar.★

*See also* DEATH.

**Elvish**  The language of the Elves,★ invented by Tolkien and inspired in its chief variants by Finnish and Welsh. Many of the names of beings and places in Middle-earth are Elvish in origin, which explains their aesthetic quality. The title of Tolkien's famous book, *The Silmarillion*,★ derives from an Elvish word. The chief variants of Elvish—variants accounted for historically and geographically by Tolkien— are Quenya,★ Sindarin★ and Silvan. Elvish enriched the speech of the Edain★ (*see* WESTRON). Tolkien invented a number of languages in making Middle-earth (*see* PHILOLOGY, TOLKIEN AND).

Elvish can be studied with the aid of Jim Allan's *An Introduction to Elvish* (1978), Ruth S. Noel's *The Languages of Middle-earth* (1980), and glossaries to the volumes of *The History of Middle-earth* and other unfinished material by Tolkien edited by his son, Christopher Tolkien.★

**Elwing**  In *The Silmarillion*, daughter of Dior★ and princess of Doriath,★ who escaped from there with the Silmaril after her parents were murdered by the sons of Fëanor.★ She married Eärendil★ at the Mouths of Sirion,★ and they had two sons, Elrond and Elros. While Eärendil was at sea the sons of Fëanor attacked, and Elwing cast herself into the ocean with the Silmaril. Ulmo★ the Vala★ saved her by transforming her into a bird, allowing her to fly to her husband. The Silmaril helped them to sail through the protective shadowy seas to Valinor.★ Being Half-Elven she was allowed to choose the fate of an Elf or human, and chose the former. When Eärendil with the Silmaril was allowed to sail in the sky, Elwing lived in a tower on the northern coast of Valinor, from where she flew as a bird to meet him as he drew near.

**Ents** Herders who were originally given the task, by Yavanna,★ of being guardians of the flora of Middle-earth. Trees★ were the chief among plant life and Ents described in *The Lord of the Rings*★ resembled trees, though they had the power of speech and movement, and were about fourteen feet tall.

Ents came into being around the same time as Elves★ and were taught to speak by them. In the First Age★ Ents and Entwives★ were found throughout Beleriand★ and to the east. As time went on, male and female became separated, as Entwives favoured agriculture and gardens, and Ents tended the great forests. In the Third Age★ Ents were associated with the Forest of Fangorn,★ where they entered the War of the Ring★ after meeting the hobbits★ Merry and Pippin.

Ents had their own slow language, reflecting the tree-like timescale of their being. Those other than Ents were unable to learn this complex language, with the exception of Tolkien himself. Ents also spoke Quenya,★ but in an Entish style.

**Entwives** Herders who were originally given the task, by Yavanna,★ of being guardians of the flora of Middle-earth. They came into being around the same time as Elves★ and were taught to speak by them. In the First Age★ Ents★ and Entwives were found throughout Beleriand★ and to the east. As time went on, male and female became separated, as Entwives favoured agriculture and gardens, and Ents tended the great forests. Entwives were said to have taught men the skills of agriculture. Tragically, their gardens were destroyed and they vanished before the end of the Second

Age.★ Ents encountered during the events recorded in *The Lord of the Rings*★ lamented the disappearance of the Ent-wives. Their loss is part of the poignant sense of fading and impermanence in the tales of Middle-earth,★ particularly the tales of the Third Age★ (*see* DEATH).

**Éowyn**  In *The Lord of the Rings*,★ a beautiful woman of Rohan,★ niece of King Théoden.★ She was golden-haired, slim and graceful. Her height allowed her to pass as a man when she disguised herself in order to fight in the great battle before Minas Tirith.★ With the aid of Merry she slew the Lord of the Nazgûl.★ Wounded, she found healing★ at the hands of Aragorn.★ At first her heart had been lost in hopeless love for him, but she was won over, and her will to live restored, by Faramir.★ After marrying him, she became Lady of Ithilien.★

**Erebor**  In *The Hobbit*,★ a Dwarf★ kingdom under a mountain possessed by Smaug★ the dragon. Later the restored kingdom played a part in the War of the Ring.★

*See also UNFINISHED TALES.*

**Ered Luin**  The vast mountain chain, the 'Blue Mountains', running North to South which marked the eastern boundary of Beleriand★ in the First Age.★ At that time the Dwarf cities of Belegost and Nogrod were located there. The southernmost part of the Ered Luin survived the catastrophic changes in the terrain of the world at the end of the First Age. They then lay to the west of Middle-earth,★ west of Arnor★ and Eriador.★

**Eregion**  This 'Land of Holly' was called Hollin in Westron,★ and lay at the western feet of the Misty Mountains★ in the Second Age,★ when it was a realm of Noldorin★ Elves.★ The Elven Rings★ were made here. Eregion lay between the rivers Glanduin and Bruinen. Moria★ lay nearby, connected by a tunnel travelled in a later Age by the Company of the Ring.★

**Eriador**  The area between the Ered Luin★ to the west and the Misty Mountains★ to the east, in which lay Arnor★ and where later the Shire★ was settled.

**Escape**   *See* 'ON FAIRY-STORIES'.

**Esgaroth**   The lake town of *The Hobbit*,★ where Men lived on the Long Lake south of the Lonely Mountain. It was an excellent commercial centre, trading with the Woodland Realm★ and Erebor.★

*Eucatastrophe*   *See* CONSOLATION.

**Evil**   *The Lord of the Rings*,★ according to Tom Shippey, attempts to reconcile two views of evil, the Manichaeist (associated with Boethius) and the Judeo–Christian (represented by Augustine). One is a subjective view of evil, and the other objective. The Augustinian view can be called subjective in the sense that evil is a negation, not being in itself. For Augustine, all God's creation was pronounced by him to be good. Tolkien, believes Shippey, tries to take account of both sides, each of which is true to our experience. He sees this happening with the symbol of the Ring borne by Frodo.★ It is an objective reality, the power of which is to be resisted. It also however appeals subjectively to a person's weakness. For instance, the Ring appeals to possessiveness in Bilbo,★ fear in Frodo,★ patriotism in Boromir★ and pity in Gandalf.★

But is Tolkien's portrayal of the objective reality of evil through the Ring Manichaeist? Such a view sees evil as part of the very nature of the universe. Tolkien's Ring, however, is not the creation of Ilúvatar,★ but of a creature, Sauron,★ a Maia.★ The description of Manichaeist might be more true of Tolkien's cosmological myth. In this, the fall★ of Melkor, or Morgoth,★ takes place before the creation of the world. In his music of creation, on which the making of the world is founded, Ilúvatar incorporates the discord of evil as a lesser theme, ultimately overcome in the conduct of the music. This might show a lack of reconciliation of good and evil in Tolkien's thinking imagination. Such a lack could suggest Manichaeism. However, the whole beautiful myth of the creation music of the *Ainulindalë*★ actually rejects a dualism of good and evil. A greater problem, philosophically and theologically, is the existence of the Valar★ before creation. This conflicts with Tolkien's depiction of the Valar as angels, servants of Ilúvatar, rather than deities. This can be reconciled by seeing the world, Eä,★ within which is Middle-earth,★ as only part of creation, the larger reality of which includes the being of the Valar. In achieving a realistic tension between subjective and objective evil, Tolkien's fertile imagination creates many embodiments of evil—Balrogs,★ dragons,★ Orcs,★ the fallen Valar, Morgoth, and his servant, the Maia Sauron, the ringwraiths, spiders such as Shelob★ or Ungoliant,★ werewolves and trolls.★

John Milton, in his great epic *Paradise Lost*, has often been charged with unwittingly making Satan the hero of his poem. To fallen human beings, evil is fatally attractive, and bad characters are easier to create in fiction than good. Are evil beings such as Morgoth, Sauron or Saruman,★ and Elves and Men who fall into evil like Fëanor★ and Denethor,★ more convincing than Gandalf, Aragorn, Frodo, Beren or Galadriel? Colin Manlove tends to find the moral struggles of Frodo lacking in depth, but many would not agree with him. Good beings as well as evil are ably created by Tolkien, as well as the objective aspects of both good and evil. We are delighted by the vision of Valinor,★ the earlier days of Númenor,★ or Rivendell,★ and the goodness of Lúthien,★ Aragorn★ or Frodo.★ We understand the tragedy of Fëanor, Túrin★ or Boromir.

Set against evil in Tolkien's world are many elements, but rarely physical force (as in the overthrow of Morgoth at the end of the First Age,★ the destruction of Númenor,★ or Gandalf's fight with the Balrog★). One important element is healing.★ Another is art, in many forms of creativity, such as song. Another is the renunciation of possession.★ A further element is sacrifice.★ Underlying them all is faith in providence,★ hope in the ultimate happy ending even if a person does not him or herself live to see it.

Because of his theology of Middle-earth, Tolkien is able to portray evil as utterly real, without falling into a dualism of good and evil. The many occasions of tragedy★ within his tales (pre-eminently in the story of Túrin★) emphasise the reality of evil in the world; evil originated by the fall★ of Melkor (Morgoth).

Evil is only possible to creatures capable of creativity and freewill. The Orcs,★ to the contrary, are programmed to inflict evil; tools rather than agents of Morgoth and Sauron. Much of Tolkien's invented mythology concerns creativity and art, the foundation of language and culture. The making of the world by the demiurgic Valar, the fashioning of the Silmarils, and the forging of the Rings,★ shape all events. For Tolkien, a study of evil necessarily has to do with the use and misuse of creativity and freewill. Both salvation and damnation involve moral choices. Thus evil is indivisible: its implications are applicable to the real world, as well as to Tolkien's invented, secondary world (itself one example of creativity).

**Further reading**

T.A. Shippey, *The Road to Middle-earth* (1982); Paul H. Kocher, *A Reader's Guide to 'The Silmarillion'* (1980); C.N. Manlove, *Modern Fantasy: Five Studies* (1975).

# F

**Fair Elves**  In *The Silmarillion,*★ these were the first group of Elves★ to set out on the Great Journey to the West from Cuiviénen, where they first awoke. They were golden-haired.

**Fairies**  Beings from myth and folklore represented as Elves★ in Tolkien's fiction.

*See also* 'ON FAIRY-STORIES'.

**Fall**  Tolkien isolates the theme of fall as one of the central concerns of his mythology of Middle-earth.★ His theology of the fall is taken from the Bible (*see* CHRISTIANITY, TOLKIEN AND), but he shapes it according to his artistic purposes. There is no direct equivalent of the biblical fall of mankind and some angels★ as (1) Tolkien is writing fiction; and (2) there are races other than mankind. Fall is experienced in both aspects of the human, however, the Elvish and the Mannish. Elves are not fallen as a race, and only rarely turn to wickedness individually, so they have no original sin. The position of humans is different. Tolkien introduces the idea of Re-formation to cover the good human beings in his tales of Middle-earth. These are distinguished from Black Númenóreans (Númenor has its own, second fall), and other wicked people, such as the Haradrim.★ Tolkien explains:

Men have 'fallen'—any legends put in the form of supposed ancient history of this actual world of ours must accept that—but the peoples of the West, the good side are Re-formed. That is they are the descendants of Men that tried to repent and fled Westward from the domination of the Prime Dark Lord, and his false worship, and by contrast with the Elves renewed (and enlarged) their knowledge of the truth and the nature of the World.

In this way Tolkien pictures a pagan, pre-Christian, naturally monotheistic group of people. To them has been revealed part of God's purposes, inklings of what is to come in the gospel story, a revelation to which they have faithfully responded according to their light. C.S. Lewis makes a similar exploration of what might be called enlightened paganism on a smaller scale in his beautiful historical novel, *Till We Have Faces*.

The fall in the Garden of Eden does not come into Tolkien's tales—it happens off-stage, as it were. Tolkien regarded the events of Eden as part of actual human history, accounting for the darkness of the world. In his fantasy, he explored the fall theme primarily in the fall of Morgoth★ (Melkor) before the making of the world, and in the disobedience of the Númenóreans in breaking the Ban of the Valar against setting foot on the shores of the Undying Lands.

These moral falls, which like the fall of Lucifer and the fall of Adam are related, account for the separation of Elves and mankind (*see* ELVEN QUALITY). More dramatically, they account for the destruction of Beleriand★ and Númenor,★ and the change in the shape of the world, making it normally impossible to reach the Uttermost West, the lost Eden. On an individual scale, the story of Túrin★ explores the effects of evil★ on a good man who has a tragic flaw. Other explorations include the fall of

Saruman★ and the more tragic Denethor,★ and the corrosive effect of the One Ring★ on Gollum★ and, to a lesser extent, on Bilbo★ and Frodo.★ There is denial of fall, too, in the faithful of Númenor like Elendil,★ and those who refuse possession★ of the Ring like Gandalf★ and Galadriel.★

Though original sin is muted in the good humans of Middle-earth, there is a powerful image of it in the Orcs (who, like Elves, symbolise an aspect of human beings). Orcs were bred into evil by Morgoth, originally from captured Elves (as the Ainur do not have the power to create conscious beings). They were programmed by this breeding, and thus had no moral choice. Their inability to do good is applicable to the concept of original sin. In speaking of human beings in relation to fall and to sin, Tolkien argued that we are still moral, freewilled beings, to whom is revealed something of God's purposes (see NATURAL THEOLOGY, TOLKIEN AND). As he wrote to C.S. Lewis, in the poem 'Mythopoeia':

> Although now long estranged,
> Man is not wholly lost nor wholly changed.
> Dis-graced he may be, yet is not de-throned,
> and keeps the rags of lordship once he owned . . .

See also EVIL.

**Fall of Gondolin** The earliest part of *The Silmarillion*★ in terms of composition, this tale tells of Morgoth's invasion of the hidden Elven city of Gondolin, the heroism of its defenders and the escape of Tuor,★ Eärendil★ and others.

**Fangorn Forest** In *The Lord of the Rings*,★ an ancient woodland east of the southern tip of the Misty Mountains,★ and home of its guardian, the Ent★ Fangorn, encountered by Merry and Pippin.

**Fantasy** *See* IMAGINATION.

**Faramir** In *The Lord of the Rings*,★ brother of Boromir★ and son of Denethor,★ Steward of Gondor.★ A Dúnadan,★ Faramir was Captain of the Rangers of Ithilien★ when he encountered the Ring-bearer Frodo★ and Sam on their quest★ to destroy the One Ring.★ Though a brave warrior, Faramir had a gentle and courteous disposition, and was like Aragorn the ideal Christian hero.★ He also loved music and tales from the ancient days of Middle-earth.★ While recovering from his wounds in the War of the Ring★ he fell in love with Éowyn, the battle-maiden of Rohan,★ later marrying her.

**Farmer Giles of Ham (1949)** This light-hearted short story is subtitled 'The Rise and Wonderful Adventures of Farmer Giles, Lord of Tame, Count of Worminghall and King of the Little Kingdom'. It begins with a mock-scholarly Foreword about its supposed authorship, translation from Latin, and the extent of the 'Little Kingdom' in 'a dark period of the history of Britain'. Tolkien concludes that the setting is before the days of King Arthur, in the valley of the Thames.

Farmer Giles, of the village of Ham, had a dog named Garm. One night a rather deaf and short-sighted giant wandered by mistake near Farmer Giles' farm, trampling his fields and animals. The nervous farmer let fly with an anachronistic blunderbuss stuffed with wire, stones and other bits. The giant, not hearing the bang, supposed himself stung and quickly left that place with its apparently unpleasant horseflies. Farmer Giles was now the village hero.★ Even the king of the Little Kingdom heard of his deed and sent him the gift of a long sword.

The farmer enjoyed his reputation until a dragon★ heard of the rich kingdom from the giant, and times were hard. The name of the dragon was Chrysophylax Dives, and he came to investigate the land. The fiery dragon made a nuisance of himself, but the king's knights were unwilling to take him on.

Meanwhile, the scaly beast got closer and closer to Ham. It turned out that the sword given to Giles was called Tailbiter, and had belonged to a renowned dragon-slayer.

The pressure was on for the reluctant hero to go dragon-hunting, so the farmer set off with Garm, his dog, and his old grey mare.

Much to Giles' surprise, the wily dragon greeted him with a 'Good morning', thinking of his next meal. (He had earlier eaten a stringy parson, whereas Giles was large and fat.) The sword, Tailbiter, however, nonplussed the dragon—with good reason, for, after challenging the dragon, Farmer Giles wounded his wing, making him unable to fly.

Instead he ran, pursued by the fat farmer on his grey mare. The folk of Ham cheered at the pursuit. Eventually the exhausted dragon bargained to save his skin. If Farmer Giles would let him go home, the dragon would return with treasure. The farmer agreed, and the dragon left for home in the far-off mountains, with no intention of returning.

The king, hearing of the events, decided that the dragon's wealth should be his. He encamped with his entourage in Farmer Giles' field, draining the local economy. The day soon came when the dragon had agreed to return, but of course he didn't. The furious king ordered Giles to come to his court and lead his knights to punish the dragon.

After four tiring days, Farmer Giles on his grey mare and the king's knights on their horses, they reached the far-away mountains. The mare became lame, so she and Giles found themselves behind the party as it reached Chrysophylax's territory. Suddenly the dragon leapt out of his cave. Farmer Giles rushed to give battle, holding the eager sword, Tailbiter. The knights were either killed or fled, but the old mare stood her ground. The dragon became nervous at the sight of his old enemy with the fearful sword. As Giles insisted to the dragon on having treasure the old grey mare began to worry about how it was going to be carried. However, Farmer Giles forced the dragon to carry a great load of it on his back.

Instead of returning to the king's court, the odd procession made its way to Ham. The king was outraged and made his way to the village, not realising that the dragon was still there. He was unable to insist that Giles give him the treasure, and from that time the farmer was Lord of the region around the village, backed up by his tamed dragon—or, Tame Worm—who was housed in a 'hall', a barn. Giles was called Lord of the Tame Worm, and eventually Lord of Tame. This title led to the name Thame, as Ham and Tame became conflated. The humbled dragon was eventually allowed by Giles to return home to the mountains.

This humorous story, though on the surface very different from the tales of Middle-earth,★ is characteristic of Tolkien in its themes. The story's inspiration is linguistic: it provides a spoof explanation for the name of an actual village east of Oxford★ called Worminghall, near Thame. An uneaten parson in the story is a grammarian (the equivalent of a philologist), making him shrewd and wise (*see* PHILOLOGY, TOLKIEN AND). The Little Kingdom has similarities with the Shire,★ particularly the sheltered and homely life of Ham. Farmer Giles is like a complacent hobbit,★ with unexpected qualities. The humour—with its mock scholarship—is similar to that in the collection of hobbit verses, *Adventures of Tom Bombadil.*★

**The Father Christmas Letters (1976)** This is a collection of letters, edited by Baillie Tolkien (wife of Christopher Tolkien★), that Tolkien wrote to his children in the 1920s and 30s. They were written as from Father Christmas. The book contains many illustrations that Tolkien made to accompany the letters.

**Father Morgan** *See* MORGAN, FATHER FRANCIS.

**Fëanor** In *The Silmarillion,*★ an Elven prince of the Noldor★ and genius in skill of mind and hands. His tragic flaw was a quickness to anger, possession★ and pride. His great inventions included adapting the Tengwar script of Elvish★ and the making of the Silmarils, incorporating the holy light of the Two Trees.★ When Morgoth stole the Silmarils and murdered his father, Fëanor decided to return to Middle-earth in defiance of the wishes of the Valar. He swore the dreadful Oath of Fëanor, which led to catastrophy for him, his household and the region of Beleriand★ (*see* DOOM OF MANDOS). One of his notorious deeds was the slaughter of fellow Elves at Alqualondë.★ Fëanor died after conflict with Morgoth's Balrogs.★ His name in Sindarin★ Elvish means 'spirit of fire'.

**The Fellowship of the Ring** (1954)   The first volume of *The Lord of the Rings*,★ comprising Books One and Two. It tells of Gandalf's discovery that the magical Ring★ poss-essed by Frodo★ the hobbit★ is in fact the One Ring,★ controlling all the other Rings of Powers. It records the formation of the Company of the Ring★ to support the Ring-bearer, and its perilous journey on the way to destroy the Ring.

Book One tells of Bilbo's farewell party, as he leaves for retirement in Rivendell; Gandalf's account of the history of the Ring to Frodo★ long after; Frodo's sad departure from Hobbiton★ with Sam and Pippin; encounters with Sau-ron's★ Black Riders; their arrival at Buckland;★ the journey through the Old Forest, and visit to the House of Tom Bombadil;★ the capture of Frodo by a barrow-wight; their stay at Bree,★ where Aragorn★ joins them; and the attacks by Black Riders, where Frodo is badly wounded.

Book Two narrates Frodo's healing★ in Rivendell. It tells of the great Council of Elrond, in which it is decided to form the Company of the Ring, and to take what seems a foolish course of bearing the Ring to Mordor.★ It recounts the dangerous journey south, and through Moria,★ where Gandalf is lost fighting the Balrog.★ It describes the passage of the Company through Lórien, and its meeting Gala-driel.★ Leaving Lórien, the Company travels south once again on the River Anduin,★ until it reaches the Falls of Rauros. Here Boromir tries to seize the Ring from Frodo, the Company is divided, as Sam and Frodo set out alone for Mordor, and the remainder are scattered by a sudden Orc attack.

**Finduilas**  In *The Silmarillion*,★ a Noldorin★ princess of Nargothrond★ who fell in love with the tragic Túrin and was murdered by Orcs★ who captured her.

Finduilas is also the name of the wife of Denethor.★

*See also* 'TÚRIN TURAMBAR, THE TALE OF'.

**First Age**  This is the Age of the great period of the Elves,★ though their creation preceded it. The First Age is dominated by events shaped by the existence of the Silmarils, and by the theme of light★ and darkness. *The Silmarillion*★ concerns this Age, though as published the book contains material from later Ages, and from before the First Age.

The First Age came to an end with the Great Battle (*see* BATTLES OF BELERIAND) and the defeat of Morgoth,★ which resulted in the devastation of Beleriand★ and northern Middle-earth.★

**Firstborn, The**  In *The Silmarillion*,★ the name given to the Elves,★ created before the other Children of Ilúvatar,★ mankind. It particularly referred to the Eldar.★

**Forelithe**  In *The Lord of the Rings*,★ the sixth month of the Shire★ Reckoning, approximating our June. Lith, or Lithe, is Mid-Year's Day in the Shire.

**Foreyule**  In *The Lord of the Rings*,★ the last month of the Shire★ Reckoning, approximating our December.

**Fourth Age**  In Tolkien's Middle-earth,★ the Age which began the dominance of mankind, and the virtual fading of the Elves★ and even hobbits★ (who are human). The Christian era of the *evangelium* in which we now live comes after the Ages chronicled by *The Silmarillion*,★ *The Hobbit*★ and *The Lord of the Rings*.★ Many of Tolkien's stories are set beyond the Fourth Age, including *The Lost Road*,★ *Farmer Giles of Ham*★ and *Smith of Wootton Major*,★ but usually were not intended to be part of his invented mythology. *The Lost Road*★ and *The Book of Lost Tales*★ are exceptions.

The Fourth Age began with the passing of the Three Rings★ after Sauron's★ defeat. Most of the Elves,★ especially those of the Eldar,★ passed over the sea to Valinor.★

**Frodo Baggins**   *See* BAGGINS, FRODO.

# G

**Galadriel**  In Tolkien's mythology, an Elven princess and sister of Finrod Felagund. Galadriel's name in Sindarin★ means 'maiden crowned with gleaming hair'. She was given this name in her youth because she had long hair which glistened with gold but was also diffused with silver. At that time her disposition was like an Amazon (*see* HALETH), and when she took part in athletic events she bound up her hair as a crown.

With Elrond★ and Glorfindel,★ Galadriel is the only significant figure from the First Age,★ prominent in *The Silmarillion*,★ to appear in *The Lord of the Rings*.★

Galadriel was implicated in the Noldorin rebellion against the Valar.★ Hence at first she was forbidden to return to Valinor★—the Valar only relented and let her return at the end of the Third Age.★ When in Middle-earth★ she at first lived with her brother on Tol Sirion;★ when he went to Nargothrond★ she moved to Doriath. There she was taught by Queen Melian. In a later Age, she modelled Lórien★ on Doriath.

It was in Doriath that she married Celeborn. She remained with him in Middle-earth after the First Age.★

In the Second Age★ Galadriel lived for a while in Lindon and Eregion★ before founding Lórien. She became keeper of one of the Elven Rings,★ Nenya, the Ring of Water.

A significant moral moment is the temptation of Galadriel when offered the One Ring★ by Frodo★ in *The Lord of the Rings*. She contemplated the possibility of successfully wielding the Ring against Sauron★ (*see* EVIL).

For some readers, the devotion of Sam and Gimli to Galadriel undeniably evokes the veneration for Mary the mother of Jesus that Roman Catholics have. Tolkien was a devout member of that denomination.

In a letter in 1971 Tolkien commented on the religious association of Galadriel:

> I think it is true that I owe much of this character to Christian and Catholic teaching and imagination about Mary, but actually Galadriel was a penitent: in her youth a leader in the rebellion against the Valar (the angelic guardians). At the end of the First Age she proudly refused forgiveness or permission to return. She was pardoned because of her resistance to the final and overwhelming temptation to take the Ring for herself.

Also significant is Galadriel's desire for the Uttermost West of Valinor.★ This desire was fulfilled when she was allowed to go over the sea with the Ring-bearers.

Her longing was what C.S. Lewis called 'Joy' or *sehnsucht*, characteristic of so much of his writing, a concept taken up by Tolkien in his essay 'On Fairy-Stories'.★ Such longing is captured in Galadriel's song, which also laments the eventual passing of Lórien:

> O Lórien! The Winter comes, the bare and leafless Day;
> The leaves are falling in the stream, the River flows away.
> O Lórien! Too long I have dwelt upon this Hither Shore
> And in a fading crown have twined the golden elanor.
> But if of ships I now should sing, what ship would come to me,
> What ship would bear me ever back across so wide a Sea?
> (*The Fellowship of the Ring*, Bk Two, ch. 8)

Something of the development of Galadriel's important place in the history of Middle-earth★ can be seen in *Unfinished Tales*.

**Gamgee, Samwise ('Sam')**   In *The Lord of the Rings*,★ the loyal companion of the Ring-bearer Frodo Baggins★ and the real hero★ of the quest.★ He was chosen as one of the Companions of the Ring,★ a hobbit★ of the Shire★ like Frodo. Bilbo in earlier years had taught him his letters and put in his head a love and longing for Elves.★

Samwise is a translation into Old English of his name in hobbitish★ and means 'half-wit' (which is fitting for a shrewd, honest and heroic figure considered a fool by the great and powerful). Even Tolkien's attitude to Sam is at times condescending. Like Christ himself, Sam is a fool-figure (*see* HERO).

In a letter to his son Christopher, Christmas Eve 1944, Tolkien speaks revealingly of Sam: 'Cert.[ainly] Sam is the most closely drawn character [in *The Lord of the Rings*], the successor to Bilbo of the first book, the genuine hobbit. Frodo is not so interesting, because he has to be highminded, and has (as it were) a vocation.' Elsewhere (Letter 131) Tolkien calls Sam 'the chief hero'.

Sam has an acute sense, awakened by the events of the quest, of what Tolkien calls 'the seamless web of story'. He is an essential part of the narrative frame of *The Lord of the Rings* and thus the older tales of *The Silmarillion*. Sam senses, because of an intuitive feeling of providence,★ that he and Frodo are part of a larger story (*see* STORY, THEOLOGY OF). He also is integral to the structure of the book in representing homeliness (*see* NATURE). His love for Rosie★ is an 'untold story', yet regarded as an essential backdrop to the heroic story. Tolkien writes in a letter probably sent in 1951:

> I think the simple 'rustic' love of Sam and his Rosie (nowhere elaborated) is *absolutely essential* to the study of

his (the chief hero's) character, and to the theme of the relation of ordinary life (breathing, eating, working, begetting) and quests, sacrifice, causes, and the 'longing for Elves', and sheer beauty.

## Brief chronology

(Dates are in Third Age★ years unless marked F.A.—Fourth Age.)

2960 Hamfast Gamgee becomes gardener at Bag End.

2980 Birth of Samwise Gamgee in the Shire, youngest son of Hamfast Gamgee and Bell (née Goodchild).

2984 Birth of Rosie Cotton.

3018 Sam selected by Gandalf to accompany Frodo to Rivendell.

3019 Frodo and Sam break from the Company of the Ring to head for Mordor.

3020 Marriage of Sam and Rosie★ Cotton.

3021 Bag End given to Sam by Frodo when he goes over the Sea. Birth of Sam and Rosie's first child, Elanor the Fair.

7 (FA) Sam elected Mayor of the Shire.

62 (FA) Death of Rosie.

82 (FA) Sam sails over the Sea as former Ring-bearer.

**Gandalf**   In *The Hobbit*★ and *The Lord of the Rings*,★ Gandalf appears as an old man. He is a wizard,★ one of the Maiar★ sent by the Valar★ to Middle-earth★ in the Third Age★ to encourage the resistance of Sauron.★ In his youth in Valinor he was called Olórin (Letter 325, in Tolkien's *Letters*★).

In his fatal conflict with the Balrog★ in Moria★ he is one of the supreme examples of sacrifice★ in Tolkien's writings. In laying down his life he gave up (as he thought) the chance to play his central part in the resistance of Sauron when those who opposed him were at their most vulnerable. His sacrifice was accepted and he was allowed to return to Middle-earth in a resurrected body.

Faithful to his calling as a wizard, Gandalf is a prime mover in the fight against Sauron. On his coronation Aragorn★ states about Gandalf: 'He has been the mover of all that has been accomplished, and this is his victory.'

Gandalf is also important to the narrative of *The Hobbit*★ and *The Lord of the Rings*.★ This is because he interprets the place of providence★ in events. For example, he reveals the key part that the pity of Frodo★ and Sam for Gollum★ played in the unfolding of events. He also foresaw what could be accomplished by the 'foolish' act of sending weak hobbits★ into the stronghold of Sauron (*see* THE HERO).

Gandalf himself was a Ring-bearer. He bore Narya,★ the Ring of Fire, the Kindler, which aspect of himself he represented to hobbits in a childlike way as a love of fireworks.

**Geography of Middle-earth**   Two geocatastrophic events affected the geography of the world of Tolkien's sub-creation.★ The first was the ruin of Beleriand★ at the end of the First Age.★ The second was the even more dramatic drowning of Númenor★ in the Second Age,★ which resulted in a change in the world. It is only after the destruction of Númenor that the world is our familiar sphere. Aman★ is removed from the physical world, and is only to be found by the Straight Road.★

At different times in the history of Tolkien's invented world there are significant land masses: Aman, Númenor,★ Beleriand (to the north of Middle-earth) and Middle-earth★ (as it existed at the time of the events recorded in *The Hobbit*★ and *The Lord of the Rings*★). These areas can be described geographically (as has been done in *The Atlas of Middle-earth*).

Aman was a great western continent. It lay between the great sea of Belegaer and the outer sea of Ekkaia, which was the boundary of the world. Parallel to the eastern coast of Aman ran the great mountain chain of the Pelóri. Valinor★ was to be found west of the Pelóri, and Eldamar between the mountains and the sea, near the pass of the Calacirya. North and south lay vast wastelands. The island of Tol Eressëa★ lay off the coast. To the east of the great sea of Belegaer lay Middle-earth. In the First Age★ the northern region of Beleriand was significant, with settlements of Elves★, Dwarves★ and Men. After its destruction, the more southerly regions became important. The star-shaped island of Númenor★ was raised in the middle of the great sea for a habitation for the Dúnedain.★ These are the lands that are described in *The Silmarillion*★ and *Unfinished Tales*.★

The southern regions of Middle-earth are those regions which are familiar to the readers of *The Lord of the Rings* and *The Hobbit*. Because of the growing importance of Men, and gradual decline of the Elves,★ regions generally express the political boundaries of Men rather than Elves. Physically, the north-south presence of the Misty Mountains★ and the River Anduin★ is significant. In the south the White Mountains of Gondor★ and the mountain chains of Mordor★ impose themselves. To the west, the Blue Mountains are a feature. The most important western feature is the long coastline of the sea of Belegaer. Politically, the kingdoms of Gondor and Arnor★ are important, as well as the southern lands of the Haradrim.★

The Elven region of Eregion★ was important in the Second Age,★ with Grey Havens,★ Rivendell★ and Lórien★ retaining their importance into the Third Age.★ There were significant Dwarf realms, including Khazad-dûm,★ abandoned at the time the Company of the Ring★ passed through the Misty Mountains.

The Shire was located in the old realm of Arnor. It was preserved from danger by its guardians, the Rangers of the North.★

**Further reading**

Karen Wynn Fonstad, *The Atlas of Middle-earth* (1981).

104

**Gil-galad**   The last High King of the Noldorian* Elves* in Middle-earth. His name in Sindarin* means 'star of radiance'. After the end of the First Age* he remained in Lindon. With Elendil* he led the Last Alliance of Men and Elves against Sauron when he grew to power again after the destruction of Númenor.* Though Sauron was defeated Gil-galad was burned to death by his heat.

Sam recites part of a lay called 'The Fall of Gil-galad', translated by Bilbo Baggins.* It begins:

> Gil-galad was an Elven-king.
> Of him the harpers sadly sing:
> the last whose realm was fair and free
> between the Mountains and the Sea.

**Gilson, R.Q. 'Rob'**   A close friend of Tolkien's youth, and member of the T.C.B.S.* Like another member, G.B. Smith,* he was killed on active service in World War I. Gilson was the son of the headmaster at King Edward's School, Birmingham, which Tolkien and the others attended. He was artistic and intelligent, and attended Cambridge before being swallowed up by war.

**Glorfindel**   In *The Silmarillion*,* a noble Elf* of Gondolin* who fell to his death in combat with a Balrog* after escaping Morgoth's sack of the city. His name means 'golden-haired' in Sindarin.* Tolkien suggests that an Elf of the same name, who appears in the Third Age* in *The Lord of the Rings*,* was almost certainly a reincarnation of the same person. Glorfindel seemed to be the second most important Elf, after Elrond,* in Rivendell.* He fought the Nazgûl,* protecting Frodo* and his companions as they drew near to Rivendell.

**God**   *See* ILÚVATAR; PROVIDENCE; NATURAL THEOLOGY, TOLKIEN AND; CHRISTIANITY, TOLKIEN AND.

**Goldberry**   In *The Lord of the Rings*,* the River-daughter, child of the River-woman of the Withywindle, which ran through the Old Forest to the east of the Shire.★ She was the wife of Tom Bombadil.★ Her race is not clear. As a Maia,★ Tom may be able to marry one of another race (as the Maia Melian★ married an Elf,★ and her daughter, Lúthien,★ married a human). She shared Tom's affinity with nature,★ symbolising the hippie ideal in the 1960s when *The Lord of the Rings* had a cult following. The courtship and marriage of Tom and Goldberry is described in *Adventures of Tom Bombadil*.★

**Gollum**   In *The Lord of the Rings*,★ a once-hobbit★ who bore the marks of long centuries underground guarding yet possessed by the One Ring★ which he called 'my precious', and which he had deluded himself into thinking was a birthday present to him.

He originally had been a Stoor★ hobbit, before hobbits migrated westwards over the Misty Mountains★ and settled in the Shire.★ His original name was Sméagol. He had acquired the Ring by murdering his cousin Déagol, who found it while fishing in the River Anduin.★ The name Gollum was given to him because of his filthy habit of noisily clearing his throat.

After possessing the Ring, Gollum hid for centuries in the roots of the Misty Mountains. Seemingly by luck (*see* PROVIDENCE) Bilbo Baggins★ stumbled across the underground lake where Gollum dwelt (as recorded in *The Hobbit*★). After losing the Ring to its new bearer, Gollum ventured out into unfamiliar daylight to seek out Bilbo, falling into Sauron's★ hands. Anxious to discover the Ring for himself, Sauron found the clue from Gollum that it lay in the Shire. The events after this, culminating in the War of the Ring,★ are chronicled in *The Lord of the Rings*.★

Gollum picked up the trail of Frodo,★ the new Ring-bearer, and the Company of the Ring★ before they entered Moria.★ After Frodo and Sam parted from the Company Gollum fell into their hands and led them towards Mordor.★ Treacherously, he guided them into Shelob's Lair,★

106

where the quest* to destroy the Ring was nearly foiled. Later, when Frodo failed to cast the Ring into the Cracks of Doom, Gollum seized the Ring but fell into the fires of Mount Doom with it.

Gollum is of crucial importance to the movement and resolution of events. This is not only because of the contrast between his ravished appearance after centuries possessed by the Ring, and the appearance of a normal, well-rounded hobbit. He is also important morally because of pity shown to him first by Bilbo, then Frodo and, finally, the less soft-hearted Sam. Their pity proves to be a key action in the outworking of providence.* The character of Gollum also reveals Tolkien's concern for repentance in human life. Despite his depravity, a side of Gollum struggles to rise above the overwhelming demands of the Ring which possesses him. There are times in the story when it seems possible that Gollum will be saved. He retains the moral character of a hobbit. The two sides of his nature are so marked that Sam, characteristically, dubs them Slinker and Stinker. The former, expressed in his fawning attitude to Frodo, showed hope of something better, despite Sam's cynicism.

## Brief chronology

(Dates in Third Age.)

2430 Sméagol (Gollum) born around this time.

2463 Approximate date Ring found by his cousin in the Anduin.

2941 Bilbo Baggins possesses the Ring after Gollum loses it deep under the Misty Mountains.

3017 Sauron releases the captured Gollum after extracting the name 'Baggins' from him.

3018 Gollum escapes from the Woodland Realm during an Orc raid.

3019 Perishes in the Cracks of Doom after biting the Ring off Frodo's hand.

**Gondolin** In *The Silmarillion*,* a great city whose name in Sindarin* means 'the hidden rock'. It was built in a secret and protected realm by the Elf* king Turgon,* surrounded by the Encircling Mountains. For centuries it lay hidden from Morgoth* who eventually sacked it with the help of Balrogs,* Orcs* and dragons.* Among survivors were Tuor,* Idril* and the young Eärendil.*

*See also* 'TUOR AND THE FALL OF GONDOLIN'.

**Gondolin, Fall of** *See* 'TUOR AND THE FALL OF GONDOLIN'.

**Gondor** Founded in the Second Age* by Elendil,* the realm of Gondor plays a significant part in the events chronicled in *The Lord of the Rings*.* At its founding it was the south kingdom in Middle-earth, the north kingdom being Arnor,* of which only ruins remained in Frodo's* day.

**Gordon, E.V.** A Canadian, who had been a Rhodes Scholar at Oxford,* he was appointed to teach in the English Department at Leeds University soon after Tolkien. The two men became firm friends, and were soon collaborating on a major piece of scholarship. It was a new edition of a favourite Middle English poem of Tolkien's, *Sir Gawain and the Green Knight*.* Further projects came to nothing, with Tolkien moving to Oxford and Gordon eventually moving to Manchester University. In 1938 he died suddenly, at the age of forty-two, and Tolkien lost a friend and much needed collaborator.

**Green-elves** In *The Silmarillion*,* Elves* who remained in Ossiriand to the east of Beleriand.* They were skilled woodmen who lived secretly. The Green-elves tended to wear green and loved to sing. The bow was their favoured weapon.

**Grey-elves** *See* SINDAR.

**Grey Havens**    A town and harbour founded by Círdan★
after the destruction of Beleriand.★ Those leaving Middle-
earth★ for the Uttermost West sailed from there, like Bilbo★
and Frodo★ in *The Lord of the Rings*.★
**Gríma**    *See* WORMTONGUE.

# H

**Hador**  In *The Silmarillion*,★ the greatest Chieftain among Men in the First Age.★ He was given the dominion of Dor-lómin,★ gathering together the Third House★ of the Edain.★

**Haladin**  In *The Silmarillion*,★ the second group of humans to enter Beleriand.★ They lived in the Forest of Brethil. They were granted habitation there by King Thingol★ of Doriath★ in return for guarding the region, especially the Crossings of Teiglin. Túrin★ Turambar dwelt with them for a time, becoming their leader.

**Haleth**  In *The Silmarillion*,★ she was the first chief of the Haladin,★ leading them to Brethil to settle. Haleth was a renowned Amazon, who had a select bodyguard of women.
  *See also* GALADRIEL.

**Halflings**  *See* HOBBITS.

**Halimath**  The ninth month in the Reckoning of the Shire.★ It is approximately September. It is from the Old English *halig-monath*, holy month—the month of sacrifice.

**Hallow of Eru**  The sole temple in Númenor,★ to be found on the top of Meneltarma. It had no roof. As devotion to Ilúvatar★ (Eru) declined, worship at the Hallow was neglected. Ar-Pharazôn finally banned it altogether. After the overwhelming of Númenor by the sea it was thought that the Hallow rose above the waves.

The Hallow is a rare reference to religious practice in Tolkien's Middle-earth (*see* CHRISTIANITY, TOLKIEN AND).

**Halls of Mandos (Houses of the Dead)** In *The Silmarillion*,★ a waiting place for the spirits of Elves★ and Men after death. Lúthien, in the tale of Beren and Lúthien the Elf-maiden,★ came here to plead for her lover, Beren. The Halls of Mandos are situated on the far western shores of Aman.★

**Haradrim** In Middle-earth,★ the people of Harad (meaning 'the South'), the area south of Mordor.★ They fought for Sauron★ during the War of the Ring,★ some of their number using elephants in battle. They have some similarity to the Calormenes in C.S. Lewis' *The Chronicles of Narnia*.

**Harfoots** The most numerous of the three branches of hobbits.★ They were the first to migrate over the Misty Mountains★ from the River Anduin★ region. They persisted with the custom of living underground longer than the other types of hobbit.

**Havard, R.E. 'Humphrey' (1901–85)** Affectionately known as the 'Useless Quack', he was the doctor of Tolkien and C.S. Lewis,★ and a member of The Inklings.★ The son of an Anglican clergyman, 'Humphrey' Havard was received into the Roman Catholic Church when aged thirty. He studied medicine after reading Chemistry and became a doctor. In 1934 he took over a medical practice in Oxford★ with surgeries in Headington and St Giles (near the Eagle and Child public house, haunt of The Inklings).

**Healing** As a counter to the ever-present effects of evil★ and the fall★ in Tolkien's fiction is the persistence of this theme. Healing powers are often a quality of gifted people, whether Maiar,★ Elves★ or mankind—such as Melian,★ Gandalf,★ Lúthien,★ Beleg (in the tale of Túrin★ Turambar), or Aragorn.★ It is also a property of certain places such as the Pools of Ivrin, Lórien★ or Fangorn Forest.★ Healing can also be instituted as an expression of care, as in the Houses of Healing in Minas Tirith.*

When Beren* was grey and exhausted by his journey to Doriath* across the Nan Dungortheb* the sight of Lúthien's beauty, and her singing, brought healing to him—the power of romantic love.

> Enchantment healed his weary feet
>    That over hills were doomed to roam;
> And forth he hastened, strong and fleet,
>    And grasped at moonbeams glistening.
> (*The Fellowship of the Ring*, Bk One, ch. 11)

Lúthien's healing powers are often exercised (*see* BEREN AND LÚTHIEN THE ELF-MAIDEN, THE TALE OF), as when she healed Beren of the evil wound he received from Carcharoth.* Her greatest healing deed was when, by her sacrifice,* she brought Beren back from the dead.

One of the principal healers in *The Lord of the Rings** is the future king, Aragorn. The power of healing was part of his true kingship, a kingship that was Christ-like (*see* CHRISTIANITY, TOLKIEN AND). One of his ancient names was *Envinyatar*, the Renewer. His healing hands are laid on Faramir,* the Lady Éowyn* and the hobbit* Merry. The healing process took great skill and persistence. In this restoration an old prophecy was fulfilled:

> Life to the dying
> In the king's hand lying!

**Helcaraxë** The strait separating Aman* from Middle-earth* in *The Silmarillion** before the great change in the world after the destruction of Númenor.* Many of the Elves* returning to Middle-earth crossed here after the theft of the Silmarils by Morgoth.*

It was also referred to as 'the Grinding Ice'.

**The hero** Modern fiction tends to concern itself with the anti-hero rather than the hero, as traditionally understood.

Tolkien's choice of fantasy however, and in particular heroic romance such as *The Lord of the Rings*,★ allows a use of the hero. Traditional heroes are expected by the reader, as part of the genre.

Tolkien, however, knew his readership, and knew that he could not write like the author of *The Odyssey*, *Morte d'Arthur*, or *Beowulf*. The original audience for these works believed that evil★ could be dealt with by a superhero. A hero like that today would be an unconvincing picture-strip hero like Indiana Jones or James Bond, where believability depends on motion.

Tolkien's concept of heroism deserves careful study. He has been able (for those who can enter his imaginary world) to create convincing heroes that are more biblical than superhuman. In Tolkien's Middle-earth,★ ultimately the meek inherit the world. C.S. Lewis puts his finger on the main characteristic of heroism in Tolkien's mythology, that apparent foolishness is the method of providence,★ that imagination wins over brute strength. The model of heroism is a God who becomes a humble carpenter. In his review of *The Fellowship of the Ring*, Lewis observed:

> Almost the central theme of the book is the contrast between the Hobbits (or 'the Shire') and the appalling destiny to which some of them are called, the terrifying discovery that the humdrum happiness of the Shire, which they had taken for granted as something normal, is in reality a sort of local and temporal accident, that its existence depends on being protected by powers which Hobbits dare not imagine, that any Hobbit may find himself forced out of the Shire and caught up in that high conflict. More strangely still, the event of that conflict between strongest things may come to depend on him, who is almost the weakest.

Sam the hobbit is the 'real hero' (as Tolkien calls him) of

*The Lord of the Rings*. In a letter to his son, Christopher, in 1944, Tolkien wrote that certainly 'Sam is the most closely drawn character, the successor to Bilbo of the first book, the genuine hobbit. Frodo is not so interesting, because he has to be highminded, and has (as it were) a vocation.'

In both *The Hobbit* and *The Lord of the Rings*, the ways of providence, often managed and interpreted by Gandalf, are to use unheroic, humble figures like Bilbo, Frodo, Sam and Merry, in a heroic manner. The world is to be saved by humble, ordinary people, not the mighty, powerful and wise. But there are 'heroic' heroes as well, with qualities that redefine greatness. Aragorn★ is a figure who can stand with the great heroes of legend. Yet he is marked by gentleness, humility and a gift of healing.★ Though the setting is pre-Christian, he is a Christian hero and king. In him high qualities more often than not associated with the Elves★ are softened and humanised.

Significantly, Tolkien's heroes are not autonomous and individualistic. (Where they are, as in Túrin,★ this is accounted a tragic flaw.) They are helped by providence, and by Gandalf the wizard; Frodo is helped by Sam; Beren by Lúthien. The virtue of healing, redressing the effects of the fall★ and thus striking a blow against the enemy, is a constant theme in the tales of Middle-earth. One can think of the healing hands of Melian, Aragorn, Gandalf, Lúthien and many others.

Aragorn combines many heroic qualities. He is a Christ-like true king, whose return is heralded in ancient prophecy. He is healer, guardian (as Ranger★) and wise man as well as warrior, whose command even the dead acknowledge. That he is more than just a good king can be seen by contrast with Théoden. Théoden gives leadership in battle, and expresses love and fatherliness to his warriors. But Aragorn excells him by being primarily a healer.

Stewardship is also a heroic quality valued in Tolkien's world. So is sacrifice.★ Aragorn and the free defenders of

Minas Tirith★ are willing to sacrifice their lives in hopeless battle to distract Sauron's attention from Frodo, the Ring-bearer, and Sam. Frodo and Sam are willing to give their lives to destroy the Ring.★ Lúthien and Arwen are willing to renounce natural immortality for love of humans, sharing their fate beyond death.

Servanthood and loyalty are also heroic qualities. Aragorn for years serves the hobbits as unappreciated guardian, with other Rangers. Sam serves Frodo, helping him achieve his task. Another aspect of the hero in Tolkien, helpfully set out by Jane Chance Nitzsche, is the 'Elf-knight' as a figure of Christ. Tolkien, Nitzsche demonstrates, takes his symbolism here from Edmund Spenser's *The Faerie Queene*, and from the imagery of Christ as knight in *The Ancrene Wisse*. Here knights or heroes have an Elven quality★ of goodness. For Tolkien, the Elves symbolise the higher, desirable side of human nature, and he felt that he was picking up this tradition from Spenser and the author of the *Ancrene Wisse*.

The later idea of Elves and fairies as dainty, diminutive figures Tolkien regarded with distaste as being degenerate. It led to George MacDonald's★ fantasies eventually falling into disfavour with Tolkien, even though his debt to the Scotsman is great. MacDonald, for example, represents elvishness through the recurring figure of the wise woman, or great-great-grandmother. For him, as for Tolkien, this Elvish quality represented what is noble in human nature. As with Tolkien, the greatness of this quality is often feminine. For MacDonald's wise woman there are Tolkien's Galadriel★ and Lúthien. On the even higher level of the Valar★ and the Maiar★ there are Varda★ (Elbereth) and Queen Melian.★

According to Jane Nitzsche, in Tolkien, the Christian symbolism of the faerie hero or faerie king comes strongly in his story *Smith of Wootton Major*.★ She again finds Tolkien's inspiration in the *Ancrene Wisse*. She writes of Smith in Tolkien's story:

Here suffering is valuable because God may reward it—may 'turn towards it with His grace, and make the heart pure and clear-sighted, and this no one may achieve who is tainted with vices or with an earthly love of worldly things, for this taint affects the eyes of the heart so badly that it cannot recognize God or rejoice in the sight of him' . . . This quotation from 'Love', the seventh section of the Ancrene Wisse, beautifully summarises the pure spiritual condition of the child Smith. Because free of vice and filled with charity he is 'graced' with the gift of the star, his passport into the other world of Faerie, but one which simultaneously endows him with a recovery of insight and perception because of his visits to the other world. And the love of Smith for his family and for his fellow man and ultimately for God stems from a pure heart: 'A pure heart, as St. Bernard says, effects two things: it makes you do all that you do either for the love of God alone, or for the good of others for His sake' . . . an Augustinian pronouncement springing from the pages of the Ancrene Wisse (*Tolkien's Art*, page 67).

The faery king in disguise—Alf (=Elf)—serves as a humble apprentice to the graceless Nokes, and thus is able to pass the star of inheritance to the worthy Smith. Thereafter Smith has an Elven quality.

**Further reading**

Jane Chance Nitzsche, *Tolkien's Art* (1979); C.S. Lewis, *Of This and Other Worlds* (1982).

**High Elves**   In *The Silmarillion*,⋆ the name given to Elves of Aman⋆ and to Elves who dwelt at some time there.

**History of Middle-earth**   Strictly, Middle-earth is only part of the world, or Eä. Before the change in the world, after the destruction of Númenor,★ the Undying Lands of the West, including Valinor,★ were physically part of the world. The history of Elves and humans incorporates events in Valinor. The history can be divided into many Ages (see AGES OF MIDDLE-EARTH).

Much of Tolkien's invention concerned the history, annals, languages, chronology and geography of Middle-earth. He was concerned to make an inwardly consistent sub-creation.★ There were a number of major tales which stood (or were intended to stand) independently of the history, with that history as an imaginatively appealing backdrop. The tales were those of Beren and Lúthien the Elf-maiden,★ Túrin Turambar,★ Tuor and the Fall of Gondolin,★ the Voyage of Eärendil★ the Mariner, *The Hobbit*★ and *The Lord of the Rings*.★

Tolkien may of course have intended to create others. Tolkien also invented a beautiful cosmological myth, portraying events before the creation of the world (see *AINULINDALË*).

**History of Middle-earth**   The title of a series of volumes of unfinished or preliminary material edited and published after Tolkien's death by his son, Christopher, who also provides a detailed commentary. The volumes are *The Book of Lost Tales*,★ *The Lays of Beleriand*,★ *The Shaping of Middle-earth*,★ *The Lost Road*★ and the four books of *The History of The Lord of the Rings*.★

**History of The Lord of the Rings**   A series of four books, part of *History of Middle-earth*,★ which collects early drafts of *The Lord of the Rings*.★ The books are *The Return of the Shadow*,★ *The Treason of Isengard*,★ *The War of the Ring*★ and *Sauron Defeated*.★

**Hithlum**   In *The Silmarillion*,★ the region to the north-west of Beleriand,★ to the south of which was Dor-lómin★ (associated with Túrin★ Turambar). The name, which is Sindarin,★ means 'Land of Mist'.

***The Hobbit*** **(1937)**   This children's story belongs to the
Third Age★ of Middle-earth, and chronologically precedes
*The Lord of the Rings.*★

   Mr Bilbo Baggins,★ then a peace-loving middle-aged
hobbit,★ is the hero of this tale, the bare bones of which are
as follows: a party of Dwarves,★ thirteen in number, are on
a quest★ for their long lost treasure, which is jealously
guarded by a dragon.★ Their leader is the great Thorin★
Oakenshield. They employ Bilbo Baggins as their burglar
to steal it, at the recommendation of the wizard★ Gandalf★
the Grey. The reluctant Mr Baggins would rather spend a
quiet day with his pipe and pot of tea in his comfortable
hobbit-hole than partake in any unrespectable adventure.

   The Dwarves become increasingly thankful for the fact
that they employed him, despite initial misgivings, as he
gets them out of many scrapes. He seems to have extraordinary luck, but there is an underlying sense of providence★
at work in events.

   After near disaster with three trolls,★ the party find
refreshment at The Last Homely House at Rivendell,★ kept
by Elves★ under the leadership of Elrond★ Half-elven. They
continue further up the slopes of the Orc★ infested Misty
Mountains.★ Sheltering from a thunder battle between
giants in a seemingly deserted cave they are suddenly
overwhelmed by the goblin hordes, with the exception of
the quick-witted Gandalf. The wizard rescues them as they
are brought before the fat goblin chief. As they make their
escape, Bilbo is knocked unconscious and left behind in the
darkness.

   Reviving, Bilbo discovers a Ring★ lying beside him in the
tunnel. It is the ruling Ring that forms the subject of *The
Lord of the Rings*, but Bilbo is to discover only its magical
property of invisibility at this stage. After putting the Ring
in his pocket, Bilbo stumbles along the black tunnel.
Eventually, he comes across a subterranean lake where
Gollum★ dwells, a large-eyed corruption of a Stoor★

hobbit, his life preserved over centuries by the Ring he has now lost for the first time.

After a battle of riddles, Bilbo escapes, seemingly by luck, by slipping on the Ring. Following the vengeful Gollum, who cannot see him, he finds his way out of the mountains on the other side.

Reunited with Gandalf and the Dwarves, Bilbo sets off with them on the next stage of their journey: across the forbidding forest of Mirkwood.★ They are almost burned alive by Orcs, only to be rescued by eagles,★ who whisk them aloft to safety high in the mountains. After rest and food, they are lifted on their way, and soon encounter Beorn,★ who can assume animal or human shape. His house is near the fringe of Mirkwood.

Beorn gives them provisions for their journey through the dangerous forest, and warns them not to leave the Elvish path that runs through it. At this point Gandalf leaves them for pressing 'business in the south' of Mirkwood. The power of the Necromancer—revealed in *The Lord of the Rings* as Sauron★—is growing. He tells them that they have no cause to worry while they have the resourceful Mr Baggins with them. As so often, Gandalf interprets the underlying pattern of providence in the world of Middle-earth.★

After a long, dark and cheerless journey★ through the evil-ridden growths of Mirkwood, the party is enchanted off the path by the sight of mysterious lights. They desperately hope for food for their shrunken stomachs. Thorin is taken by the Wood-elves. The remainder, except Bilbo, are captured and cocooned by hideous and bloated spiders. The plucky hobbit rescues them, and rises in the esteem of the Dwarves, who had regarded him as an unlikely hero.★

By slipping on the Ring, Bilbo narrowly escapes capture by the Wood-elves, who are suspicious of the trespassers in their part of the forest. The Elves are ruled by Thranduil,★

father of Legolas★ (who doesn't appear in this story). Bilbo trails the Elves and their prisoners to their stronghold built into a rocky hill. The hobbit's resourcefulness is tested to the full in rescuing them.

After a cramped and foodless journey (for the Dwarves) in empty barrels down a river, and (for Bilbo) a cold, wet, virtually foodless journey on a barrel, the party arrives at Lake-town, or Esgaroth,★ on the Long Lake, south of the Lonely Mountain where Smaug★ the dragon dwelt, jealously guarding his hoard of lost treasure.

Reaching the Lonely Mountain Bilbo and the Dwarves search fruitlessly for the secret back door into the dragon's lair. With the help of their map, and apparent luck, the door is discovered. The reluctant hobbit is despatched down the dark tunnel. A little afterwards, a white-faced Bilbo reappears, clutching a stolen trophy. He urges the Dwarves to enter the comparative safety of the tunnel before the vengeful dragon can blast fire and destruction on that part of the mountain.

Bilbo, invisible now wearing the Ring, ventures once more to the dragon's hoard. The dragon awakes and there ensues a conversation between the two which, like the earlier riddles with Gollum, requires all Bilbo's quick wits. He escapes with singed ankles and head to tell the Dwarves that the dragon is out to destroy them. After blasting the mountainside, Smaug wings off to devastate Lake-town. Here, a well-aimed arrow from Bard the Bowman pierced the dragon in his only vulnerable spot—a weakness discovered by Bilbo and passed on to Bard by a messenger bird.

In Smaug's absence, Bilbo and the Dwarves are able to cross his lair and emerge from the mountain by the main entrance. To the dismay of the Dwarves, both the Wood-elves and the Men of Lake-town make a claim to a share in the treasure. Bilbo desperately tries to mediate as battle threatens.

Just as all looks at its worst, the sky darkens with evil birds, foreshadowing the arrival of a great army of goblins and wolves. Against this common enemy the Dwarves are reunited with Men and Elves. Thus begins the 'Battle of Five Armies', in which the forces of evil are dominant. At the moment when all seems lost, the noble eagles—symbols of providence—intervene and save the day.

Bilbo and Gandalf—who returned before the battle—journey back to the peaceful Shire. Bilbo has refused most of his share of the treasure, having seen the results of greed. The events have changed him for ever, but even more, the Ring he secretly possesses will shape the events recorded in *The Lord of the Rings*.

Significant information about the background to 'The quest of Erebor' (the events of *The Hobbit*) is found in *Unfinished Tales*.★ There we learn of the reluctance of the Dwarves to take along a hobbit, the great persuasion Gandalf had to muster for Thorin, and the part that providence played in the unfolding of events.

**Hobbitish**   In *The Lord of the Rings*,★ a dialect of Westron★ (or Common Speech) belonging to hobbits★ settled in the Shire.★ It has many resemblances to the speech of Men of the Anduin★ region, to which the people of Rohan★ were related. Tolkien revealed dialect differences in the style of English into which he 'translated' them. Ideally, some would have been represented in Old English.

**Hobbiton**   A village in the Shire★ made famous by events recounted in *The Lord of the Rings*.★ Hobbiton was the home of Bilbo★ and Frodo★ Baggins, as well as Sam Gamgee.★ Its features such as Bagshot Row, the Mill and The Ivy Bush pub are part of its homeliness.★

**Hobbits**   Many people have been acquainted with hobbits through J.R.R. Tolkien's children's story, *The Hobbit*.★ The title of that book refers to its hero,★ Mr Bilbo Baggins.★ A critic in the *New Statesman* remarked of Tolkien: 'It is a triumph that the genus *Hobbit*, which he himself has invented, rings just as real as the time-hallowed genera of Goblin, Troll, and Elf.'

C.S. Lewis believed that the hobbits 'are perhaps a myth that only an Englishman (or, should we add, a Dutchman?) could have created'. Instead of a creation of character as we find it in novels, much of what we know of Bilbo, Frodo, Sam and other hobbits we know because we know them in character as hobbits, as we know Gandalf★ in character as a wizard★ or Treebeard in character as an Ent.★ Tolkien sustains the character of these different races with great skill.

Bilbo's house was a typical dwelling place of a wealthy hobbit. It was not a worm-filled, dirty, damp hole, but a comfortable, many-roomed underground home. Its hall, which connected all the rooms, had 'panelled walls, and floors tiled and carpeted, provided with polished chairs, and lots and lots of pegs for hats and coats—the hobbit was fond of visitors.' Hobbits generally liked to be thought respectable, not having adventures or behaving in an unexpected way.

At the time of *The Hobbit* and *The Lord of the Rings* in the Third Age★ hobbits mainly lived in the Shire,★ but they had migrated from the East, from the other side of the Misty Mountains★ in the Vale of Anduin.★ Originally, they were closely related to mankind, created in the First Age.★ Gollum★ was originally a Stoor★ hobbit of the Anduin region.

Hobbits such as Bilbo and Frodo and their contemporaries spoke hobbitish,★ a provincial form of Westron,★ the Common Speech. They were called a variety of names by other races, such as Halfling or, in Rohirric,★ *holbytla* ('hole-builder'). The term 'hobbit' is Tolkien's English equivalent for their name for themselves, *kuduk*.

Hobbits are a little people, about half the height of mankind, and even smaller than the bearded Dwarves. Male hobbits themselves have no beards (though Stoors have down on their faces) and are inclined to be rather fat in the stomach, but not as much as the Dwarves. They dress in bright colours (chiefly green and yellow) and wear no shoes—for, as Tolkien tells us, 'their feet grow natural leathery soles and thick warm brown hair like the stuff on their heads (which is curly)'. Also they have 'long clever brown fingers, good-natured faces, and laugh deep fruity laughs (especially after dinner, which they have twice a day when they can get it)'. Nowadays, one could be forgiven for thinking that the race is extinct. They are now much less numerous, and are able to hide quickly when a man comes blundering along. Hobbits recover quickly from falls or bruises, as well as having a fund of sayings that they consider wise. Some hobbits reveal a gift for lyrics and poetry, as evidenced in the collection gleaned from the Red Book of Westmarch,★ *The Adventures of Tom Bombadil.*★

Bilbo Baggins was undoubtedly one of the most scholarly of the hobbits, being a main contributer to the Red Book, which was composed by hobbits. In attributing this as his source for *The Hobbit* and *The Lord of the Rings*, Tolkien was able to account for the style and perspective of their narration. It also provided him with some kind of solution to the vexed question of the narrative framework of *The Silmarillion.*★ Attached to the Red Book were a number of other chronicles, including the three volumes of Bilbo's *Translations from the Elvish*, which, as translations, retained the high style which makes *The Silmarillion* so different a narrative from *The Hobbit* and *The Lord of the Rings*. One could imagine a hobbit chronicler treating a tale such as Beren and Lúthien★ in the humbler, homelier style of *The Lord of the Rings*, and creating a similar masterpiece. But, alas, no such chronicle survives.

**Homeliness**  *See* NATURE.

**Huan**  In *The Silmarillion,*★ the noble wolfhound of Valinor★ given to Celegorm★ by the Vala★ Oromë.★ He features in The Tale of Beren and Lúthien the Elf-maiden,★ killing the foul werewolf, Carcharoth. Huan had much of the nature of an Elf,★ being ageless and tireless. Three times he was allowed to speak.

**Húrin**   In *The Silmarillion*,★ the father of the tragic Túrin★ and Nienor. Captured by Morgoth,★ he was set upon Thangorodrim for many years to view the outworkings of Morgoth's curse on his family. What he saw was twisted by the malice and deceit of the enemy of Elves★ and Men. After his release he unintentionally gave Morgoth a clue as to the whereabouts of the hidden kingdom of Gondolin.★ Húrin recovered the blessed Nauglamír,★ which he brought to King Thingol★ in Doriath★ where Queen Melian★ exerted her healing★ power to free him from Morgoth's deceits.

# I

**Idril** In *The Silmarillion*,★ the Elven daughter of King Turgon★ of Gondolin.★ In one of only three marriages of Elves★ and humans, she chose Tuor,★ one of the Edain.★ Their son was Eärendil.★ The family escaped from the fall of Gondolin to the Mouths of Sirion★ in Arvernien in the south of Beleriand.★ When Tuor became old, she sailed with him into the Uttermost West. The Line of Gondolin passed to their son, Eärendil.

**Illustrator, Tolkien as an** *See PICTURES* (1979).

**Ilúvatar** In *The Silmarillion*,★ the name of God, creator of the world, also called Eru, 'the One'. Ilúvatar means 'Father of All'. In the *Ainulindalë*★ is recorded how, when he created the angelic beings, he revealed to them the themes of creation in music. As his agents they helped to realise the vision in the making of the world.

Though superficially, God seems absent from the events of Middle-earth,★ in fact its history is the outworking of the themes of the music at the beginning of creation. Consequently, providence★ is a constant reality throughout the tales of Middle-earth. The presence of the will of Ilúvatar, the creator, emphasises Tolkien's idea of sub-creation.★ In reading the fiction, the reader is aware of the mind and will of the teller and maker of the tale (Tolkien). In making and telling stories, Tolkien believed, we exercise a God-given right to be a sub-creator. If done with skill and integrity, our creation parallels the primary world. It is part of 'the seamless web of story'. The human creator parallels the divine creator, though on a sub-scale.

In Tolkien's mythology, Elves and mankind are called 'the Children of Ilúvatar' as they were the special and direct creations of God, not the handiwork of the demiurgic angels. Their destiny had an element of mystery to it. The Elves were to be for ever tied up with the world, whereas the destiny of mortal man beyond death was to be greater.

These sorts of theological and philosophical themes constantly preoccupied Tolkien as he invented his mythology. They contributed to his inability to complete his work.

*See also* CHRISTIANITY, TOLKIEN AND; NATURAL THEOLOGY, TOLKIEN AND.

**Imagination** In Tolkien, imagination is an integrating concept affecting both his thought and fiction. The same is true of C.S. Lewis,★ his friend, and the nineteenth-century author, George MacDonald,★ whose ideas on the imagination anticipated those of Lewis and Tolkien. Laying the foundation for many of Tolkien's ideas was the romantic poet and thinker Samuel Taylor Coleridge.

1. Central to S.T. Coleridge's radical view of the imagination was the importance of metaphor, and 'the perception of similitude in dissimilitude'. At its best and most natural, imagination is expressed in language. Metaphor is imagination in action.

The mind, believed Coleridge, is active in making sense of the world. The mind imposes itself on reality, shaping it. Imagination has a central role, therefore, in knowledge, shaping and adapting it. The poet is the epitome of this process, using a 'synthetic and magical power' which Coleridge calls imagination.

The imagination is 'esemplastic', unifying and shaping. Its pattern, sharply revealed in poetry, is set out by Coleridge:

This power, first put into action by the will and understanding, and retained under their irremissive, though gentle and unnoticed control . . . reveals itself in the balance or reconcilement of opposite or discordant qualities: of sameness, with difference; of the general with the concrete; the idea with the image; the individual with the representative; the sense of novelty and freshness with old and familiar objects; a more than usual state of emotion with more than usual order; judgement ever awake and steady self-possession with enthusiasm and feeling profound or vehement; and while it blends and harmonizes the natural and the artificial, still subordinates art to nature; the manner to the matter; and our admiration of the poet to our sympathy with the poetry.

Like Tolkien, Coleridge tries to distinguish a primary and secondary imagination. The primary imagination is concerned with, and operates in, the primary or 'ordinary' world. The secondary imagination, employing language and metaphor, reworks and reshapes this primary or ordinary world. It captures the inscape, rather than visual surface, of reality. Tolkien sees the most exalted function of imagination as sub-creation* in linguistic form, creating, if successful, a secondary world.

2. Coleridge's thought is subtle and complex. Though not as good a thinker as Coleridge, George MacDonald explored the concept of the imagination in great depths, particularly in his essays, 'The imagination: its functions and its culture' (1867) and 'The fantastic imagination' (1882). His views remarkably foreshadow those of Tolkien and C.S. Lewis, and are worked out creatively in his fantasies. For example, in *The Princess and Curdie* (1882) he

creates a convincing secondary world. This can be seen especially in the city of Gwyntystorm, which has a distinct atmosphere, and in the varied country regions that lie between it and the ancient Queen's castle. It is also possible to map Fairy Land in *Phantastes*.

MacDonald does not tie imagination to language like Tolkien and Coleridge, but like Tolkien he sees the foundation for understanding it in the relationship between God and his creation. Though he does not use the word, MacDonald sees the product of human imagination as 'sub-creation'. 'The imagination of man is made in the image of the imagination of God. Everything of man must have been of God first.' MacDonald sees the human imagination as living and moving and having its being in the imagination of God.

The human being is not creative in a primary sense. 'Indeed, a man is rather *being thought* than *thinking*, when a new thought arises in his mind . . . He did not create it.' Even the forms by which a person reveals his thoughts are not created by him in a primary sense; they belong to nature.

MacDonald had a scientific training, and is remarkably modern in pointing out the importance of imagination in science. He also, like Lewis and Tolkien, values metaphor highly: 'All words . . . belonging to the inner world of the mind, are of the imagination, are originally poetic.' He claims that in both the arts and sciences, imagination is central to knowledge: 'We dare to claim for the true, childlike, humble imagination, such an inward oneness with the laws of the universe that it possesses in itself an insight into the very nature of things.'

A central function of the imagination (an idea developed by C.S. Lewis) is the making of meaning. This making is strictly subordinate to the primary meanings put into his created reality by God. However, in 'the new arrangement of thought and figure . . . the new meaning contained is presented as it never was before'. He writes:

Every new embodiment of a known truth must be a new and wider revelation. No man is capable of seeing for himself the whole of any truth: he needs it echoed back to him from every soul in the universe; and still its centre is hid in the Father of Lights.

He sees the operation of the imagination as choosing, gathering and vitally combining the material of a new revelation.

Such embodiments are not the result of the man's intention, or of the operation of his conscious nature. His feeling is that they are given to him; that from the vast unknown, where time and space are not, they suddenly appear in luminous writing upon the wall of his consciousness.

That there is always more to a work of art than the producer himself perceived while producing it, seemed to MacDonald a strong reason for 'attributing to it a larger origin than the man alone—for saying at the last, that the inspiration of the Almighty shaped its ends'. Somewhat similar ideas are found in Tolkien (*see* NATURAL THEOLOGY, TOLKIEN AND).

MacDonald's view of the imagination is squarely based on the view that all meanings are put into reality by their primary creator, God. All meaning refers to him, and thus is objective rather than subjective. He expresses this view eloquently in the following passage, anticipating Tolkien and C.S. Lewis:

One difference between God's work and man's is that while God's work cannot mean more than he meant, man's must mean more than he meant. For in everything that God has made, there is layer upon layer of ascending significance; also he expresses the same thought in higher and higher kinds of that thought: it is God's things, his embodied thoughts, which alone a man has to use, modified and adapted to his own purposes, for the

129

expression of his thoughts; therefore he cannot help his words and figures falling into such combinations in the mind of another as he had himself not foreseen, so many are the thoughts allied to every other thought, so many are the relations involved in every figure, so many the facts hinted in every symbol. A man may well himself discover truth in what he wrote; for he was dealing all the time with things that came from thoughts beyond his own.

3. Intuitively, MacDonald dwells upon the importance of meaning. The question of meaning (both of reality itself and of language) is central in the twentieth century. It is a key theme running throughout the writings of C.S. Lewis, who was influenced by the ideas of Tolkien, and had much in common with him (*see* INKLINGS, THE). For Lewis, meaning was intimately tied up both with the role of the imagination, and with the fact that the entire universe is a dependent creation of God. He saw reason as the organ of truth, and imagination as the organ of meaning. Reason and imagination each had their own integrity. He particularly stressed the dependence of even the most abstract of thinking upon imagination.

C.S. Lewis, like Tolkien, believed that in some tangible sense the products of imagination in the arts could be true. Myth★ could become fact. In writing fantasies like *The Chronicles of Narnia* and *The Hobbit*★ they felt that they were discovering inevitable realities that were not the product of theories of the conscious mind (even though rational control is not relinquished in the making of good fantasy). It was this attitude which prompted both men to create consistent secondary worlds, or sub-creations, like Middle-earth and Perelandra. Fiction, for C.S. Lewis, was the making of meaning. It reflects the greater creativity of God when he originated and put together his universe and ourselves. Meaning is at the core of real things and events.

Natural objects are not mere facts. Human beings are not merely personalities. Objects, events and people are real in so far as they are in relationship to other objects, events and persons, and ultimately in relationship to God. With persons, this relationship is more than that of an object to God its creator; it involves personal characteristics like choice. The complex web of relationships that is the hallmark of reality confers objects, events and people with meaning. In themselves, they do not mean: they refer elsewhere to their meaning.

The heart of Lewis' Christian view of meaning is captured by a Dutch Christian philosopher:

> Meaning is the mode of being of all that is created. This universal character of referring and expressing, which is proper to our entire created cosmos, stamps created reality as meaning, in accordance with its dependent non-self-sufficient nature. Meaning is the being of all that has been created and the nature even of our selfhood. It has a religious root and a divine origin (Herman Dooyeweerd).

A similar view seems to have been held by the brilliant thinker, Michael Polanyi, at least in equating meaning and being as a consequence of a theistic view of the universe.

It is on the relationship between concept and meaning, and thought and imagination, that C.S. Lewis makes his most distinctive contribution to understanding the imagination. He argues that good imagining is as vital as good thinking, and either is impoverished without the other.

C.S. Lewis set out some key ideas, which owed much to his friend Owen Barfield,★ in an essay in his book *Rehabilitations*:

> It must not be supposed that I am in any sense putting forward the imagination as the organ of truth. We are not talking of truth, but of meaning: meaning which is the

antecedent condition both of truth and falsehood, whose antithesis is not error but nonsense. . . . For me, reason is the natural organ of truth; but imagination is the organ of meaning. Imagination, producing new metaphors or revivifying old, is not the cause of truth, but its condition. It is, I confess, undeniable that such a view indirectly implies a kind of truth or rightness in the imagination itself . . . the truth we [win] by metaphor [can] not be greater than the truth of the metaphor itself; and . . . all our truth, or all but a few fragments, is won by metaphor. And thence, I confess, it does follow that if our thinking is ever true, then the metaphors by which we think must have been good metaphors. It does follow that if those original equations, between good and light, or evil and dark, between breath and soul and all the others, were from the beginning arbitrary and fanciful—if there is not, in fact, a kind of psycho-physical parallelism (or more) in the universe—then all our thinking is nonsensical. But we cannot, without contradiction, believe it to be nonsensical. And so, admittedly, the view I have taken has metaphysical implications. But so has every view.

There are a number of suggestive ideas here, many of which Lewis developed and refined in later years, leading to his definitive statement about literature, *An Experiment in Criticism*. Some of the basic ideas are as follows: (a) There is a distinction between reason and imagination as regards roles—reason is to do with theoretical truths, imagination is to do with meanings. (b) There are standards of correctness, or norms, for the imagination, held tacitly and universally by human beings. (c) Meaning is a condition of the framing of truth; poor meanings make for poor thoughts. (d) The framing of truths in propositions necessitates the employment of metaphors supplied by the imagination. Language and thought necessarily rely upon metaphor.

One of the most controversial and difficult points here is that meaning is somehow a condition of thought. It is a condition in a manner obviously different from the way the physical brain is. A footnote in Barfield's *Poetic Diction* sheds light on this, particularly if the term 'the imagination' is substituted for 'poet': 'Logical judgments, by their nature, can only render more explicit some one part of a truth already implicit in their terms. But the poet makes the terms themselves. He does not make judgments, therefore; he only makes them possible—and only he makes them possible.' Imagination is the maker of meaning, the definer of terms in a proposition, and as such is a condition of truth.

The place of metaphor in thinking was central to C.S. Lewis' beliefs. Like Tolkien, he had a high view of human language and the authority of the word. In his book *Miracles*, he points out that to speak of anything beyond the perceptions of our five senses, metaphorical expression is required, this is as true in the fields of psychology, economics, philosophy and politics as it is in the fields of religion and poetry. To speak of super-sensibles, he argues, is inevitably to talk

as if they could be seen or touched or heard (e.g. must talk of 'complexes' and 'repressions' as if desires could really be tied up in bundles or shoved back; of 'growth' and 'development' as if institutions could really grow like trees or unfold like flowers; of energy being 'released' as if it were an animal let out of a cage).

4. Tolkien's view of the imagination centres around his idea of 'sub-creation'. This is most clearly set out in a famous essay (*see* 'ON FAIRY-STORIES'), and reveals his affinity with the ideas of Coleridge, MacDonald and Lewis. There he speaks of creating secondary worlds with an 'inner consistency of reality', and of the relationship between works of imagination and truth. He also stresses the central importance of human language. It was typical of him to

write elsewhere in a similar vein: 'Language has both strengthened imagination and been freed by it.'

See also PHILOLOGY, J.R.R. TOLKIEN AND; STORY, THEOLOGY OF; ROMANTICISM; NATURAL THEOLOGY, TOLKIEN AND.

**Immortality** *See* DEATH.

**Imrahil** In *The Lord of the Rings*,★ Prince of Dol Amroth in southern Gondor.★ He played an important part in the War of the Ring.★ During Faramir's★ illness, after the suicide of the Steward Denethor,★ he ruled Minas Tirith.★

**'Imram'** A poem concerning the voyage of St Brendan. Tolkien altered the story to fit his invented mythology. The poem was intended to be part of the (unfinished) 'The Notion Club Papers',★ which was to feature time travel like *The Lost Road*.★ 'Imram' is Gaelic for 'voyage'. The poem mentions the Lost Road,★ a 'shoreless mountain' (Meneltarma) marking 'the foundered land' (Númenor★), a mysterious island (Tol Eressëa★) with a white Tree (Celeborn★), and a beautiful star (Eärendil★) marking the old road leading beyond the world.

'Imram' was published in *Time & Tide*, 3rd December 1955.

**Inklings, The** J.R.R. Tolkien was a central figure in The Inklings, a literary group of friends held together by the zest and enthusiasm of C.S. Lewis. Tolkien described it in a letter as an 'undetermined and unelected circle of friends who gathered around C.S.L[ewis]., and met in his rooms in Magdalen. . . . Our habit was to read aloud compositions of various kinds (and lengths!). . .'

As Tolkien's description suggests, there is a problem of definition. The group called The Inklings was so informal and casual, such a wide variety of writers passed through it, that very little common entity remains. However, along with Tolkien and Lewis, Charles Williams was a focal person. These three men were united in the defence of reason, romanticism★ and Christianity.★

Tolkien points out that 'The Inklings had no recorder and C.S. Lewis no Boswell'. However, glimpses of meetings can be seen in the letters of Tolkien* and Lewis, and in the diaries of Lewis' brother, Major Warren Hamilton Lewis. The preface of *Essays Presented to Charles Williams* is also informative.

There also exists a lively and vivid description of the group by someone who was once a member of it, but had gradually realised that the aims and sympathies of his life and writings were out of keeping with it. There is a convincing overlap between this 'outsider's' description of the group and the insights into The Inklings given by those heartily in favour of its aims, however informal.

The novelist and poet John Wain's description of the Oxford* group occurs in his autobiography *Sprightly Running*. He remembers that, though admiring Lewis and his friends tremendously, 'already it was clear that I did not share their basic attitudes. The group had a corporate mind, as all effective groups must. . .' He defined it like this: 'Politically conservative, not to say reactionary; in religion, Anglo- or Roman Catholic; in art, frankly hostile to any manifestation of the "modern spirit".'

He admits however that he would be giving quite a false picture of Lewis and his friends if he presented them as merely reactionary, as if they were putting all their energies into negatively being *against* things. This is far from the truth, he says. As he put it: 'This was a circle of instigators, almost of incendiaries, meeting to urge one another on in the task of redirecting the whole current of contemporary art and life.'

According to Wain, after Charles Williams' death in 1945, Tolkien and Lewis became the two most active members of the group. Wain writes: 'While Lewis attacked on a wide front, with broadcasts, popular-theological books, children's stories, romances, and controversial literary criticism, Tolkien concentrated on the writing of his colossal "Lord of the Rings" trilogy. His readings of each successive instalment were eagerly received, for "romance" was a pillar of this whole structure.' Writers admired by Tolkien and Lewis ('the literary household gods' of the group, Wain calls them) included George MacDonald,★ William Morris ('selectively') and E.R. Eddison. They all had in common the fact that they *invented*. According to Wain, 'Lewis considered "fine fabling" an essential part of literature, and never lost a chance to push any author, from Spenser to Rider Haggard, who would be called a romancer.' John Wain points out that during the time he was involved with The Inklings (around 1944 or 1945 to 1946), he was surprised by the 'unexpected alliances' it was capable of forming. (Wain tends to describe the group of friends in martial terms.) Yet he felt that the key to this unexpectedness lay in C.S. Lewis' character: 'Lewis . . . is basically a humble man. While he will fight long and hard for his beliefs, he is entirely free of the pride which refuses reinforcement for the sake of keeping within its hands the sole glory of conquer or, if need be, of heroic defeat.' The 'unexpected alliances' included Dorothy L. Sayers, the children's author Roger Lancelyn Green, and the right-wing poet Roy Campbell. Wain concludes: 'Lewis, during these years, had very much the mentality of a partisan leader: anyone who would skirmish against the enemy—the drab, unbelieving, sneering, blinkered modern world—should be his brother, be he ne'er so vile.'

C.S. Lewis himself gives an insight into The Inklings almost incidentally in his preface to *Essays Presented to Charles Williams*, to which Tolkien contributed. Lewis points out that three of the essays in the collection are on literature and, specifically, one aspect of literature, the 'narrative art'. That, Lewis says, is natural enough. Charles Williams' '*All Hallows Eve* and my own *Perelandra* (as well as Professor Tolkien's unfinished sequel to *The Hobbit*) had all been read aloud, each chapter as it was written. They owe a good deal to the hard-hitting criticism of the circle. The problems of narrative as such—seldom heard of in modern critical writings—were constantly before our minds.'

The Inklings embodied the ideals of life and pleasure of Tolkien and Lewis, especially Lewis, who spoke of good evenings full of 'the cut and parry of prolonged, fierce, masculine argument'. Both Tolkien and Lewis were club-able—Tolkien had been in the T.C.B.S.★ group of school friends and in The Kolbitar★ (along with Lewis) in previous years. The Inklings' most important years were the 1940s, especially the war years when Charles Williams was resident in Oxford.

The group was no mutual admiration society. They mainly felt deeply the truth of the poet Blake's aphorism: 'Opposition is true friendship.' Lewis himself was 'hungry for rational opposition'. His friend Professor John Lawlor thinks that to attack Lewis in this way was probably the first step towards friendship with him. Tolkien remembered how much Lewis felt at home in this kind of company. 'C.S.L. had a passion for hearing things read aloud, a power of memory for things received in that way, and also a facility in extempore criticism, none of which were shared (especially not the last) in anything like the same degree by his friends.'

Other members of the informal group included Lewis' brother (Major W.H. 'Warnie' Lewis), Owen Barfield★ (author of a key book, *Poetic Diction*) and Charles Williams. Charles Williams wrote poetry, novels, plays, literary criticism and thought-provoking theology. He powerfully influenced Lewis, though Tolkien was not so taken with him, while respecting him.

Tolkien occasionally refers to the group in his *Letters*.★ Writing approvingly to his publisher about Lewis' science-fiction story, *Out of the Silent Planet*, he speaks of it 'being read aloud to our local club (which goes in for reading

137

things short and long aloud). It proved an exciting serial, and was highly approved. But of course we are all rather like-minded.' It is clear from his letters that The Inklings provided valuable and much-needed encouragement as he struggled to compose *The Lord of the Rings*.

A letter written in 1944 to his son Christopher, away with the RAF in South Africa, is typical:

> Monday 22 May. . . . It was a wretched cold day yesterday (Sunday). I worked very hard at my chapter—it is most exhausting work; especially as the climax approaches and one has to keep the pitch up: no easy level will do; and there are all sorts of minor problems of plot and mechanism. I wrote and tore up and rewrote most of it a good many times; but I was rewarded this morning, as both C.S.L[ewis]. and C[harles]. W[illiams]. thought it an admirable performance, and the latest chapters the best so far. Gollum continues to develop into a most intriguing character . . .

Other members not so far mentioned, and chronicled in Humphrey Carpenter's authoritative study *The Inklings* (1978), were J.A.W. Bennett, Lord David Cecil, Nevill Coghill,* Commander Jim Dundas-Grant, Hugo Dyson,* Adam Fox, Colin Hardie, Dr 'Humphrey' Havard,* Gervase Mathew, R.B. McCallum, C.E. ('Tom') Stevens, Christopher Tolkien* and Charles Wrenn.

One of the favourite haunts of The Inklings was The Eagle and Child public house in St Giles (known more familiarly as The Bird and Baby). Many a discussion or friendly argument was washed down with beer.

W.H. Lewis, C.S. Lewis' brother, was sceptical of the idea of The Inklings representing a school of literature or theology. He is probably right to be so in view of the diversity of its members at one time or another. However, Lewis hankered for others who shared his core beliefs, and some of the main Inklings like Williams, Tolkien and even

Barfield did, though Barfield never became an orthodox Christian. Even though he was baptised into the Anglican Church he remained committed to anthroposophism.

Speaking in America, Owen Barfield tried to define The Inklings as an entity. He wondered if something was not happening to 'the Romantic Impulse' during its life. He could discern four important strands, each mainly identified with Lewis, Tolkien, Williams, or himself: (a) the yearning for the infinite and unattainable—Lewis' *sehnsucht* or joy;★ (b) in Barfield's own words, 'The conviction of the dignity of man and his part in the future history of the world conceived as a kind of progress towards increasing immanence of the divine in the human' (Barfield's own position); (c) the idealisation of love between the sexes, as in Charles Williams' thought and writings; and (d) the opposite of tragedy, the happy ending, Tolkien's idea of the *eucatastrophe*.

**Further reading**

Humphrey Carpenter, *The Inklings: C.S. Lewis, J.R.R. Tolkien, Charles Williams and their friends* (1978); John Wain, *Sprightly Running: Part of an Autobiography* (1962); Rand Kuhl, 'Owen Barfield in Southern California', *Mythlore*, Vol. 1, No. 4, 1969.

**Isengard** In *The Lord of the Rings*,★ the stronghold of the wizard★ Saruman.★ There a great tower, Orthanc, lay in the centre of a broad plain, which was surrounded by a natural circle of stone wall. The only gate into Isengard faced south. Isengard was built by men of Gondor★ in its golden age. Later, Saruman was given permission to dwell there, after which he fortified it, replacing grass and trees with stone and technology (*see* POSSESSION). Secretly, Orcs★ and wolves were brought there to bolster Saruman's increasing power and desire for domination. His stronghold was destroyed by Ents★ led by Fangorn at the time of the War of the Ring.★

**Isildur**   A Dúnadan★ of Númenor★ referred to in *The Lord of the Rings*★ on account of his cutting the One Ring★ from Sauron's hand, and then losing it in the River Anduin★ while fleeing from Orcs★ who killed him. The lost Ring was eventually found by Gollum's★ cousin, whom Gollum murdered for it.

Isildur was the older son of Elendil,★ the leader of the faithful in Númenor. He bravely stole a fruit of the threatened Tree Nimloth★ and thus preserved the line of the White Tree when he escaped the drowning of the great island. He helped to found the Númenórean realms in exile, Gondor★ and Arnor.★

**Istari**   *See* WIZARDS.

**Ithilien**   In *The Lord of the Rings*,★ an area of Gondor between the River Anduin★ and the western mountain range of Mordor, the Mountains of Shadow. Here the Ring-bearer, Frodo,★ with Sam and Gollum,★ encountered Faramir.★ Because the influence of Sauron★ had not been long in the region, it still retained its beauty at the time of the War of the Ring.★

**Ivrin**   In *The Silmarillion*,★ a lake at the source of the River Narog, to the north of Beleriand.★ There were beautiful falls here. Ulmo★ the Valar★ guarded the purity of the water. However, the area was polluted and desecrated by Glaurung★ as the dragon★ moved south to ravish Nargothrond.★

# J

**Journey**  *See* THE ROAD; QUEST.

**Joy**  Tolkien refers to the quality of joy in his essay 'On Fairy-Stories'.★ It is a key feature of such stories, he believes, related to the happy ending, or *eucatastrophe,* part of the consolation★ they endow. Tolkien believes that joy in the story marks the presence of grace from the primary world. 'It denies (in the face of much evidence, if you will) universal final defeat and in so far is *evangelium,* giving a fleeting glimpse of Joy, Joy beyond the walls of the world, poignant as grief.' He adds: 'In such stories when the sudden "turn" comes we get a piercing glimpse of joy, and heart's desire, that for a moment passes outside the frame, rends indeed the very web of story, and lets a gleam come through.'

In an epilogue to the essay, Tolkien gives more consideration to the quality of joy, linking it to the gospel narratives, which have all the qualities of an other-worldly fairy-story, while at the same time being primary world history. This doubleness intensifies the quality of joy, identifying its objective source.

Tolkien's friend, C.S. Lewis, explored the quality of joy, both in his quest, which led to his Christian conversion, and in his writings. The two men were very much at one in seeking to define and embody this quality, so Lewis' view deserves some mention.

Joy, thought Lewis, inspired the creation of fantasy. The creation of another world is an attempt to reconcile human beings and the real world. It tries to embody the fulfilment of imaginative longing. Imaginative worlds, wonderlands, are 'regions of the spirit'. Such worlds of the numinous★ may be found within science fiction, poetry, fairy-stories, novels, myths, even within a phrase or sentence. Lewis claimed in *Of Other Worlds*: 'To construct plausible and moving "other worlds" you must draw on the only real "other world" we know, that of the spirit.'

In a dissertation, *The Dialectic of Desire*, Corbin Carnell explored the theme of joy in Lewis' work. He argued that Lewis illuminates a state of mind which has been a recurrent theme in literature. This is the compulsive quest★ 'which brings with it both fleeting joy and the sad realization that one is yet separated from what is desired'. Joy, for C.S. Lewis, is the key both to the nature of human beings and their Creator (whom Lewis called 'the glad creator').

C.S. Lewis saw this unquenchable longing as a sure sign that no part of the created world, and thus no aspect of human experience, is capable of fulfilling fallen humankind. We are dominated by a homelessness, and yet by a keen sense of what home means.

For Lewis, joy is a foretaste of ultimate reality, heaven itself, or, the same thing, our world or home as it was meant to be, unspoiled by the fall★ of humankind, and one day to be remade. 'Joy,' wrote C.S. Lewis, 'is the serious business of Heaven.'

In Tolkien, there is not only the quality of joy linked to the sudden turn in the story, the sense of *eucatastrophe*, but also this joy as inconsolable longing in Lewis' sense. Dominating the entire cycle of his tales of Middle-earth★ is a longing to obtain the Undying Lands of the Uttermost West. The longing is often symbolised by a longing for the sea, which lay to the west of Middle-earth, and over which lay Valinor,★ even if by a hidden road.

Such longing is sharply portrayed in Galadriel, who, since the rebellion of the Noldor,★ had been forbidden to return to the West from Middle-earth. Her longing is poignantly captured in her song (*see* GALADRIEL). Though a Wood-elf, Legolas★ grows to long for the sea and the West. In *The Silmarillion*, Turgon★ of Gondolin★ instructs mariners to seek a way to the West in the hope that the Valar,★ the lords of the West, might help him. One of them, Voronwë, is gripped by the longing of his people and, in the purposes of providence,★ leads Tuor★ to Gondolin. On a more homely level, Sam is gripped with longing for all things Elvish★ before he is chosen to aid Frodo★ in the quest to destroy the One Ring.★

# K

**Khazad–dûm**  Also called Moria, the greatest of the Dwarf realms, carved under the Misty Mountains★ in the First Age.★ It consisted of many vast halls on various levels. In the Second Age★ a connecting tunnel was made to Eregion.★ *The Lord of the Rings*★ records how the Company of the Ring★ disturbed a Balrog★ deep underneath Khazaddûm. Gandalf★ sacrificed his life fighting the monster.

**Kíli**  In *The Hobbit*,★ a member of the company of Dwarves★ for which Bilbo Baggins★ was the official burglar. He was nephew of Thorin★ Oakenshield and, with his brother Fíli, died defending Thorin's body during the great Battle of the Five Armies.

Tolkien obtained his name from the Poetic Edda (*see* THE KOLBITAR).

**Kinslaying**  In *The Silmarillion*,★ the slaying of the Elves★ of Alqualondë★ by the Noldor,★ led by the rebellious Fëanor.★ They refused to give ships to the Noldor to return to Middle-earth. One consequence of the Kinslaying was the alienation of Thingol★ and Doriath★ from the family of Fëanor.

*See also* DOOM OF MANDOS.

**The Kolbitar**  An informal reading club initiated by Tolkien soon after he became a Professor at Oxford★ to explore Icelandic literature such as the Poetic Edda. The name

144

meant those who crowd so close to the fire in winter that they seem to 'bite the coal'. C.S. Lewis★ attended meetings, as did Nevill Coghill.★ It predated The Inklings.★

**Kortirion**   *See* WARWICK.

# L

**Lamps of the Valar**  In *The Silmarillion*,⋆ two great globes set on top of great pillars of stone in the North and South of Middle-earth by the Valar⋆ to light the world. The malicious destruction of the Lamps by Morgoth⋆ (Melkor) marked the end of the spring of the world.

   *See also* LIGHT.

**Last Battle, The**  In Tolkien's mythology, the final conflict against evil at the end of the world; an end which will mark a new beginning.

   *See also* APOCALYPTIC, TOLKIEN AND.

**Laurelin**  In *The Silmarillion*,⋆ one of the Two Trees⋆ of Valinor.⋆ She was also called the Golden Tree, and her name means 'the song of gold' in Elvish.⋆ Her light-green leaves were edged with gold, her flowers were dazzling yellow and her dew seemed like a golden rain.

***The Lays of Beleriand***  This is the third volume of *The History of Middle-earth*, edited by Christopher Tolkien⋆ from his father's unfinished writings. It mainly consists of substantial unfinished narrative poems, one telling the story of Túrin Turambar,⋆ and the other the tale of Beren and Lúthien.⋆ These are two of what Tolkien regarded as the four narratives that stood independently of the complex annals of the First Age⋆ of Middle-earth. (The others were the tale of Tuor★ and the Fall of Gondolin,★ and the story of Eärendil the mariner.★

The Túrin poem, entitled 'The Lay of the Children of Húrin', consists of two versions, both unfinished. It was a bold experiment in alliterative verse, which Tolkien confessed he wrote 'with pleasure'. Unlike the summary tale published in *The Silmarillion*★ it has vividness and what C.S. Lewis elsewhere called 'realism of presentation'. The poem is early, begun around 1918, so some names differ from the final *The Silmarillion*. Gwindor for instance is called Flinding go-Fuilin.

It is valuable to read this poem in conjunction with the long prose version (alas, also incomplete) in *Unfinished Tales*. These, along with the summary in *The Silmarillion*, will help the reader to have a fuller enjoyment of one of Tolkien's greatest stories.

The Beren and Lúthien poem, entitled 'The Lay of Leithian' (meaning, 'release from bondage'), is also in two versions, the first much longer than 'The Lay of the Children of Húrin', and the other quite brief. It is written in octosyllabic couplets, a form Tolkien uses with great power and effectiveness. Tolkien abandoned the first version in 1931, returning to it in 1949 or 1950 and beginning the second version. At this time he still hoped that *The Silmarillion* might be published. As with the Túrin poem, this beautiful poem telling the love story of Beren and Lúthien and the quest★ for the Silmaril adds reality to the summary version in the published *The Silmarillion*.

C.S. Lewis,★ in the early days of his friendship with Tolkien, provided diplomatic and ingenious criticism of the unfinished poem. Lewis' commentary is reproduced as an appendix in this book. It was Lewis' encouragement that kept Tolkien writing *The Lord of the Rings* which otherwise might too have remained unfinished. A.N. Wilson vividly describes the development of friendship between Lewis and Tolkien in his biography *C.S. Lewis*, and speaks highly of

'The Lay of Leithian': 'Though at times the verse is technically imperfect, it is full of passages of quite stunning beauty; and the overall conception must make it, though unfinished, one of the most remarkable poems written in English in the twentieth century.'

**'The Lay of Leithian'** A long, unfinished poem telling the tale of Beren and Lúthien the Elf-maiden,★ published in *The Lays of Beleriand.*★

**'The Lay of Aotrou and Itroun' (1945)** A narrative poem published in the *Welsh Review* (Vol. 4, No. 4, December 1945). The title means 'Lord and Lady', and the poem was inspired by the Celtic legends of Brittany (which has close linguistic links with Wales). A childless Lord obtains a potion from a Corrigan, a fairy enchantress. Twins result, but in payment the Corrigan demands that he marries her. He refuses, and there is no happy ending. Sin has real consequences.

***Leaf by Niggle* (1945)** First published in January 1945 in *The Dublin Review*, this short allegory was republished in *Tree and Leaf.*★ The allegory, an unusual form for Tolkien, is also untypical in having autobiographical elements.

Niggle, a little man and artist, knew that he would one day have to make a journey. Many matters got in the way of his painting, such as the demands of his neighbour, Mr Parish, who had a lame leg. Niggle was soft-hearted and rather lazy.

Niggle was concerned to finish one painting in particular. This had started as an illustration of a leaf caught in the wind, then became a tree. Through gaps in the leaves and branches a forest and a whole world opened up. As the painting grew (with other, smaller paintings tacked on) Niggle had had to move it into a specially built shed on his potato plot.

Eventually Niggle fell ill after getting soaked in a storm while running an errand for Mr Parish. Then the dreaded Inspector visited to tell him that the time had come for him to set out on the journey.

Taking a train, his first stop (which seemed to last for a century) was at the Workhouse. Niggle had not brought any belongings. He worked very hard there on various chores. At last, one day, when he had been ordered to rest, he overheard two voices discussing his case. One of them spoke up for him. It was time for gentler treatment, he said.

Niggle was allowed to resume his journey in a small train which led him to the familiar world depicted on his painting of long ago, and to his tree, now complete. 'It's a gift!' he exclaimed. Niggle then walked towards the forest (which had tall mountains behind). He realised that there was unfinished work here, and that Parish could help him—his old neighbour knew a lot about plants, earth and trees. At this realisation he came across Parish, and the two of them worked busily together.

At last, Niggle felt that it was time to move on into the mountains. Parish wished to remain behind to await his wife. It turned out that the region they had worked in together was called Niggle's Country, much to their surprise. A guide led Niggle into the mountains.

Long before, back in the town near where Niggle and Parish had lived before the journey, a fragment of Niggle's painting had survived and been hung in the town museum, entitled simply 'Leaf by Niggle'. It depicted a spray of leaves with a glimpse of a mountain peak.

Niggle's Country became a popular place to send travellers as a holiday, for refreshment and convalescence, and as a splendid introduction to the mountains.

Tolkien's little story suggests the link between art and reality. Even in heaven there will be a place for the artist to add his or her own touch to the created world.

The allegorical element could be interpreted as follows, much as suggested by Tom Shippey in his *The Road to Middle-earth*:

The journey★ = death.
Niggle the painter = Tolkien the writer.

Painting leaves rather than trees = Tolkien's perfectionism, and ability to be easily distracted.

Niggle's leaf = *The Hobbit*.

Niggle's tree = *The Lord of the Rings* (and *The Silmarillion*).

The country that opens up = Middle-earth.★

Other pictures tacked on = poems and other works.

The neglected garden = Tolkien's professorial responsibilities.

Parish's excellent potatoes = 'proper' work.

The Workhouse = Purgatory.

Niggle = creative element in humans (*see* ELVEN QUALITY).

Parish = practical element in humans.

The mountains = heaven, and the resolution of Niggle's two sides 'art and life'.

Potatoes = scholarship.

Trees★ = fantasy.

This interpretation emphasises the autobiographical aspect of the story. The tale has equal applicability to the artist in general, however. In particular, there is a poignancy to the unfinished nature of Niggle's work. There are very few artists (or indeed other people) who can say at the end of their lives, 'It is finished.'

**Legolas**    In *The Lord of the Rings*,★ an Elf★ of the Woodland Realm, son of King Thranduil,★ who was a member of the Company of the Ring.★ His friendship with Gimli★ the Dwarf symbolised the resolution of an ancient animosity between the two races. When Legolas first saw the sea in southern Gondor★ it awoke a longing for the Elvenhome in the Uttermost West (*see* JOY). After the passing of Aragorn,★ Legolas and Gimli sailed together to the West on the Straight Road.★

Legolas and a number of the Woodland-Elves were notable for restoring the land of Ithilien,★ despoiled in the War of the Ring.★

**Lembas**    In Tolkien's Middle-earth,★ the waybread of the

Elves.★ In Sindarin★ Elvish this means 'journey-' or 'way-bread'; in Quenya★ it means 'life-bread'. Some readers have seen a sacramental echo in the function of lembas (*see* CHRISTIANITY, TOLKIEN AND). Many travellers were sustained by it, including Frodo★ and Sam in *The Lord of the Rings.*★

***The Letters of J.R.R. Tolkien* (1981)** This substantial 463-page book is a selection of Tolkien's letters from the mid-1930s (when he was in his mid-forties), as *The Hobbit*★ was being prepared for the press, to just before his death in 1973 at the age of eighty-one. Only eight letters come from the period before that. The collection was edited by Humphrey Carpenter, Tolkien's biographer, with the assistance of Christopher Tolkien,★ Tolkien's son, to whom a number of the letters are addressed. The letters greatly concern Tolkien's fictional works, including their development and inter-relationship. Much is also revealed of the life and personality of this remarkable and complex man. Far from mentally inhabiting an 'unreal' world of imagination,★ the letters unveil Tolkien's sharp observation and critique of the foibles of the modern age (*see* POSSESSION).

Much like his close friend C.S. Lewis,★ Tolkien probably would have been happy to be seen as a specimen or even relic of the almost lost age of 'Old Western Man'. Like Lewis, he was able successfully to look at, and write for, our modern age with command and pertinence. The letters constantly give clues to Tolkien's thought and worldview, unlike Lewis almost totally expressed in his fiction (but *see* 'ON FAIRY-STORIES'). His deep Christian faith is evident in the letters, where he in one place answers a child's letter (Letter 310) about 'the purpose of life' (*see* CHRISTIANITY, TOLKIEN AND).

As deep as his Christian insight is his love for language. He was a philologist★ by profession. His genius with language is nowhere more evident than in his creation of names for people and places in Middle-earth.★ Many of the letters concern his invented languages, including Elvish.★

Mainly since the cult popularity of Tolkien's fiction in the 1960s, numerous interpretations of his work have appeared in journals and books. These letters have embedded in them Tolkien's own interpretation of, and commentary on, his work. An author's own view of his or her work is not necessarily the final say, or the best, but because of the unique nature of Tolkien's invention, his comments provide a framework and standard for understanding his work. Without the *Letters* interpretation would be much more difficult, especially as so much of Tolkien's work is unfinished. The *Letters* reinforce the fact that Tolkien's work demands to be taken seriously, in the terms in which it was written, including its linguistic inspiration.

There are many memorable letters in the corpus, a few of which are as follows:

Letter 131—A letter of around 10,000 words to Milton Waldman, of the publisher Collins, demonstrating the integral relationship between *The Silmarillion*★ and other matter from the first two Ages★ of Middle-earth, and *The Hobbit*★ and *The Lord of the Rings*★ set in the Third Age.★ The letter reveals a great deal about the development of Tolkien's work. It was written around 1951, when Tolkien hoped that *The Silmarillion* and *The Lord of the Rings* might be published together.

Letter 144—Addressed to the author Naomi Mitchison in 1954, this letter answers key questions about *The Lord of the Rings*.

Letter 153—A bookseller challenged the metaphysics of *The Lord of the Rings*, and Tolkien wrote this careful and revealing letter, which he never finished. He thought he was taking himself too seriously, but it illustrates the theological seriousness of his fiction.

Letter 163—This letter to W.H. Auden★ in 1955 casts light on Tolkien's life in relation to the development of his fiction.

Letter 165—What remains of a letter written to Tolkien's US publisher, Houghton Mifflin Co., to provide publicity material about what 'made him tick'. It was used as the basis for this information.

Letter 212—This is a draft, never sent, continuing a previous letter to Rhona Beare. It speaks of the difference between Tolkien's invented mythology and the biblical narrative, for instance, on the nature of the fall.★

Letter 257—This letter, written in 1964, reveals much about Tolkien's development.

**Lewis, C.S. (1898–1963)**  Tolkien's deep friendship with C.S. Lewis was of great significance to both men. Tolkien found in Lewis an appreciative audience for his burgeoning stories and poems of Middle-earth,★ a good many of which were not published until after his death. Without Lewis' encouragement over many years, *The Lord of the Rings*★ would probably have never appeared in print. Lewis equally had cause to appreciate Tolkien. His views on myth★ and imagination,★ and the relation of both to reality, helped to convince Lewis (who had not long before been a convinced atheist) of the truth of Christianity.★ Seeing mind to mind on both imagination and the truth of Christianity was the foundation of their remarkable friendship. The Inklings,★ the group of literary friends around Lewis, grew out of this rapport between Lewis and Tolkien. A.N. Wilson, in his biography *C.S.Lewis*, remarks that at the very beginning of the association between Lewis and Tolkien, 'it must have seemed clear to him at once that Tolkien was a man of literary genius'. On Tolkien's side, thinking with sadness in 1929 of his marriage, he wrote: 'Friendship with Lewis compensates for much.'

Known to his friends as 'Jack' (he didn't like 'Clive Staples'), C.S. Lewis was born in the outskirts of Belfast on 29th November 1898, and died in his Oxford home, The Kilns, almost sixty-five years later. Like Tolkien, he was equally a scholar and a storyteller. The story of his early life, his conversion from atheism to Christianity and his awareness of joy* and longing for a fulfilment outside of his own self, is told in his autobiography *Surprised by Joy* and his allegory *The Pilgrim's Regress*.

Jack Lewis was devoted to his brother W.H. 'Warnie' Lewis. The two brothers were brought together by their common interest in creating imaginary worlds as boys, and also by the death of their mother of cancer. Mrs Flora Lewis died when Jack was nine. Their father never got over the loss, and relations between father and sons became more and more strained as time went on. C.S. Lewis portrays his father, Albert Lewis, as having little talent for happiness, and withdrawing into the safe monotony of routine. A.N. Wilson, however, believes the picture Lewis painted of his father as a 'comic character' to be one-sided. The richest heritage Albert Lewis gave to Jack was, literally, a houseful of old books which the gifted boy explored unimpeded. In the year of his mother's ghastly death, the young C.S. Lewis was sent off to Hertfordshire to join his brother at a school he later in life dubbed 'Belsen'. This title seems no great exaggeration. The brutal headmaster was several years later certified insane.

In 1910 Jack was moved first to Campbell College, Belfast, and next year to 'Chartres' (Cherbourg House) in Malvern, and later Malvern College ('Wyvern'), Worcestershire. He was never happy, however, until he was finally sent to a private tutor in Bookham called W.T. Kirkpatrick. His brother Warnie wrote, in his introduction to *Letters of C.S. Lewis*:

The fact is he should never have been sent to a public school at all. Already, at 14, his intelligence was such that he would have fitted in better among undergraduates than schoolboys; and by his temperament he was bound to be a misfit, a heretic, an object of suspicion within the

154

collective-minded and standardising Public School system.

His private tutorage under the Irishman W.T. Kirkpatrick was one of the happiest periods of his life. Not only did he rapidly mature and grow under the stringent rationality of this teacher, but he discovered the beauty of the English countryside and fantasy writers such as William Morris, also beloved of Tolkien. Full of the discovery of George MacDonald's★ *Phantastes*, Lewis wrote about its power to Arthur Greeves, his life-long Ulster friend, in 1915: 'Of course it is hopeless for me to try to describe it, but when you have followed the hero Anodos along the little stream of the faery wood, have heard about the terrible ash tree . . . and heard the episode of Cosmo, I know you will agree with me.' In *Surprised by Joy*, Lewis describes the effect as 'baptising his imagination'.

The Great War had broken out. Warnie was already on active duty. Lewis was not old enough to enlist until 1917. He spent his nineteenth birthday on the front-line. In spring 1918 Lewis was wounded in action and was eventually discharged after a spell in hospital. During all this time he, like Tolkien, had been writing poetry. By 1923 Lewis had confirmed his brilliance by gaining a Triple First at Oxford★ University. He won a temporary lectureship in Philosophy at University College. Then Magdalen College appointed him as a Fellow, lecturing and tutoring in English. He was an Oxford Don until 1954, when Cambridge University invited him to the new Chair of Medieval and Renaissance Literature, where he described himself as an 'Old Western Man' in his inaugural lecture.

In the early Oxford days Tolkien became one of C.S. Lewis' life-long friends. They would criticise one another's poetry, drift into theology and philosophy, pun or talk university English School politics. Tolkien helped to force Lewis to reconsider the claims of Christianity. He was first 'cornered' by theism and then biblical Christianity.

In 1952 Lewis met an American lady, Helen Joy Davidman, with whom he had corresponded for some time. She was a poet and novelist who had been converted from atheism and Marxism to Christianity. When she was free to remarry, and was dying of cancer, Lewis married her. She came home to The Kilns to die in the summer of 1957, but had a miraculous stay of execution. In fact she lived until 1960. The happiness that had come to him so late in life, and subsequent bitter bereavement, is recorded in his *A Grief Observed*.

As well as *The Chronicles of Narnia* for children, C.S. Lewis wrote a classic science-fiction trilogy, a novel (*Till We Have Faces*), other fiction, literary criticism, cultural criticism, ethics, theology and poetry.

## Further reading

C.S. Lewis, *The Pilgrim's Regress* (1933, 1943); *Surprised by Joy: The Shape of My Early Life* (1955); *Letters of C.S. Lewis* (1966); (Ed.) Walter Hooper, *They Stand Together: The Letters of C.S. Lewis to Arthur Greeves* (1979); W.H. Lewis (Ed. Clyde S. Kilby and Marjorie L. Meade) *Brothers and Friends: The Diaries of Major Warren Hamilton Lewis* (1982); Humphrey Carpenter, *The Inklings: C.S. Lewis, J.R.R. Tolkien, Charles Williams and their friends* (1978); Roger Lancelyn Green and Walter Hooper, *C.S. Lewis: A Biography* (1974); Lyle W. Dorsett, *And God came in: The extraordinary story of Joy Davidman—her life and marriage to C.S. Lewis* (1983); Brian Sibley, *Shadowlands: The Story of C.S. Lewis and Joy Davidman* (1985); William Griffin, *C.S. Lewis: The authentic voice* (1988); George Sayer, *Jack: C.S. Lewis and his times* (1988); Douglas Gresham, *Lenten lands: My childhood with Joy Davidman and C.S. Lewis* (1989); Colin Duriez, *The C.S. Lewis Handbook: A Comprehensive Guide to his Life, Thought and Writings* (1990); A.N. Wilson, *C.S. Lewis: A Biography* (1990).

**Light**   Light, and its contrast with darkness, is a key motif in
Tolkien's mythology of Middle-earth. Through the tales he
builds up a precise and careful meaning to light. Rather than
a modern, New Age meaning or, say, an intellectual
concept of humanistic enlightment, Tolkien's inspiration
and model is biblical (*see* CHRISTIANITY, TOLKIEN
AND).

Verlyn Flieger has made a major study of the relationship
of light, language and biblical content in Tolkien. In
*Splintered Light: Logos and Language in Tolkien's World* (1983)
she writes that *The Silmarillion*

> is a vast, fantasy mythology with the familiar mytholo-
> gical themes—gods and men, creation, transgression,
> love, war, heroism, and doom. But more than anything
> else, and more than most mythologies, it is a story about
> light. Images of light in all stages—brilliant, dim, whole,
> refracted—pervade the songs and stories of Tolkien's
> fictive world, a world peopled by sub-creators whose
> interactions with the light shape Middle-earth and their
> own destinies. Tolkien's use of light in The Silmarillion
> derives from his Christian belief . . .

Clyde Kilby, who was able to discuss Tolkien's fiction
with him, speaks of the contrast of light and darkness
always being emphasised in *The Lord of the Rings.*★

In *Tolkien and the Silmarillion*, Clyde Kilby points out
some of the many affinities between Tolkien's and the
biblical imagination. This affinity is startlingly evident in the
case of the creation of light. Like the Bible, in Tolkien light
is created before the existence of the sun and moon. The sun
and moon are creatures, not deities.

Light itself is associated, Flieger points out, with the
divine logos, the light of the world, Christ himself. We see
by him. Light in Tolkien's world is a sign of providence,★
accomplished by the agency of the Valar★ and defiled by the
primal enemy of Elvish and human life, Melkor (or

Morgoth★), the equivalent of Lucifer, who became darkened as Satan.

As in George MacDonald's powerful children's story, 'The Day Boy and the Night Girl', gradations of light are employed symbolically. Tolkien shows the process of the fall★ by a diminuation of the light. First there are the Two Lamps lighting the whole world, then the Two Trees★ lighting only the Undying Lands, and then the vastly diminished light of sun and moon, made from tiny vestiges of the light of the Trees. In MacDonald's story there is a beautiful description of how the Night Girl sees at night by light of moon and star—the only reality she knows. True reality is known only gradually. First there is dim light of night, then broad daylight, then the deeper light of true reality.

Other famous uses of the image of light include Plato's myth of the cave—where those in it have known only flickering representations of true forms in the world out-side—and the dialogue between the green witch and Pudd-leglum, with the children, in her Underworld, in *The Silver Chair* by C.S. Lewis. There she tries to persuade them that the sun and the world it shines upon don't exist; they are a fantasy based around the existence of lamps which light her gloomy world.

The abiding image of light in Tolkien's world is the Two Trees,★ extinguished by the visible darkness of Ungoliant.★ Some of the light of the Trees had, however, been captured in the Silmarils fashioned by Fëanor.★ Fëanor's desire to recover the Silmarils, stolen by Morgoth, is a prime element in the events of the First Age★ of Middle-earth.

As part of the theme of gradation and splintering of light, Tolkien creates the beautiful period of twilight in Middle-earth before the rising of sun and moon (the time when humans appear). The Elves, created in the twilight, looked upon and saw the dazzling stars associated with Varda.★ They are called to the light that exists in the Undying

Lands—the light of the Two Trees.* Consequently, they journey in quest* of those lands, some unwillingly. Not all complete the journey, and some remain in Middle-earth, in the twilight. This division affects the history, and thus the language, of the Elves, Quenya* being the language of the Elves of Valinor* and Sindarin* the speech of those in Middle-earth.

Tolkien's portrayal of the twilight is haunted with a sense of the numinous,* and the presence of Varda. 'A Elbereth Gilthoniel'* is an Elvish hymn or prayer to her. After the rising of the sun and moon, the stars in the night sky continued to comfort and give hope to those faithful to Ilúvatar. The Seven Stars, the Sickle of the Valar, had been placed in the sky by Varda as a sign of the ultimate defeat of Morgoth.

As well as the delicate symbolism of the gradation of light, darkness is a powerful image in Tolkien, again biblical, of all that is the enemy of human life in its full purpose. From the darkness that moved with the arachnoid Ungoliant to the blackness of Shelob's Lair,* from the burning black of Morgoth's hands by the Silmarils he clutched to the threat of the Black Riders in the long protected Shire,* darkness is present through the tales as a palpable image of evil. Sam in Mordor,* well-versed in the history of Middle-earth, was able to see that 'in the end the Shadow was only a small and passing thing: there was light and beauty for ever beyond its reach'.

A powerful image related to that of light is fire. In *The Silmarillion* we learn that there is a Secret Fire at the heart of real (rather than only envisaged) being. The Secret Fire has its biblical equivalent in the Holy Spirit. Gandalf (who goes in title from 'The Grey' to 'The White') declares himself the servant of the Secret Fire, and bears the Ring of Fire, Narya.* This Ring was passed on to Gandalf by Círdan* when the wizard arrived in Middle-earth: 'Take this ring, Master,' he said, 'for your labours will be heavy; but it will support you in the weariness that you have taken upon yourself. For this is the Ring of Fire, and with it you may rekindle hearts in a world that grows chill.'

Fëanor,★ like Gandalf, is associated with fire. His name, given to him by his mother, is prophetic and means 'spirit of fire'. He is the epitome of Elvish creativity and craftsmanship. Yet instead of being a servant of the Secret Fire like Gandalf, he desired possession★ of it, like Morgoth before him. Thus he was unwilling to give back the Silmarils after the destruction of the Two Trees so that their light might be used. His pride in his achievement led him to foolishly pursue Morgoth into Middle-earth, which led to the exile of the Noldor.★

A very early part of Tolkien's invented mythology, the story of Eärendil,★ displays the theme of light with great power. In Eärendil, the human who became the brightest star in the night sky over Middle-earth, Tolkien succeeded in making a Christ-figure, a prefiguration of the Saviour. The light came from the Silmaril on Eärendil's brow, as a sign of hope to the faithful in the world below. The story of Eärendil the intercessor was inspired by the Old English word 'Eärendel' in the poem *Crist*.

**The Lord of the Rings (1954–55)**   This great tale of the Third Age★ of Middle-earth★ is written in six parts. Each of the three volumes published contains two of the parts. The volumes are: *The Fellowship of the Ring*,★ *The Two Towers*★ and *The Return of the King*.★ The evolution of the work is traced in the four parts of *The History of The Lord of the Rings*,★ edited by Christopher Tolkien.★

*The Lord of the Rings* is a heroic romance, telling of the quest★ to destroy the one, ruling Ring★ of power, before it can fall into the hands of its maker, Sauron,★ the dark lord of the title. As a consistent, unified story, it stands independently of the invented mythology and historical chronicles of Middle-earth. Events of the past provide a backdrop and haunting dimension to the story.

As a work of literature, the merits and demerits of *The Lord of the Rings* have been extensively discussed by scholars (see the end section of this handbook, BOOKS ABOUT J.R.R. TOLKIEN). Among its admirers were the poet W.H. Auden* and Tolkien's friend C.S. Lewis.* In a review written upon the publication of the third volume, Lewis pointed out the beauty of the structure of the work:

> There are two Books in each volume and now that all six are before us the very high architectural quality of the romance is revealed. Book I builds up the main theme. In Book II that theme, enriched with much retrospective material, continues. Then comes the change. In III and V the fate of the company, now divided, becomes entangled with a huge complex of forces which are grouping and regrouping themselves in relation to Mordor. The main theme, isolated from this, occupies IV and the early part of VI (the latter part of course giving all the resolutions). But we are never allowed to forget the intimate connection between it and the rest. On the one hand, the whole world is going to the war; the story rings with galloping hoofs, trumpets, steel on steel. On the other, very far away, miserable figures creep (like mice on a slag heap) through the twilight of Mordor. And all the time we know the fate of the world depends far more on the small movement than on the great. This is a structural invention of the highest order: it adds immensely to the pathos, irony, and grandeur of the tale (*Of This and Other Worlds*).

Some critics less enthusiastic than C.S. Lewis have pointed out what they regard as flaws in the work: the change of tone from *The Hobbit*-like opening to the seriousness of the quest; a lack of moral seriousness (in that the good characters do not wrestle with evil*); the adolescent quality of many of the characters, who never grow up;

unconvincing battle scenarios; the distraction of having to read half a volume before the tale of Frodo and Sam continues; and so on.

Considered structurally, however, the opening is not a flaw, but sets the scene of homeliness★ so important to Tolkien. Out of this humble context, the unexpected heroes★ Frodo and Sam arise. The charge of a lack of moral seriousness does not hold once the subtlety and range of Tolkien's examination of evil is explored. On Tolkien's character portrayal, it is important to realise that this is not meant to be novelistic. *The Lord of the Rings* is a heroic romance. Characters are known according to type, and in Tolkien type can be Dwarf, hobbit,★ Ent★ and Elf,★ as well as varieties of the human. And so the discussion can go on.

One mark of the quality of *The Lord of the Rings* as literature is its linguistic basis. Tolkien makes use of his invented languages in names, and also in imaginative possibility. Language is the basis of the background mythology. Another mark of its literary quality is Tolkien's success in integrating the wealth of symbolism of his work. Quest, the journey, sacrifice,★ healing,★ death★ and many other symbolic elements are beautifully incarnate in the book. The very landscapes through which the travellers pass are symbolic, suggesting moods which correspond to the stage of the journey, and to the phase of the overall story. The terrors of Moria, the archetypal underworld,★ contrast for example with the refreshment to the spirit of Lórien.★ Always, these landscapes are fully part of the movement of the book, aesthetically shaped and integrated.

Tolkien's greatest achievement is the embodiment of myth★ in literature. It was an amazing achievement to create living myth. Tolkien shared this ability with George MacDonald.★ It is a further achievement to successfully make myth incarnate in literary form. In MacDonald the myth remains outside literary form—extraliterary, as C.S.

Lewis points out. Had Tolkien completed his work on *The Silmarillion*, all the evidence suggests that there would have been several stories in which this literary achievement of embodying myth was repeated; stories like 'The tale of Beren and Lúthien the Elf-maiden'.* In a long letter to a publisher in 1951 (Letter 131, *see LETTERS OF J.R.R. TOLKIEN* ), Tolkien attempted to sum up the meaning of the then unpublished *The Lord of the Rings* as he saw it. He had been speaking of its predecessors, *The Silmarillion* and *The Hobbit*:

The sequel, *The Lord of the Rings*, much the largest, and I hope also in proportion the best, of the entire cycle, concludes the whole business—an attempt is made to include in it, and wind up, all the elements and motives of what has preceded: Elves, Dwarves, the Kings of Men, heroic 'Homeric' horsemen, Orcs and demons, the terrors of the Ring-servants and Necromancy, and the vast horror of the Dark Throne, even in style it is to include the colloquialism and vulgarity of Hobbits, poetry and the highest style of prose. We are to see the overthrow of the last incarnation of Evil, the unmaking of the Ring, the final departure of the Elves, and the return in majesty of the true King, to take over the Dominion of Men, inheriting all that can be transmitted of Elfdom in his high marriage with Arwen daughter of Elrond, as well as the lineal royalty of Númenor. But as the earliest Tales are seen through Elvish eyes, as it were, this last great Tale, coming down from myth and legend to the earth, is seen mainly through the eyes of Hobbits: it thus becomes in fact anthropocentric. But through Hobbits, not Men so-called, because the last Tale is to exemplify most clearly a recurrent theme: the place in 'world politics' of the unforeseen and unforeseeable acts of will, and deeds of virtue of the apparently small, ungreat, forgotten in the places of the Wise and Great (good as well as evil). A moral of the whole (after the primary symbolism of the Ring, as the will to mere power, seeking to make itself objective by physical force and mechanism, and so also inevitably by lies) is the obvious one that without the high and noble the simple and vulgar is utterly mean; and without the simple and ordinary the noble and heroic is meaningless.

The basic story of *The Lord of the Rings* is briefly as follows. The wizard★ Gandalf★ discovers that the Ring★ found by Bilbo★ (as recounted in *The Hobbit*) is in fact the One Ring controlling the Rings of Power forged in the Second Age★ in Eregion.★ Frodo,★ inheritor of the Ring, flees from the comfort of the Shire★ with his companions. On his trail are the Black Riders sent from Mordor★ by Sauron. With the help of the Ranger, Aragorn,★ they succeed in reaching the security of Rivendell. There Elrond★ holds a great council where it is decided that the Ring must be destroyed, and that Frodo should be the Ring-bearer. The Company of the Ring★ is also chosen to help him on the desperate quest.★ The Ring can only be destroyed in the Mountain of Fire, Mount Doom, in Mordor.

Frustrated in its attempt to cross the Misty Mountains★ in the snow, the Company is led by Gandalf into the underground ways of Moria. Here dwells a dreadful Balrog.★ Gandalf, in great sacrifice, gives his life fighting the spirit of the underworld to allow the others to escape. The Company is led on by Aragorn, revealed as the secret heir of the ancient Kings of the West. They pass through the blessed realm of Lórien and then down the great River Anduin. The creature Gollum★ is by now on their trail, seeking back his lost Ring.

Boromir★ tries to seize the Ring by force to use against the enemy. A party of Orcs attack, killing him as he defends Merry and Pippin the hobbits. Frodo and Sam have by now parted from the rest of the Company, heading eastwards, their destination Mordor. The remainder of the Company follow the track of the Orcs who have captured Merry and Pippin, going westwards.

The story now follows the progress of Frodo and Sam, and the others remaining in the Company, in parallel.

Frodo and Sam move slowly towards Mordor, now led by the treacherous Gollum, intent on betrayal, yet held back by the rags of his lost nature. Finding the main entrance to Mordor impassable, Frodo accepts Gollum's offer to lead them to a secret entrance. There he leads them into Shelob's Lair.★ After many perils (including the near death of Frodo) the two make their hopeless way to Mount Doom. At the final moment Frodo cannot throw the Ring into the Cracks of Doom. Gollum bites off the ring-finger, but falls to his death with the Ring. The quest is over. As Mordor disintegrates, and the wraith of Sauron fades, the two are rescued by eagles★ and reunited with their friends, where they are hailed as heroes.

In the parallel story, after their capture Merry and Pippin are tracked by Aragorn, Legolas★ and Gimli★ to the Forest of Fangorn, into which they have disappeared after escaping the Orcs. In the forest, the hobbits meet the Ent★ Treebeard, guardian of the woodland. The Ents assault and capture Isengard,★ the stronghold of the traitor Saruman.★ Here the hobbits are reunited with the others of the Company, as well as Gandalf,★ returned from the dead.

Gandalf and the others had healed the aged King of Rohan,★ Théoden,★ and revealed the poisonous deception of Wormtongue,★ secret servant of Saruman. With Théoden's forces, most of the Company move towards Minas Tirith,★ now under threat from Sauron's forces. Aragorn, Legolas and Gimli, however, pass through the Paths of the Dead to gather the spirits of long-dead warriors bound by a dreadful oath. These they lead southwards to attack the enemy there.

Without the destruction of the Ring, the alliance against

Mordor would have failed. Though there was no certainty of the success of the quest of Frodo and Sam, the people of Gondor and Rohan, and the other allies, were prepared to fight to the death against the formidable enemy.

The story ends with the gradual healing of the land, preparing the way for the domination of mankind. The fading of the Elves is complete as the last ships pass over the sea to the Undying Lands of the West. On them are the Ring-bearers Bilbo and Frodo. Sam follows later, after a happy life in the Shire with his beloved Rosie.★

*See also* THE WAR OF THE RING.

**Lórien** In *The Lord of the Rings*,★ the Elvish★ realm of Celeborn★ and Galadriel★ between the rivers Celebrant and Anduin.★ It was modelled upon Doriath★ of the First Age,★ where Galadriel learned of Melian.★ It is also called Lothlórien ('Lórien of the blossom'). Lórien was one of a few Elvish areas left in Middle-earth★ in the Third Age★ (*see* GREY HAVENS; RIVENDELL). It best preserved the beauty and timelessness of Valinor.★ The chief city of Lórien was called Caras Galadon.

**The Lost Road** *see* THE STRAIGHT ROAD.

***The Lost Road and Other Writings*** **(1987)** This is the fifth volume in the series *The History of Middle-earth*, in which Christopher Tolkien★ has collected together and edited unfinished material by his father.

Under pressure to produce a sequel to the popular *The Hobbit*★, Tolkien at the end of 1937 reluctantly set aside his mythology and tales of the First and Second Ages★ of Middle-earth.★ This fifth volume completes the presentation and commentary on his invention up to that time.

At this point, Tolkien had composed later versions of 'The Annals of Valinor' and 'The Annals of Beleriand', and a greatly amplified version of 'The Silmarillion' was nearly complete. He had also started work on the history of the Downfall of Númenor★ and the change in the world which resulted from this. All this material is included. There is also an account of the development of the Elvish★ languages, 'The Lhammas' ('Account of Tongues'), supposedly written by Rúmil.★

Tolkien was also wrestling with the problem of the narrative framework of 'The Silmarillion'. One of the most interesting sections of this book is his unfinished tale of time-travel, 'The Lost Road', which, if it had been successful, would have provided such a framework. Tolkien tried to absorb his earlier framework, whereby the traveller Aelfwine★ was told the tales of the First Age, into the story of 'The Lost Road'. As it happened, the telling of *The Lord of the Rings*★ provided some kind of resolution to the problem of the narrative framework for 'The Silmarillion'.

Tolkien never prepared a sustained Elvish vocabulary, but did construct an etymological dictionary of word relationships. This is included in the book under the title 'The Etymologies'.

*See also* PHILOLOGY, J.R.R. TOLKIEN AND.

**Lothlórien** *See* LÓRIEN.

**Loyalty** We have only to think of Sam's loyalty to Frodo to realise that this is an important quality in Tolkien's world of Middle-earth. This is a quality Tolkien was glad to borrow from medieval literature. He explored many permutations of loyalty, some good some bad.

The negative aspect of loyalty is considered in *The Homecoming of Beorhtnoth Beorhthelm's Son[r. In The Lord of the Rings*,★ Denethor, Steward of Gondor,★ preferred his elder son Boromir, even dead, to the younger, Faramir, because of Boromir's loyalty to him: 'Boromir was loyal to me and no wizard's pupil. He would have remembered his father's need, and would not have squandered what fortune gave. He would have brought me a mighty gift.'

On the positive side, there is not only Sam's loyalty to Frodo, but Merry's to King Théoden,★ and Pippin's to Denethor, as well as the bizarre and fascinating loyalty that

Gollum★ has to Frodo; a loyalty that might possibly, it is hinted, have been his redemption. There is also Gandalf's loyalty to the workings of goodness in providence★. He is able to declare that he is servant of the Secret Fire, the divine creativity behind all things that have been made.

Loyalty is most of all associated in Tolkien with heroism. In figures such as Frodo and Sam, and in Beren★ and Lúthien★ of old, there is sacrifice★ for the sake of others, as a basic principle of goodness and setting the world right. Tolkien appreciated this quality in the world of *Beowulf*. In his famous essay 'Beowulf: The Monsters and the Critics',★ he observes: 'Man alien in a hostile world, engaged in a struggle which he cannot win while the world lasts, is assured that his foes are the foes also of Dryhten [The Lord], that his courage noble in itself is also the highest loyalty.'

**Lúthien**   In *The Silmarillion*,★ the Elven★ daughter of King Thingol★ and Queen Melian★ in Doriath, the most beautiful of Elf and human. She had great powers, including music,★ and courage. The story of her sacrifical love for Beren★ the mortal is recorded both in *The Silmarillion*★ as published, and in an unfinished poetic version published in *The Lays of Beleriand*.★ Hers was the most significant union of an Elf with a human being and illustrates Tolkien's central theme of immortality and death.★

*See also* BEREN AND LÚTHIEN THE ELF-MAIDEN, THE TALE OF.

# M

**MacDonald, George (1824–1905)** The Scottish writer George MacDonald was born in Huntly in rural Aberdeenshire, the son of a weaver. C.S. Lewis regarded his own debt to him as inestimable. Tolkien's attitude to the fantasist was more ambivalent, and often critical. Yet there were many affinities. The theme of death★ is central to the fiction of both Tolkien and MacDonald. The Scot's thinking about the imagination★ has a number of striking similarities with Tolkien's. The goblins in Tolkien's children's story *The Hobbit* are reminiscent of the goblins in MacDonald's *Curdie* stories for children, not as terrifying and malicious as the Orcs★ of *The Lord of the Rings* and *The Silmarillion*. There are hints of rudimentary 'sub-creation'★ in MacDonald. His distinctive great-great-grandmother figures have an Elven quality★ that could belong to Tolkien's world. He has powerful feminine images of spirituality and providence★ that are akin to Tolkien's Galadriel★ and Varda.★

Like Tolkien and C.S. Lewis, MacDonald lost his mother in boyhood; a fact that touched his thought and writings. His views on the imagination anticipated those of Lewis as well as Tolkien, and inspired G.K. Chesterton. He was a close friend of Charles Dodgson (Lewis Carroll) and John Ruskin, the art critic. His insights into the unconscious mind predated the rise of modern psychology. Like Lewis and Tolkien he was a scholar as well as a story-teller. Lewis regarded him as his 'master'.

MacDonald's sense that all imaginative meaning originates with the Christian Creator became the foundation of C.S. Lewis' thinking and imagining. Such a view is also central to Tolkien. Two key essays, 'The imagination: its functions and its culture' (1867) and 'The fantastic imagination' (1882), remarkably foreshadow Tolkien's famous essay 'On Fairy-Stories'.★ Tolkien's views on imagination persuaded C.S. Lewis of the truth of Christianity on a windy night in 1931. Many years before Lewis had stumbled across a copy of MacDonald's *Phantastes* (1858), resulting in what he famously described as a baptism of his imagination.

George MacDonald wrote nearly thirty novels, several books of sermons, a number of abiding fantasies for adults and children, short stories and poetry. His childhood is beautifully captured in his semi-autobiographical *Ranald Bannerman's Boyhood* (1871). He never lost sight of his humble childhood and adolescence, living in a cottage so small that he slept in an attic. He was a happy boy, riding, climbing, swimming and fishing—and reading while lying on the back of his beloved horse. We catch many glimpses of the countryside he knew and loved in his writings.

George MacDonald entered Aberdeen University in 1840, and had a scientific training. For a few years he worked as a tutor in London. Then he entered Highbury Theological College and married. He was called to a church in Arundle, where he fell into disfavour with the deacons, who reduced his small salary to persuade him to leave. Some of the poorer members, however, rallied around with offerings they could ill afford. Then he moved to Manchester for some years, preaching to a small congregation and giving lectures. The rapidly growing family was always on the brink of poverty. Fortunately, the poet Byron's widow, recognising MacDonald's literary gifts, started to provide financial help. The family moved down to London, living in a house then called 'The Retreat' near the Thames at Hammersmith, later owned by William Morris.

Many famous writers and artists came to visit the MacDonalds, as well as people who shared a concern for London's desperate and crowded poor. One friend was Charles Dodgson, who let the MacDonald children hear his story *Alice in Wonderland*. As a result of their enthusiasm he decided to publish it. One of MacDonald's sons, Greville, remembered calling a cab for the poet Tennyson.

For a time George MacDonald was Professor of Literature at Bedford College, London. Because of continued ill health the family eventually moved to Italy, where Mac-Donald and his wife were to remain for the rest of their lives. There were, however, frequent stays in Britain during the warmer months, and a long and successful visit to the United States on a lecture tour. One of his latest books, *Lilith* (1895), is among his greatest: a fantasy with the same power to move and to change a person's imaginative life as *Phantastes*.

### Further reading

Greville MacDonald, *George MacDonald and his wife* (1924); C.S. Lewis, *George MacDonald: an anthology* (1946); R.N. Hein, *The Harmony Within: The Spiritual Vision of George MacDonald* (1982); Kathy Triggs, *The Stars and the Stillness: A Portrait of George MacDonald* (1986); William Raeper, *George MacDonald* (1987); Michael Phillips, *George MacDonald: Scotland's Beloved Storyteller* (1987); Elizabeth Saintsbury, *George MacDonald: A Short Life* (1987).

**Maedhros**   In *The Silmarillion,*★ the eldest son of Fëanor,★ a Noldorin Elf. He is one of Tolkien's tragic heroes★ (*see*

TRAGEDY). He resisted the excesses of his father and brothers, even though he swore the Oath★ of Fëanor. Morgoth★ captured him and cruelly hung him upon Thangorodrim by his right wrist. He was rescued by his friend, Fingon, with the help of the great eagle★ Thorondor.★ Maedhros cleverly resisted the onslaughts of Morgoth. After the passing of Beren★ and Lúthien★ Maedhros succumbed to the Oath of Fëanor. This culminated in his stealing a Silmaril along with Maglor★ his brother. Suffering from his moral guilt, and the physical pain of the Silmaril burning his hand, Maedhros threw himself and the gem into a volcanic chasm.

**Maglor** In *The Silmarillion*,★ a Noldorin Elf and son of Fëanor.★ Though he swore the Oath★ of Fëanor, he later tried, unsuccessfully, to reverse his claim to the Silmarils. His brother Maedhros persuaded him to join in stealing the Silmarils. He cast the tormenting gem into the sea in remorse. Maglor was one of the great singers (*see* MUSIC) among the Eldar.★

**Maiar** In *The Silmarillion*,★ angelic beings, or Ainur,★ of lesser degree than the Valar.★ The singular form is Maia. They stewarded the world under the direction of the Valar. The loyal of the Maiar included Olórin (Gandalf★), Melian★ and perhaps Tom Bombadil.★ They were capable of various incarnations. Those who rebelled against Ilúvatar★ (God) with Morgoth★ (Melkor), expressed degrees of depravity, and included Sauron★ (once striking in appearance) and the Balrogs.★

**Mandos** In *The Silmarillion*,★ one of the Valar,★ who impassively kept the Houses of the Dead (the Halls of Mandos★). He judged the fates of Elves★ and humans in knowledge of the will of Ilúvatar★ (God). He is only recorded as being moved to pity by the plea of Lúthien★ for Beren.★

*See also* DOOM OF MANDOS.

**Manwë** In *The Silmarillion*,★ the chief of the angelic

Ainur,★ brother of the fallen Melkor (Morgoth★), and husband of Varda.★ Of the Valar★ he had the greatest understanding of the will and designs of Ilúvatar★ (God). He was particularly concerned with the ideas of air, clouds and wind, and with the birds of the air—eagles★ being especially significant. He is Lord of the world and the West.

**Melian** In *The Silmarillion*,★ one of the Maiar,★ who took on human form for love of the Elven-king, Thingol.★ The two of them founded Doriath★ and had a single child, Lúthien.★ After the passing of Lúthien, who chose mortality for love of Beren★, and the murder of Thingol, Melian abandoned Middle-earth★ and her human form.

**Melkor** *See* MORGOTH.

**Menegroth** The underground halls of the Elven-king Thingol★ in Doriath,★ also called the Thousand Caves. Menegroth was built in a rocky hill beside the River Esgalduin, accessible by a stone bridge.

**Meriadoc ('Merry') Brandybuck** In *The Lord of the Rings*,★ one of the Company of the Ring;★ a hobbit★ of the Shire.★ Merry was a friend of the young Frodo Baggins,★ growing up in Buckland.★ He accompanied him from Bag End when Frodo departed with the Ring.★ When the Company was divided by an Orc attack, Merry and Pippin were captured. They escaped into Fangorn Forest★ and there encountered Ents.★ This eventually led to reunion with others in the Company. Merry took service with King Théoden,★ rode with Éowyn★ to battle, and in it Merry and Éowyn killed the dread Lord of the Nazgûl. Both found healing★ at the hands of Aragorn. After the War of the Ring,★ Merry in later years became Master of Buckland. He wrote several scholarly works, such as *Old Words and Names in the Shire*.

**Michel Delving** A town in the Shire,★ essentially the capital and located in the Westfarthing. It was the seat of the Mayor, the Shire's main dignitary.

**Middle-earth** Tolkien's sub-created world (*see* SUB-CRE-ATION) that features in *The Silmarillion*,★ *The Hobbit*★ and

173

*The Lord of the Rings*.★ Middle-earth can refer to the whole world, or only the land-mass east of the great sea of Belegaer.★ The world of the First Age★ seems to be flat—Tolkien envisaged a complex cosmology. The blessed realm of Aman,★ west of the great sea, could be reached by sea from the east, from Beleriand★ and other regions. This became increasingly difficult, because of the disobedience of the Noldor,★ the Elves★ swayed by Fëanor.★ In the Second Age,★ after the destruction of Númenor,★ the shape of the world changed. It became the sphere we know. Aman was removed from the physical geography of the world, though still a real place.

Middle-earth is the planned habitation of mankind. Though Elves★ awoke here they were called on the Great Journey to Aman to be with the Valar.★ Those who stayed in Middle-earth, or returned to it from Aman, enriched the life and language of mankind (*see* ELVEN QUALITY). Eventually, most Elves passed from Middle-earth, but left their mark genetically on mankind, most especially through the marriage of the Elf-maiden Lúthien★ to the mortal Beren.★

*The Atlas of Middle-earth* provides a guide to the geographies of Tolkien's world.

*See also* GEOGRAPHY OF MIDDLE-EARTH.

**Minas Tirith**   The name means 'tower of guard'. In *The Silmarillion*,★ Minas Tirith is a fortress built on the river island of Tol Sirion★ by Finrod, later occupied by Sauron.★ In *The Lord of the Rings*,★ Minas Tirith is the great and beautiful city of Gondor,★ having the significance of Byzantium in Christendom. It combined strength with architectural beauty. Minas Tirith was built on seven levels and contained many features, such as the Houses of Healing.

**Mirkwood**   In *The Hobbit*,★ a great forest to the east of the Misty Mountains★ and the River Anduin.★ In earlier times it had been called Greenwood the Great—until the shadow of Sauron fell on it. Like Dorthonion★ in the First Age,★ it became a place of evil. Mirkwood was polluted with great spiders, the presence of Orcs, and other terrors. Bilbo,★ with Thorin and Company,★ passes through it in the quest★ for dragon's★ treasure. After the War of the Ring,★ Mirkwood was cleansed and restored, and renamed Eryn Lasgalen, 'wood of green leaves'.

**Misty Mountains** A major feature of the geography★ of Middle-earth★ in the Third Age.★ The Misty Mountains were a great chain of mountains running from north to south like a spine. They ran about 900 miles, from the Northern Waste to the Gap of Rohan.★ In *The Lord of the Rings*,★ the Company of the Ring★ is unable to cross the mountains because of a fierce snowstorm, and goes underneath via Moria.★ In *The Hobbit*, Bilbo★ and the Dwarves with him cross through by Orc★ tunnels. Bilbo encounters Gollum★ far underground.

*See also* UNDERGROUND PLACES AND JOURNEYS.

**Mithril** A valuable metal that was both light and strong, and which shone like silver. It was jealously prized by the Dwarves and could only be found in Khazad-dûm,★ where it provided the basis for the Dwarf-region's economy.

***The Monsters and the Critics and Other Essays* (1983)** A collection of general essays on linguistic or literary topics. They are all lectures given over a long period of time, from the mid-1930s to Tolkien's retirement in 1959 as Merton Professor of English Language and Literature. The essays are as follows:

'Beowulf: The monsters and the critics',★ the now famous essay defending the artistic unity and integrity of the great Old English poem.

'On translating Beowulf'. Tolkien defends a prose translation of the poem as an aid to study. He points out that 'Old English (or Anglo-Saxon) is not a very difficult language . . . But the idiom and diction of Old English verse is not easy. Its manner and conventions, and its metre, are unlike those of modern English verse. Also it is preserved fragmentarily and by chance. . .' Tolkien later discusses alliterative verse, in which he was skilled.

'Sir Gawain and the Green Knight'. This presents Tolkien's main thinking about a medieval English poem that was a particular favourite of his, and which he translated. He devoted a great deal of study to it. He states:

> It is indeed a poem that deserves close and detailed attention, and after that . . . careful consideration, and re-consideration. It is one of the masterpieces of fourteenth-century art in England, and of English literature as a whole . . . It belongs to that literary kind which has deep roots in the past, deeper even than its author was aware. It is made of tales often told before and elsewhere, and of elements that derive from remote times, beyond the vision or awareness of the poet: like *Beowulf*, or some of Shakespeare's major plays, such as *King Lear* or *Hamlet*.

'On Fairy-Stories'.★ This was an Andrew Lang lecture delivered at the University of St Andrews on 8th March 1939. It presents the heart of Tolkien's thinking about fantasy, sub-creation★ and the nature of fiction. It provides a key into his work, and that of C.S. Lewis★ and George MacDonald.★

'English and Welsh'. In this lecture, given at Oxford★ the day after the publication of *The Return of the King*,★ Tolkien speaks of the attraction that the Welsh language has for him (*see* ELVISH). He also mentions its preference for a hard 'c' over 'k'. Tolkien also speaks of the growth of his love of language, in which Welsh played an important part (*see* PHILOLOGIST, TOLKIEN AS A).

'A secret vice'. This lecture is of particular interest because of its autobiographical elements. Tolkien speaks of the pleasure of inventing languages, and believes that this 'hobby' is natural in childhood. He gives examples of his own invention, including Elvish.

'Valedictory address to the University of Oxford'. In this lecture, Tolkien reflects back over the more than thirty years in which he had held two Chairs in the University. He is particularly interested in the relationship between the teaching of language and literature.

**Mordor**  The name means 'black land' because of the effects of its possession by Sauron.★ Lying to the east of the lower reaches of the River Anduin,★ Mordor is bounded on three sides by mountain chains. Sauron possessed Mordor in the Second Age.★ He left it for a long period during his sojourn in Númenor.★ After his defeat, Gondor★ drove out the evil inhabitants of Mordor and built strongholds to prevent their return. In the Third Age,★ the Nazgûl★ entered Mordor and prepared for the return of Sauron, then hidden in Dol Guldur★ (where he was at the time of the events in *The Hobbit*★) *The Lord of the Rings*★ tells of the War of the Ring★ and the heroic quest to destroy it in the very heart of Mordor at Mount Doom.★

**Morgan, Father Francis**  The guardian of Tolkien and his brother Hilary,★ appointed by their mother, Mable Tolkien.★ Father Morgan was a Roman Catholic parish priest, attached to the Birmingham★ Oratory, founded by John Henry Newman. He provided friendship and counsel for the fatherless family. Half-Welsh and half-Spanish, he was an extrovert, whose enthusiasm helped to better the lot of the Tolkien family. With the boys often ill, and the mother developing diabetes, Father Morgan hit on the plan of moving them to Rednal, in the countryside, for the summer of 1904. It was like being back at their beloved Sarehole.★ Mabel Tolkien died there later that year and Father Morgan was left with the responsibility of the boys. He helped them financially, found them lodgings in Birmingham and took them on holiday. An improvement in lodgings meant that Tolkien met his future wife, Edith

Bratt, another lodger. Father Francis (like King Thingol★ with Beren★ and Lúthien★) disapproved of their love, fearful of distraction from Tolkien's studies, and ordered him to make no commitment to Edith until he was twenty-one. It meant a long separation, but Tolkien was loyal to his benefactor, the only father he had known. When Tolkien wrote of their eventual engagement, Father Francis accepted it without a fuss. When their first son was born, Father Francis travelled from Birmingham to baptise him. Sometimes he joined the growing family on their seaside holidays at Lyme Regis.

**Morgoth**   This name, 'the black enemy', was given to the Fallen Vala,★ Melkor, by Fëanor after he had stolen the Silmarils and helped to extinguish the light★ of the Two Trees.★

Morgoth is an equivalent to the biblical Satan, or Lucifer, who was originally an angel★ of high rank who rebelled against God. Satan figures large in John Milton's poem *Paradise Lost*. Milton captures the greatness of the angel, which explains the extent of the havoc he wrought after his fall. In Tolkien, the focus is on the appalling malice of Morgoth, and the effect of this malice on events concerning Elves and Men (and even the Valar). Though the emphases of Milton and Tolkien are different, their theology and explanation of evil is very close.

Morgoth figures in *The Silmarillion*★ being cast out of the world at the end of the First Age.★ In the Second★ and Third Ages★ his place is taken by his less powerful but more subtlely evil lieutenant, Sauron.★

In Tolkien's mythology, Morgoth (Melkor) was the first of the Ainur.★ He was the brother of Manwë★ of the Valar.★ He became jealous of his maker, Ilúvatar,★ seeking the secret of the creation principle, rather than merely being an agent of creation. His rebellion introduced discord into the original Great Music of creation (*see AINULINDALË*). Morgoth (Melkor) set himself in opposition to Ilúvatar and the Valar. When the world was made he particularly hated the Children of Ilúvatar—Elves★ and Men.

Morgoth used darkness and cold as a weapon, extinguishing the light of the Two Lamps and using Ungoliant★ to devour the light of the Two Trees. The latter deed was done after Morgoth had been in chains for a vast period of time, and had only been released by the Valar because he seemed repentant. After seizing the Silmarils, Morgoth returned to the icy northern wastes of Middle-earth,★ to Angband.★ Here he planned the domination of Beleriand,★ breeding Orcs★ and other monsters (*see* BATTLES OF BELERIAND). One of the greatest deeds in resistance to him was the stealing back of a Silmaril from his Iron Crown by Beren★ and Lúthien.★ Morgoth showed particular malice towards the children of Húrin★ (*see* TÚRIN TURAMBAR, THE TALE OF).

Fëanor the Elf had some of Morgoth's characteristics, and his rebellion against the wishes of the Valar, when he swore his dreadful oath after Morgoth's stealing of the Silmarils, led to the Doom of Mandos.★ The outworking of this judgement greatly aided Morgoth's purposes, and led to the eventual destruction of Beleriand.

**Moria**   *See* KHAZAD-DÛM.

**Mortality**   *See* DEATH.

*Mr Bliss* **(1982)**   This is a children's story, illustrated in colour throughout by Tolkien, about a man noted for his tall hats, who lives in a tall house. In 1932 Tolkien bought a car (he later abandoned car ownership on principle, because of the environmental effect of massive car ownership and production). The consequences of having a car suggested the story of Mr Bliss' adventures after buying a bright yellow car for five shillings. The story was shown to Tolkien's publishers in 1937 when the publication of *The Hobbit*★ had created a demand for more from the pen of the professor. Colour printing costs, however, were prohibitive. Tolkien eventually sold the manuscript to Marquette

University in the United States. It was not until after Tolkien's death that the book was published. Several of its illustrations are of high quality.

*See also PICTURES.*

**Music**  Music and song are a central theme running through Tolkien's tales of Middle-earth.★ His mythology begins with the *Ainulindalë*,★ the Music of the Ainur.★ Before the creation of the world, its character and development are expressed in music. The presence of evil★ in the world is prefigured in a discord introduced by Morgoth★ (Melkor); a discord which Ilúvatar is able to harness into a greater ultimate harmony.

*The Hobbit*★ and *The Lord of the Rings*★ are replete with songs which are integral to the story. Tolkien wrote major sections of *The Silmarillion* in verse which, though not song, is closer to music than prose is, which is true of all poetry. Modern composers like Donald Swann and Stephen Oliver have been able to set songs from Middle-earth to music with great effect. A love of song is characteristic of Elves★ and hobbits.★ Tom Bombadil's★ very speech is song.

Song is also part of the narrative action in key stories of the First Age.★ In the tale of Beren and Lúthien the Elf-maiden,★ the Elvenking Finrod Felagund battles with Sauron★ in song, and the singing of Lúthien★ destroys Sauron's tower at Tol Sirion.★ In Doriath,★ her singing had enchanted Beren, as her mother's singing had enchanted her father, Thingol,★ in earlier days. In the tale of Túrin Turambar,★ after Túrin finds healing at the Pools of Irvin, he is able to make a song for his lost friend, Beleg, and is thus able to act once more in defiance of the enemy.

In the Third Age,★ this direct power of song only seems to be retained by Galadriel.★ Her lament in Lórien,★ sung while the Company of the Ring★ were there, mentions this power:

I sang of leaves, of leaves of gold, and leaves of gold there
   grew:
Of wind I sang, a wind there came and in the branches blew.

The power of song is the magical power lying behind
creation, an idea C.S. Lewis took up in the creation of
Narnia in *The Magician's Nephew*.
   *See also THE ROAD GOES EVER ON.*

**Myth**  Myths are normally attempts to explain or understand the reality in which we find ourselves. In Tolkien's
fiction the myths belong to his secondary world of Middle-
earth.★ It is an invented mythology rather than one which
embodies a belief system (such as the Babylonian cosmology, or northern myths of creation). Yet Tolkien intended
his invented mythology to illuminate the real, primary
world. He hoped that it would bring to his reader recov-
ery★ of a true view of things, escape from the prison of
inaccurate and misleading presuppositions, and true consolation;★ consolation which pointed to the historical gospel
story. Paradoxically, Tolkien's invented mythology can
claim to be believed myth—myth in the usual sense,
pointing to an objective state of affairs.

   Tolkien sharply distinguished myth from allegory,
though he did believe in the applicability of, and need to
apply, stories. C.S. Lewis, who thought rather similarly
(though was more 'allegorical' than Tolkien), expressed this
distinction of myth and allegory. He did this when writing
to Tolkien after reading the early, unfinished poetic version
of the tale of Beren and Lúthien the Elf-maiden★: 'The two
things that come out clearly are the sense of reality in the
background and the mythical value: the essence of the myth
being that it should have no taint of allegory to the maker
and yet should suggest incipient allegories to the reader.'

   In reviewing his friend's *The Lord of the Rings*★ C.S.
Lewis describes just how Tolkien's invented mythology is
applicable to the primary, real world. Lewis concentrates on
the aspect of recovery:

The value of the myth is that it takes all the things we know and restores to them the rich significance which has been hidden by the veil of familiarity. The child enjoys his cold meat, otherwise dull to him, by pretending it is buffalo, just killed with his own bow and arrow. And the child is wise. The real meat comes back to him more savoury for having been dipped in a story; you might say that only then is it real meat. If you are tired of the real landscape, look at it in a mirror. By putting bread, gold, horse, apple, or the very roads into a myth, we do not retreat from reality: we rediscover it. As long as the story lingers in our mind, the real things are more themselves. This book applies the treatment not only to bread or apple but to good and evil, to our endless perils, our anguish and our joys. By dipping them in myth we see them more clearly. I do not think he could have done it any other way.

Tolkien's view of myth, which deeply influenced C.S. Lewis, is captured in a poem written to Lewis at the time his scepticism about Christian belief was shattered. The poem, 'Mythopoeia' (the making of myths), is reproduced in the new (1988) edition of *Tree and Leaf*.★

C.S. Lewis, like his friend J.R.R. Tolkien, placed the highest value on the making of myth—or mythopoeia—in imaginative fiction and poetry. Some stories are outright myths—as is the story of Cupid and Psyche retold by Lewis in *Till We Have Faces*. Other stories have what Lewis called a 'mythical quality'. Examples he gave were the plots of R.L. Stevenson's *Dr Jekyll and Mr Hyde*, H.G. Wells' *The Door in the Wall*, Kafka's *The Castle*, and the conceptions of Gormenghast in Mervyn Peake's *Titus Groan* and of the Ents★ and Lothlórien★ in Tolkien's *The Lord of the Rings*. Both Lewis and Tolkien aspired to myth-making in their fictional creations. They had a theology of myth.

Recognising that the term 'myth', like 'romanticism', has

many loose meanings (including 'untrue'), C.S. Lewis tried to pin down its meaning in his *An Experiment in Criticism*. A story that achieves myth has a number of characteristics. (1) It is independent of the form of words used to tell the story. (2) Narrative features such as suspense or surprise play little part in the distinctive pleasure of myth. (3) Our empathy with the characters of the story is at a minimum; we do not imaginatively transport ourselves into their lives.(4) Myth is always fantasy, dealing with the impossible and preternatural. (5) Myth is never comic; though the experience may be joyful or sad it is always grave. (6) The experience in fact is awe-inspiring, containing a numinous★ quality.

In defining myth in terms of its effect upon us, Lewis was clear that one person's myth may only be a story to another. A story may give enjoyment to a person without being perceived as myth, even though it is myth.

C.S. Lewis regarded the nineteenth-century writer George MacDonald★ as one of the greatest masters of myth-making, especially in *Phantastes* (which, Lewis says, 'baptised' his imagination long before he became a Christian believer) and *Lilith*. Tolkien did not hold MacDonald in such high regard as Lewis, although his work shows an indebtedness to him. Tolkien persuaded Lewis that, at the heart of Christianity, is a myth that is also a fact—making the claims of Christianity unique. But by becoming fact it did not cease to be myth, or lose the quality of myth. Tolkien sets out his ideas in his seminal essay 'On Fairy-Stories'.★

Tolkien spoke of the 'seamless web of story'. Human stories were interrelated, and, by God's grace, carried insights into the true nature of things. It is the gospel, however, that has broken into this web of story from the real world (*see* JOY). It is important to realise the way that Tolkien saw story (*see* STORY, THEOLOGY OF). The temptation is to source hunt Tolkien's invented mythology, for instance examining Old Norse mythology or biblical imagery. David Harvey, in *The Song of Middle-earth*, warns against this danger. Tolkien was concerned with universal mythological themes.

Tolkien's belief that God in his grace had prefigured the gospel or *evangelium* in human stories, a view shared by C.S. Lewis, was a kind of natural theology.★

## Further reading

C.S. Lewis, *An Experiment in Criticism* (1961).

# N

**Nan Dungortheb** In *The Silmarillion*,★ this 'valley of dreadful death' lay between Taur-nu-Fuin★ to the north, and Doriath★ to the south. Ungoliant★ possessed this region after darkening the Two Trees,★ and after her, her offspring and other terrible creatures continued its horror. Beren★ crossed the region on his way to Doriath, and this was considered an heroic deed because of the dangers. Such a presence of spiders is echoed, on a lesser scale, in Mirkwood★ many centuries later, as recounted in *The Hobbit*.★

**Nargothrond** In *The Silmarillion*,★ a great underground fortress consisting of many halls beside the River Narog. It was founded by Finrod Felagund the Elvenking. The name was also used to refer to the realm of the king, extending east and west of the river. Nargothrond was impregnable until Túrin★ persuaded the Elves★ to build an access bridge over the river. Glaurung the dragon crossed this stone bridge to rout the Elven caverns.

**Narya** One of the Three Rings★ of the Elves,★ known as the 'Ring of Fire', or 'the Red Ring'. Its bearer was Círdan★ until he passed it on to Gandalf.★

**Natural theology, Tolkien and** Tolkien, by confession, was a Roman Catholic. Roman Catholicism always has given a high value to natural theology. The *New Dictionary* *of Theology* defines natural theology as 'truths about God that can be learned from created things (nature, man, world) by reason alone'. The Reformation emphasised a return to Scripture alone as the source of knowledge of God, and thus all else. Nature was interpreted through the spectacles of Scripture.

In practice, Protestant apologists have tended to presuppose a common ground of reason which suggests an implicit natural theology. Roman Catholics, on the other hand, are inclined to see a continuum between natural and revealed theology. The issue is one of autonomy or neutrality in knowledge. Is there true knowledge of God without the enlightenment of Scripture? The problem with an autonomous view of human reason is the radical biblical doctrine of the fall which affected every aspect of the human, including the mind.

Tolkien's natural theology is unusual in that his stress is with the imagination rather than with reason. It is by imagination, he suggests, that there can be genuine insight into God and reality independent of the specific revelation of Scripture. However, he seeks to avoid autonomy by emphasising, in his essay 'On Fairy-Stories', that any such insights are acts of grace from the Father of Light. They are a kind of pre-revelation, opening the way to receiving the special revelation of the gospel. Furthermore, fundamental to his fiction is the theme of the fall★ of humankind.

Whereas traditional Roman Catholic thought emphasises the rational and cognitive in natural theology, Tolkien links it with imaginative meaning (*see* IMAGINATION). It is a complementary revelation to that of the propositional. The story, like language, is evidence of the image of God still remaining in fallen humankind. 'The tongue and the tale,' believed Tolkien, 'are coeval.' He also spoke of 'the seamless web of story', the interrelationship of all story-telling. Tolkien, like Lewis, believed that in a sense it was *natural* to believe in Christ our Saviour. Damnation is in fact a wilful choice against our knowledge of what is good.

For Tolkien, monotheism is 'natural religion', and is the faith of the Three Ages★ of Middle-earth (the pre-Christian era, highlighting the best of such a situation).

David Harvey, in his *The Song of Middle-earth*, argues that Tolkien employs universal motifs from mythology rather than specific sources like Old Norse mythology or the Bible. Specific borrowing from the northern imagination, and the like, is always transformed (as in the story of Kullervo in *The Kalavala* and the Túrin story). This universal emphasis, however, is not humanism (which Harvey seems to imply) but Tolkien's natural theology— which he felt pointed to the unique Christ, the sole Saviour who came in the history of the primary world.

Tolkien's natural theology is a great imaginative achievement. Natural theology is related, philosophically, to intuitionism. Tolkien's is an imaginative rather than intellectual intuitionism, perhaps like that of George MacDonald.★ One grave problem with intuitionism is illustrated in the famous Ontological Argument, which argues from a human idea of perfection to God's existence. The idea of perfection is not pure intuition, however, but formed in a tradition (Greek-Judeo-Christian), so has presuppositional, language-based, archetypal elements. The same is true of Tolkien's natural theology of the imagination—he is in fact restating and restoring an imaginative tradition, rather than inventing or 'discovering' symbols and stories that, by natural intuition, the reader knows to be in some sense true. That tradition itself, however, is making truth-claims with great power, and Tolkien allows it to be heard once again.

**Nature**   Like his close friend C.S. Lewis,★ Tolkien believed that worlds of the imagination★ are properly based upon the humble and common things of life—what Lewis called 'the quiet fullness of ordinary nature'. Both Tolkien and Lewis defended fantasy on this basis against the charge of escapism (*see* 'ON FAIRY-STORIES'). What Lewis said about *The Wind in the Willows* (the popular children's story by Kenneth Graham) could have been Tolkien's words: 'The happiness which it presents to us is in fact full of the simplest and most attainable things—food, sleep, exercise, friendship, the face of nature, even (in a sense) religion.' Such fantasy is the opposite of escapism. It deepens the reality of the real world for us—the terror as well as the beauty.

Again like Lewis, Tolkien believed that nature is better understood as God's creation. When the story-teller is building up a convincing secondary world, he or she in fact is engaged in what Tolkien called sub-creation;★ creating, as it were, in the image or as a miniaturisation of the primary world. Such story-making surveys the depths of space and time. It is the imaginative equivalent of the reason's attempt to capture reality in a single, unified theory.

The natural world of God's creating imposes a fundamental limit to the human imagination. We cannot, like God, create *ex nihilo*, out of nothing. We can only rearrange elements that God has already made, and which are already brimful with his meanings. Sub-creation, the story-telling at least of mankind (that of Elves★ is different), reflects the brokenness of God's original creation. The fall★ theme is intrinsic. Tolkien clarified this theme in the light of the claims of Christian revelation (*see* CHRISTIANITY, TOLKIEN AND). To give just one example of the effect of the fall, evil★ always results in the disruption or even the destruction of nature. Tolkien's work is full of symbolic landscapes of a spoiled world: the devastation of Ardgalen,★ the ruin of Beleriand,★ the drowning of Númenor,★ the desolation of Smaug★—to name just a few. He even takes the basis of life—light★—and employs it symbolically to show the mischief that wickedness causes, particularly the malice of Morgoth.★

Tolkien uses his own sub-creation of Middle-earth★ as a mirror of nature. There are considerable complexities in the structure of his world. Genetically, for example, there are differences between Elves and Men, even though the two races can intermarry fruitfully. As a result of these differences one race is immortal and the other must face the mystery of death.★ Elves are tied to the natural order in a way that mankind is not. Nevertheless (and, in Tolkien, because of this), Elves represent the higher aspect of human nature (see ELVEN QUALITY). Another example of complexity in Tolkien's portrayal of his world is its geography. At the drowning of Númenor the very shape of the world is changed, becoming the sphere that is familiar to us. Though an invented world, Tolkien supposes that it is our primary world in its pre-Christian history, especially as regards northern Europe.

This sense of familiar location is intensified by Tolkien in his creation of the Shire★ and of Tol Eressëa★ in early versions of *The Silmarillion.*★ The Shire, and the original Tol Eressëa, are homely places associated with Tolkien's experience of the West Midlands at the turn of the century. This identity of the West Midlands was strengthened for Tolkien by his study of medieval English literature. Favourite works such as *Pearl*★ were written in a rich West Midlands English.

As well as this large-scale 'homeliness', Tolkien was fond of creating homely places such as the Cottage of Lost Play,★ Bag End, Crickhollow, the House of Tom Bombadil,★ The Prancing Pony pub and Rivendell.★

By a powerful transposition, Tolkien portrayed a homeliness in his idea of the hero,★ an idea which he took from the Bible. His real heroes, such as Bilbo Baggins★ and Sam Gamgee,★ are taken from ordinary life. Even more 'heroic' heroes like Beren★ are in the opinion of the wise weak and frail. The great King Aragorn★ must be disguised as a humble Ranger for much of his life to be prepared for the great tasks required of him.

Tolkien had a great love for nature as a garden. His brother Hilary was a market gardener, and Tolkien was an amateur gardener. His knowledge of flora is an important element in his fiction. He of course created Elanor,★ Athelas★ and Evermind. His love for the tree★ became a central theme in his work. In Middle-earth, the tree is the crown of the flora of creation.

**Nauglamír** This is 'the Necklace of the Dwarves' spoken of in *The Silmarillion*.★ Set with many jewels, it was made for Finrod Felagund by the Dwarves.★ Húrin★ brought it out of Nargothrond★ to King Thingol★ in Doriath.★ Thingol hired Dwarves to refashion it, setting the Silmaril in it that Beren★ and Lúthien★ had wrestled from Morgoth.★

**Nazgûl** In *The Lord of the Rings*,★ spirits of Men enslaved to the Nine Rings,★ and chief servants of Sauron.★ The Men—three of them from Númenor★—had been given the Rings by Sauron in the Second Age.★ In the Third Age,★ the chief of the Nazgûl was the Witch-king. The other eight prepared Mordor★ for Sauron. The Nazgûl were also the Black Riders, sent to the Shire by the Dark Lord. After the destruction of their black horses at the Ford of Bruinen, they later appeared mounted on large flying beasts. The chief of the Nazgûl was killed by Merry and Éowyn★ during the battle before Minas Tirith, and the others disintegrated when the Ring was destroyed at Mount Doom.★

**'The New Shadow'** A story intended to be set in the Fourth Age,★ abandoned by Tolkien. It was to tell of events about 100 years after the death of Aragorn,★ where people had soon become bored with goodness. There were secret revolutionaries involved in Satanism (whether extolling Sauron★ or Morgoth★ Tolkien does not say), and boys of Gondor★ played at being Orcs.★

**Nienor** In *The Silmarillion*,★ the tragic sister of Túrin. After a spell is cast upon her by Glaurung the dragon she loses her memory. Not knowing she is his sister, Túrin marries her, after naming her Níniel. These 'twists of fate' are fashioned by the malice of Sauron★ against Húrin,★ their father. For her story, see TÚRIN TURAMBAR, THE TALE OF.

**Nimloth**   The White Tree of Númenor★ from which a fruit is secretly taken by Isildur★ before the tree is wickedly cut down. The fruit is carried to Middle-earth★ and hence the line of the tree is preserved in Gondor.★ Nimloth itself was a seedling of the white tree Celeborn.★

**Nine Rings**   The Rings of Power given to Men after being made by the Noldorin★ smiths of Eregion.★ With the forging of the One Ring, Sauron controlled these Rings, enslaving their bearers, who became the Nazgûl.★

**Níniel**   The name given to Nienor by Túrin,★ who was unaware that she was his sister.

*See also* TÚRIN TURAMBAR, THE TALE OF.

**Nogrod**   In *The Silmarillion*,★ the name of one of two cities of the Dwarves in the Blue Mountains, east of Beleriand.★

**Noldor**   Elves,★ the second group of the Eldar★ on the westward journey from Cuiviénen, led by Finwë. They had a thirst for knowledge and great skill in craftsmanship— symbolising high culture (*see* ELVEN QUALITY). Noldor means 'knowledgeable'. To the Noldor belonged the family of Fëanor,★ who became caught in the Doom of Mandos.★ Fëanor's creation of the Silmarils ranked with the work of the Valar.★ Galadriel★ also belonged to the Noldor.

**'The Notion Club Papers'**   An incomplete work due to be published in *The History of the Lord of the Rings, Part 4: Sauron Defeated*. In a letter to his publisher in July 1946, he mentioned having written three parts of this. He said that it took up material employed in the unfinished 'The Lost Road',★ but in an entirely different frame and setting. Like 'The Lost Road' it is a time-travel book, having the purpose of introducing the tales of Númenor.★ According to Tolkien's biographer, Humphrey Carpenter, The Inklings★ provide the inspiration for the setting of an informal literary group. Two of the group, Oxford★ dons, embark on a journey into the past. Carpenter believes that the unfinished work captures much of the spirit of The Inklings. One section, however, was published: the poem 'Imram'.★

**Númenor** In *The Silmarillion*,★ a great island in the middle of the sea of Belegaer. It lay between Aman★ and Middle-earth.★ Númenor, shaped like a star, was given as a home to the Edain★ by the Valar★ at the end of the First Age.★ The gift was given as a reward for their faithfulness and courage in the wars against Morgoth.★ It is equivalent to Atlantis.

In his *Letters*, Tolkien vividly explained to a publisher how Númenor was the setting for a prohibition and a fall.★

> The Númenóreans dwell within sight of the easternmost 'immortal' land, Eressëa; and as the only Men to speak an Elvish tongue . . . they are in constant communication with their ancient friends and allies . . . They become thus in appearance, and even in powers of mind, hardly distinguishable from the Elves—but they remained mortal, even though rewarded by a triple, or more than a triple, span of years. Their reward is their undoing—or the means of their temptation. Their long life aids their achievements in art and wisdom, but breeds a possessive attitude to these things, and desire awakes for more *time* for their enjoyment. Foreseeing this in part, the gods [Valar] laid a Ban on the Númenóreans from the beginning: they must never sail to Eressëa, nor westward out of sight of their own land. In all other directions they could go as they would. They must not set foot on 'immortal' lands . . . (Letter 131)

When the ban is broken, the Valar lay down their delegated powers over the world and call directly to God (Ilúvatar★). He decides to destroy Númenor and change the shape of the world. Only a faithful remnant escape to Middle-earth.

**Numinous** This is a term created by the German Lutheran theologian, Rudolf Otto (1869–1937). He was concerned to isolate the universal element in human experience that is religious. He rejected the attempts to explain away such experience by materialistic theories. The experience could be called The Holy, but he was afraid that this term might only suggest a moral category. So, as an alternative, he tried to define the numinous. He did not give a simple, rational definition, believing that the religious is ultimately inexpressible. Instead, he tried to invoke its reality. The numinous experience involves a sense of dependence upon what stands wholly other to mankind. This otherness (or other-worldliness) is unapproachable and awesome. At the same time it has a fascination and attraction. Rudolf Otto believed that Christianity has the clearest concept of the numinous.

Whatever the rights and wrongs of Otto's analysis, the implication is that the experience of the numinous is captured better by suggestion and allusion than by a theoretical analysis. It is also true that many realities captured in imaginative fiction could be described as having a quality of the numinous. C.S. Lewis realised this, incorporating the idea into his apologetic for the Christian view of suffering, *The Problem of Pain*, and cited an event from Kenneth Graham's fantasy for children, *The Wind in the Willows*, to illustrate it. Many elements in his fantasies, and in the fiction of Tolkien, convey a quality of the numinous.

Much of the numinous in Tolkien is the effect of his linguistic creativity (*see* PHILOLOGY, TOLKIEN AND). His use of Elvish names, words and phrases, which are beautiful and yet foreign, often invokes a numinous quality; similarly his employment of Runes. The uncomprehended can have great imaginative power, as in dreams, or in George MacDonald's★ *Phantastes*. Parts of *The Silmarillion*,★ using an archaic yet powerfully attractive style, also convey the numinous—the *Ainulindalë*★ is the most successful at this.

Tolkien has great ability in capturing the numinous

through the symbolic (*see* SYMBOLISM), whether in landscape (as in Doriath★ or Lórien★) or the natural elements. He uses the element of light★ with great power. The twilight which the Elves awoke to in Middle-earth, before the creation of sun and moon, has a strong significance for the imagination. Twilight is a traditional motif favoured by the Romantics (as in the link between darkness and moonlight and the sublime in Gothic literature), but Tolkien uses it with great delicacy in the world before the sun, where only the far West is lit by the light of the Two Trees.★

The numinous is embodied most of all, in Tolkien's work, in his idea of Faery (*see* SUB-CREATION)— another world in which it is possible for such beings as Elves to live and move and have a history. The world of the Elves is the focus of *The Silmarillion*, and had a powerful attraction for his imagination. Some of his Elves (like Lúthien★ or Galadriel★) are incarnations of the numinous.

Where the numinous is captured, its appeal is firstly to the imagination, which also senses it most accurately. It belongs to the area of meaning rather than concept (*see* IMAGINATION). C.S. Lewis found this when he read MacDonald's *Phantastes*, describing the effect as baptising his imagination. It was years later that he was able to reconcile this experience with his thinking. Tolkien similarly seems to have taken years of reflection (reflection often captured in his letters) to come to terms with his imaginative discoveries (*see* CHRISTIANITY, TOLKIEN AND).

# O

**Oath of Fëanor**  *The Silmarillion*★ recounts the revolt of the Noldor★ against the wishes of the guardian Valar★ in the First Age.★ This began with the far-reaching oath taken by Fëanor★ and his sons. They swore everlasting darkness on themselves if they failed to hound anyone who stole or kept a Silmaril from them. The Doom of Mandos★ was a direct consequence of the oath, and many of the tragic events in Middle-earth★ were shaped by this oath. The effects of the oath embody Tolkien's characteristic theme of the fall.★ Part of the meaning of the history of the First Age★ is the outworking of the oath in events (*see, for example*, BEREN AND LÚTHIEN THE ELF-MAIDEN, THE TALE OF).

**Old Forest**  In *The Lord of the Rings*,★ a remnant of a great forest which had once covered most of Eriador.★ It lay to the east of the Shire,★ between Buckland★ and the Barrow-downs. At the heart of the forest was the malevolent figure of Old Man Willow. The Withywindle flowed through the forest. Tom Bombadil★ had great power over the forest, and poems about him are set in the Old Forest and nearby (*see THE ADVENTURES OF TOM BOMBADIL*). Frodo★ and his companions journey through the forest after leaving the Shire.

**Olórin**  *See* GANDALF.

**'On Fairy-Stories' (1939)**  This lecture is the key source for

J.R.R. Tolkien's thinking and theology behind his creation of Middle-earth★ and its stories. He links God and mankind in two related ways. In the first, he, as an orthodox Christian, sees mankind—male and female—as being made in the image of God. This makes a qualitative difference between mankind and all other things which exist in the universe. Our ability to speak, love and create fantasy originates in this imageness of God. The second way Tolkien links God and mankind is in similarities that exist by necessity between the universe of God's making and human making. Human making derives, that is, from our being in God's image.

The actual course of Tolkien's essay does not so starkly highlight these two related links between God and mankind, but they underlie both the essay and Tolkien's fiction.

'On Fairy-Stories' was originally given as a lecture at St Andrew's University. It is concerned to rehabilitate the idea of the fairy-story, which had been relegated to children's literature, and fantasy★ in general. To regard fairy-stories as trivial, suitable only for telling to children, failed to do justice either to such stories or to real children.

The Professor, who had by then written much of *The Silmarillion*★ and published *The Hobbit*,★ attempted to set out a structure which belonged to good fairy-tales and fantasies. This structure demonstrated that fairy-tales were worthy of serious attention.

Fairy-tales, he pointed out, were stories about faerie: 'the realm or state where fairies have their being'. Listeners who had read his essay, 'Beowulf: The Monsters and the Critics',★ may have noticed a similarity here with Tolkien's portrayal of the Old English poem. Tolkien had spoken of the poet making his theme 'incarnate in the world of history and geography'. Fairy-tales were fantasy, allowing their hearers or readers to move from the details of their limited experience to 'survey the depths of space and time'. The successful fairy-story in fact was 'sub-creation',★ the ultimate achievement of fantasy; the highest art, deriving its power from human language itself. The successful writer of fairy-story 'makes a Secondary World which your mind can enter. Inside it, what he relates is "true": it accords with the laws of that world.' In addition to offering a secondary world with an 'inner consistency of reality', a good fairy-tale has three other key structural features. In the first place, it helps to bring about in the reader what Tolkien called recovery*—that is, the restoration of a true view of the meaning of ordinary and humble things which make up human life and reality; things like love, thought, trees, hills and food. (*See also* HEALING.) Secondly, the good fairy-story offers escape from one's narrow and distorted view of reality and meaning. This is the escape of the prisoner rather than the flight of the deserter. Thirdly, the good story offers consolation* leading to joy* (what C.S. Lewis called *sehnsucht*).

The consolation, argued Tolkien, only had meaning because good stories pointed to the greatest story of all. This story had all the structural features of a fairy-tale, myth or great story, with the additional feature of being true in actual human history. This was the gospel, the story of God himself coming to earth as a humble human being; a King, like Aragorn,* in disguise; a seeming fool, like Frodo and Sam; the greatest story-teller entering his own story.

Tolkien's fundamental idea of the consolation is related to his view of nature,* which was deeply theological. He saw nature in terms of a natural theology* which was sacramental. His own created Elves—which are the central concern of *The Silmarillion* and his invented languages—were natural creatures, or, at least, their destinies were tied up with the natural world. Elves* are his name for fairies, and thus are central to this essay. His main fiction, like this essay, was concerned to rehabilitate the fairy-tale, and to provide consolation for his readers. The three features of recovery, escape and consolation focus on the effect that good fairy-tales have on their readers. The effect of a work of literature on its reader is an important dimension of literary meaning. C.S. Lewis explored such effects in relation to story in his *An Experiment in Criticism*. His ideas in this late book were hammered out in meetings of The Inklings,★ and Tolkien would have been in substantial agreement with them. Thus, to explore the themes of Tolkien's essay and fiction further, it is important to read this book of Lewis'.

*See also* MYTH; ROMANTICISM; STORY, THEOLOGY OF.

**One Ring**   Also called the Great Ring, or Ruling Ring. This is the Ring treacherously made by Sauron★ to control the other Rings: the Three, the Seven and the Nine. The Three Rings of the Elves★ were, however, kept from his power, and he was unable to control the Seven Rings of the Dwarves.★ The story of the Ring shapes the events chronicled in *The Lord of the Rings*.★ After the original downfall of Sauron at the end of the Second Age,★ Isildur★ took possession of the Ring but lost it in the River Anduin.★ There it lay for centuries, until possessed, after a murder, by Gollum.★ He bore it for centuries until Bilbo Baggins★ stumbled into his part of the underground caverns north in the Misty Mountains,★ as told in *The Hobbit*.★ *The Lord of the Rings*★ records how Bilbo reluctantly dispossessed himself of the Ring, passing it to Frodo.★ Frodo took on the task of the Ring's destruction in the very heart of Mordor,★ the only way its power of evil★ could be stopped for ever.

**Orcs**   A race bred by Morgoth★ purposely for his evil, and hence having no moral choice. Because Morgoth was incapable of creating life, it seems that he made use of captured Elves★ that he had tortured for this genetic engineering. Orcs had different names in various languages; hobbits★ called them goblins. Morgoth made use of Orcs in his attempts to dominate and suppress Beleriand.★ After his downfall, and the destruction of Beleriand, Orcs survived in other parts of Middle-earth. In the Second★ and Third Ages★ Sauron★ used them in his service. The conception of the Orcs in *The Hobbit,*★ a children's book, is reminiscent of George MacDonald's goblins (as in *The Princess and the Goblin*). The Orcs of *The Silmarillion*★ and *The Lord of the Rings*★ are darker and crueller. As the Elves★ symbolise what is high and noble in human life, the Orcs represent what is base, twisted, insensitive and cruel.

It is out of the scope of this book to outline a sociology of Orcs, but there were varied types and tribes. Not all Orcs were loyal to Sauron; some served Saruman.★

**Further reading**

David Day, *A Tolkien Bestiary* (1979).

**Orodreth**  Elvenking of Nargothrond★ after the death of his brother, Finrod Felagund. His daughter, Finduilas,★ fell in love with the mortal Túrin.★

**Oromë**  In *The Silmarillion,*★ one of the Valar,★ the great hunter who discovered the awakened Elves★ and led them westwards on their Great Journey from Cuivienen.★

**Orthanc**  The stronghold built by men of Númenor★ in the Circle of Isengard★ and possessed by Saruman.★ It was built of four forked pillars of unbreakable black stone. Orthanc towered five hundred feet above the surrounding plain.

**Ossiriand**  In *The Silmarillion,*★ an area of east Beleriand,★ the name of which means 'Land of Seven Rivers' after its seven rivers (Gelion and its tributaries). Its many woods included elms. Beren★ and Lúthien★ lived here after their return from the dead. In later Ages the region was known as Lindon.

**Overlithe**  In the Shire★ Reckoning this was leap-day, occurring every fourth year with the exception of the last in the century. It was a special holiday, and occurred after Mid-year's Day.

**Oxford**    City and county town of Oxfordshire, England. It was J.R.R. Tolkien's home from 1925, when he was elected Rawlinson and Bosworth Professor of Anglo-Saxon, to his death in 1973, except for a few retirement years in Poole.

Oxford is located at the meeting of the rivers Thames and Cherwell, about fifty miles north-west of London. Its importance as early as the tenth century is evident from its mention in the *Anglo-Saxon Chronicle* for 912.

Before World War I Oxford was known as a university city and market town. Then printing was its only major industry. Between the wars, however, the Oxford motor industry grew rapidly, much to Tolkien's sorrow.

University teaching has been carried on at Oxford since the early days of the twelfth century, perhaps as a result of students migrating from Paris. The university's fame quickly grew, until by the fourteenth century it rivalled any in Europe. Tolkien was associated with three Oxford colleges: Exeter, Pembroke and Merton. Between 1911 and 1915 he was an undergraduate at Exeter College, studying first Classics then English Language and Literature. In 1925 he returned from Leeds University to become Professor of Anglo-Saxon, with Pembroke as his college. After he changed Chairs to become Professor of English Language and Literature in 1945, he became a Fellow of Merton College. A Professor's first responsibility was to the whole Oxford Faculty.

The Tolkien family lived in a succession of houses in suburban Oxford. In 1925, Tolkien bought a house at 20 Northmoor Road, in the north of the city, and then, in 1930, moved to a larger house next door, number 22. It was the mutilation of a favourite poplar tree in the street which inspired Tolkien's story 'Leaf by Niggle'.★ In 1947 the family moved to a smaller house in 3 Manor Road, as John and Michael Tolkien had now left home, but this proved too small. The house the Tolkiens moved to in 1950, in Holywell Street, had much more character, but they soon found that the Oxford traffic made living there unbearable. Tolkien wrote: 'This charming house has become uninhabitable: unsleepable-in, unworkable-in, rocked, racked with noise, and drenched with fumes. Such is modern life. Mordor in our midst.' Three years later they found a house in Headington, a quiet suburb to the east of the city, near to C.S. Lewis'* home, The Kilns. This was 76 Sandfield Road, where the Tolkiens lived until 1968 when they moved to Poole in Dorset. After Edith's death in 1971, Tolkien was able to move back to Oxford, living in College rooms in 21 Merton Street. He lived there from March 1972 until his death the following year.

# P

**Palantíri**   These were eight crystal globes, through which
could be seen events and places far off in time and space. In
conjunction, the stones could therefore be used for commu-
nication. These seeing-stones were made by the Noldor★ in
Aman.★ Like the Silmarils and the Rings,★ the palantíri
have great symbolic power in the tales of Middle-earth★ (*see*
SYMBOLISM). The master-stone was kept in Tol
Eressëa.★ The seven remaining stones were brought to
Middle-earth at the fall of Númenor★ and located at various
places. One stone, in the Tower Hills west of the Shire,★
was guarded by the Eldar. Unlike the others, it looked only
to Aman and served as a reminder to the Elves★ of the
Undying Lands. Sauron★ gained possession of a palantír
when Osgiliath was captured by his forces. When both
Saruman★ and Denethor★ made use of other palantíri,
Sauron twisted their wills and distorted their visions gained
through it. The stone from Orthanc,★ used by Saruman,
was recovered after Wormtongue★ threw it out of the
tower. By this stone, Aragorn,★ its rightful user, was able
to gain intelligence of the movements of Sauron's forces. In
later years Aragorn used it as king to aid his reign.

**Pearl**   An alliterative poem of the fourteenth century derived
from the West Midlands, the area on which Tolkien based
the Shire.★ The Christian author of this major work of

English literature is unknown, but he or she also wrote the masterpiece *Sir Gawain and the Green Knight*. Tolkien's translation into modern English, retaining the original form, was published after his death.

Pearl is the only daughter of the narrator who died at less than two years of age. The grieving father has a vision in the garden where she is buried. He sees a river. Paradise lies beyond it, where a girl is seated. It is Pearl, grown to maturity. The poet is comforted as the maiden speaks to him of her blessed state, enjoying as she is the salvation of Christ. She is a pearl lost to him.

Tolkien argues that the poem is literally autobiographical and symbolic rather than allegorical, ie it has a wideness of application.

*See also SIR GAWAIN AND THE GREEN KNIGHT, PEARL AND SIR ORFEO.*

**Peregrin ('Pippin') Took**   In *The Lord of the Rings*,★ he is one of the Company of the Ring,★ a hobbit★ of the Shire.★ Pippin was a boyhood friend of Frodo Baggins★ in Buckland.★ During the War of the Ring★ he entered into the service of Denethor★ and saved Faramir★ from his madness.

**Phial of Galadriel**   A jar of crystal given as a gift to Frodo★ by the Lady Galadriel★ during his quest★ to destroy the One Ring.★ The jar contained the light of Eärendil★ captured in the Mirror of Galadriel. Because of its source, light from the Phial brought hope and courage to a bearer who had faith. With the Phial, Frodo resisted the attraction of the Ring, and Sam was able to confront the terror of Shelob.★ The Phial has a sacramental value in the tale of *The Lord of the Rings*★ (*see* CHRISTIANITY, TOLKIEN AND).

**Philology, J.R.R. Tolkien and**   According to Professor Shippey in his book *The Road to Middle-earth*, Tolkien's fiction results from the interraction between his imagination and his professional work as a philologist. C.S. Lewis put something of his friend into the fictional character of the philologist, Elwin Ransom, in his science fiction story *Out of the Silent Planet*. In 1944, Tolkien wrote to his son Christopher: 'As a philologist I may have some part in him, and recognise some of my opinions Lewisified in him.'

The name Elwin means 'Elf friend', and is a version of the name of the central character in Tolkien's unfinished story 'The Lost Road'.* In that story he is named Alboin. From when he was a child he has invented, or rather discovered, strange and beautiful words, leading him to the theory that they are fragments from an ancient world. This slightly autobiographical story tells us much about the love which motivated Tolkien's work in philology, and how it was intimately tied up with his invented mythology of Middle-earth. Owen Barfield said of C.S. Lewis that he was in love with the imagination. It could be said of Tolkien that he was in love with language.

The academic discipline of philology, once strong, has now been absorbed into the subject area of linguistics. It combined linguistic, literary and cultural study. *Everyman's Encyclopaedia* attempts a definition: 'Philology is used either (and particularly in Europe) to include both literary scholarship and the linguistic study of literary languages, both text-oriented; or purely to mean linguistics, particularly historical or diachronic linguistics (terms to which it is losing ground).' For a taste of Tolkien's professional work, see his *The Monsters and the Critics and other Essays*★ where he remarks, 'Philology is the foundation of human letters.'

At Oxford, Tolkien taught mostly Old English, Middle English and the history of the English language. This professional work was intimately related to his construction of the languages, peoples and history of the three Ages★ of Middle-earth.★ He commented in a letter that he sought to create a mythology for England, but it might be argued that he also tried to create a mythology for the English language. The earliest expression of the mythology embodied in 'The Silmarillion',★ a poem written in 1914 about the voyage of

Eärendil,★ was inspired by a line from Cynewulf's Old English poem *Crist*, 'Ëalä Eärendel engla beorhtost' ('Behold Eärendel brightest of angels').

In his essay 'The Oxford English School' (1930), Tolkien makes clear that he regarded both literary and linguistic approaches as too narrow to gain full response to works of art. He felt that this was particularly true of early literary works, very distant from contemporary culture. Philology was a necessary dimension of both approaches. It could give a proper depth of response. Professor Shippey points out that Tolkien saw works of literary art philologically, and his own fiction came out of a philological vision.

The philological instinct is demonstrated in the quest for an Indo-European language in the deep past. As the old philologists sought for Indo-European, many Tolkien readers try to unravel a proto-Elvish language, the ancester of the two distinct branches of Tolkien's invented Elvish★—Quenya★ and Sindarin.★ It is interesting that, while Tolkien constructs a plausible family relationship between the two branches of Elvish, the two languages that inspired them—Finnish and Welsh—are not related in this way, according to linguists.

It is also interesting, as Professor Shippey points out, that the philologist Jakob Grimm produced collections of fairytales as well as learned scholarship, just as Tolkien's imaginative work sprang out of his philological study.

**Further reading**

R.A. Shippey, *The Road to Middle-earth*; Ruth S. Noel, *The Languages of Tolkien's Middle-earth*; Jim Allan, *An Introduction to Elvish*.

***Pictures* (1979)** Collected, with notes, by Christopher Tolkien.★ This large format book contains forty-eight sections of paintings, drawings and designs by J.R.R.

Tolkien, mostly relating to *The Hobbit,*★ *The Lord of the Rings*★ and *The Silmarillion.*★

Tolkien had great skills as an illustrator. His visualisation of settings from his fiction are of particular interest. Those from *The Silmarillion* (such as the illustrations of Nargothrond★) are especially valuable due to the unfinished nature of that work. Tolkien was unable to detail the stories of that period of Middle-earth★ as vividly as in *The Lord of the Rings*.

The illustrations emphasise the great care Tolkien took in visualising and creating his geography★ of Middle-earth. We glimpse Tol Sirion,★ with the shadow of Thangorodrim★ on the horizon. We see the beautiful city of Gondolin★ encircled by mountains. There is a powerful depiction of Taniquetil,★ its peak in the stars.

From the Third Age★ of Middle-earth is included Tolkien's crayon drawing of the Mallorn trees of Lórien★ in spring, capturing the numinous★ quality of the region. There are many other illustrations, including a picture of Hobbiton★ that was the frontispiece to the original edition of *The Hobbit* in 1937. One of Tolkien's illustrations of Mirkwood★ is based on an earlier painting of Taur-nu-Fuin★ illustrating Beleg's finding of Gwindor. The depiction of the Elvenking's Gate from *The Hobbit* is somewhat reminiscent of Tolkien's portrayal of Nargothrond. One of Tolkien's beautiful, stylised drawings of trees, reproduced in this book, is used on the cover of *Tree and Leaf*. A more naturalistic crayon drawing powerfully depicts Old Man Willow.

**Pippin** *See* PEREGRIN TOOK.

**Possession** Tolkien explores power in relation to possession. Possession is a unifying theme, from the desire of Morgoth★ (Melkor) to have God's power of creation, to the temptation of wielding the One Ring.★

The wrong use of power is often expressed in Tolkien in magic, the mechanical and the technological. Morgoth,

Sauron★ and Saruman★ experiment with genetic engineering, and use or encourage the use of machines. Tolkien contrasts art with magic, typified in the Elves★ (see ELVEN QUALITY), who have no desire to dominate. Tolkien, like C.S. Lewis★ and Jacques Ellul, saw a machine attitude, or technocracy, as the modern form of magic, seeking to dominate and possess nature rather than husband her. Though Tolkien tried to recreate a rural past in the Shire,★ he was not anti-cultural. He was rather opposed to a machine mentality. The Shire he portrayed could only exist because of the sacrifice and effort of its secret guardians like Aragorn★ and Gandalf.★

The magical power—the instinct to possess at any cost—of modern technocracy is recognised not only by Tolkien and Lewis (as in his science-fiction novel *That Hideous Strength*). Lord Zuckerman commented about the nuclear arms race:

> It is he, the technician, not the commander in the field, who is at the heart of the arms race, who starts the process of formulating a so-called military nuclear need . . . They have become the alchemists of our times, working in secret ways which cannot be divulged, casting spells which embrace us all (*Apocalypse Now?*, p. 25).

Domination does not necessarily imply possession in Tolkien; it is not wholly bad. Possession however is a perversion of stewardship. Denethor★ and Gandalf can be contrasted as bad and good Stewards, as they exercise responsibility over others. Tom Bombadil★ is also a good model of stewardship; the guardian of the Old Forest★ who has no desire to possess, and who is thereby invulnerable to the desire of the Ring. The earlier Ages of Middle-earth are dominated by Elves, who avoided possession. The dominance of mankind in the Fourth Age★ is intended to be modelled on Elven values, not to be a destructive territorial rivalry. Tolkien condemns the process in Númenor★ from a stewardly civilisation to one which lusted for possession and sought to enslave others.

The two central motifs of the stories of Middle-earth, the Silmarils and the Ring, focus the theme of possession. The Silmarils are wholly good and the Ring is wholly evil, yet each test those who come into contact with them. Thingol★ tragically falls morally in desiring a Silmaril; Beren★ has no desire to possess it. Rather he loves the greater treasure, Lúthien,★ who is better than any possession. Boromir succumbs to the desire of the Ring; Bilbo resists it, as does Galadriel;★ it has little power over the humble Sam.

Another powerful symbol relating to the theme of possession is the dragon★ with its hoard. Though the hoard cannot be of any use to the dragon, he is jealous over the smallest item that may be stolen, as Smaug★ is in *The Hobbit*.★

**Prancing Pony, The**   In *The Lord of the Rings*,★ the inn at Bree★ at which Frodo★ and his friends stayed on their way to Rivendell.★ It was run by Barliman Butterbur, the scatter-brained friend of Gandalf.★

**Providence**   According to Ruth S. Noel in *The Mythology of Middle-earth*, the concept of predestined fate is common in myth. In Tolkien's invented mythology, he grapples with the relationship between fate and freewill.

His solution is a Christian one which sees the hand of God, or providence, behind human history and the natural world. Working out this solution imaginatively must mean grappling with the complexity of reality. Even an invented reality is complex, for Tolkien sees it as sub-creation,★ having an 'inner consistency of reality'.

In the northern imagination to which Tolkien was so deeply indebted, fate was a fundamental principle. There is fated to be a twilight of the gods. In Greek mythology and philosophical thought, the gods are ultimately ruled by principles greater than themselves. The personal creator-god of Plato's *Timaeus* is a demiurge. It is only in the biblical narratives of Judeo-Christianity that there is a personal creator who is not conditioned, who is infinite, making an order of being out of nothing, a reality distinct from his own.

Fundamental to Tolkien's invented mythology is the fact that the demiurges or powers involved in the creation of the world are themselves creatures of Ilúvatar,★ the one God. The divine providence thus overrules all principles and powers found in created reality, including the shadow—evil. From the perspective of created beings like Elves,★ mankind and hobbits,★ it can often seem that evil★ is winning, that an indifferent or negative fate rather than providence is in command. Tolkien believed that a work of imagination like his own, an attempt at proper sub-creation, should reveal providence rather than evil or fate as the master principle. By its nature, providence (unlike evil or fate) does not do away with freewill, but respects it (*see* NATURAL THEOLOGY). Rather like John Milton writing *Paradise Lost*, Tolkien was concerned to justify the ways of God to mankind in a world spoiled by suffering and evil.

Tolkien picked up on themes of providence found in fairy-stories (*see* 'ON FAIRY-STORIES'). Frequently, bans and prohibitions are placed by the Valar★ on Elves and mankind. Fëanor refused to stay in Valinor after Morgoth's theft of the Silmarils, provoking judgement on himself and his family. The Númenóreans were forbidden to set foot on the shores of Valinor. As well as bans and prohibitions, Tolkien employed the theme of prophecy. One key prophecy in *The Lord of the Rings* was that the king, returning to Gondor,★ would be recognised by his healing★ hands. Aragorn★ also carried a sword that had been broken, fulfilling another prophecy.

The complex pattern of freewill and providence is captured in the incident where Sam, Frodo and others look in the Mirror of Galadriel.★ It showed not only what would happen, but also what might happen. Events in Middle-earth were not 'closed' but 'open'; freewill had a bearing on the outcome of events. Sam and Frodo chose to go to Mordor.★ The audacious strategy of seeking to destroy the Ring under Sauron's★ nose depended upon freely chosen sacrifice★ and a deliberate act of foolishness.

Tolkien tried to retain a mood or tone from the northern imagination; one of courage and dignity before fate or doom. Though the way forward seemed impossible of success, as with the quest★ of Frodo and Sam, or the march of the western allies to the Black Gate of Mordor, it had to be taken with full heart. Here Tolkien was emulating the Christian author of the poem *Beowulf* (*see* 'BEOWULF: THE MONSTERS AND THE CRITICS').

A characteristic symbol and presence of providence in Middle-earth are eagles.★ They can mean judgement, as in the eagle-shaped clouds before the destruction of Númenor,★ or, more usually, divine assistance.

There are numerous examples of the providential assistance of eagles in Tolkien's narratives of Middle-earth. Maedhros★ is rescued by the eagle Thorondir.★ Beren and Lúthien★ escape with the help of eagles after coming out of Angband with the Silmaril cut from the Iron Crown of Morgoth. Bilbo and the party of Dwarves are taken to the eyries of the eagles in *The Hobbit*. Gandalf★ is plucked from captivity in Isengard★ by an eagle in *The Lord of the Rings*. In the same story, the otherwise desperate Frodo and Sam are lifted from Mount Doom★ after the Ring's destruction by the great eagle. In *The Silmarillion*, eagles have their eyries in the Crissaegrim peaks south of Gondolin,★ strategically placed to view events within a wide radius. There they act as the messengers and servants of Manwë★ the Valar.★ Manwë ordained that eagles nest in mountains rather than high trees so that they could hear and report to him the voices of Men and Elves that called to him.

All means of light★ are signs of providence, placed by the Valar. Stars have a particular significance, associated with Elbereth.★ When Eärendil★ the mariner was set to sail the heavens, his star was a powerful symbol of hope to the faithful peoples of Middle-earth.

Another indication of providence was the arrival of the wizards★ in Middle-earth in the Third Age.★ Their work of guardianship was echoed to a lesser but vital extent by the Rangers★ who, for example, protected the boundaries of the Shire.★ One of the wizards, Gandalf,★ functions as a key interpreter of events (and thus of providence) in the story of *The Lord of the Rings*. Gandalf's sacrifice itself is providential. A sub-theme of providence is the place of oaths and curses, a traditional element in fairy-stories. Mandos★ puts a doom or curse on Fëanor and his family after the Kinslaying★ at Alqualondë.★ Most notable is the curse of Morgoth on the children of Húrin,★ described as one of his greatest evils. This curse is a chief element in the tale of Túrin★ Turambar. Artistically, this narrative is a great challenge to Tolkien in weaving the inter-relationship between freewill and the consequences of the curse. His greater task is to demonstrate that the great evil of this curse does not frustrate the larger purposes of providence. The creation song—the *Ainulindalë*★—reveals that the discord of Morgoth is subsumed into the musical harmony of Ilúvatar. The Túrin story is the great test of this claim. At the end of the story, despite the depths of its tragedy, Túrin is a dragon-slayer, a great hero in the battle of good against evil, light★ against dark.

In another tale, Fingon attempts to end a feud between Elves; the feud being a result of the Curse or Doom of Mandos. He traces his friend Maedhros. Maedhros begs him to kill him to end the misery of his captivity. Fingon cries to Manwë to guide his arrow. Instead, in answer to Fingon's prayer, the Vala sends one of his watching eagles, King Thorondir, to carry Fingon to rescue Maedhros.

Gandalf must be allowed to have the last word about providence, as he is so often its spokesman. At the end of *The Hobbit* he says to Bilbo:

'Surely you don't disbelieve the prophecies, because you had a hand in bringing them about yourself? You don't really suppose, do you, that all your adventures and escapes were managed by mere luck, just for your sole benefit? You are a very fine fellow, Mr Baggins, and I am very fond of you; but you are only quite a little fellow in a wide world after all!'

'Thank goodness!' said Bilbo laughing, and handed him the tobacco jar.

# Q

**Quenta Silmarillion**   Literally 'the history of the Silmarils' (*see THE SILMARILLION*).

**Quenya**   A major form of Elvish★ used in Aman,★ probably close to the original language taught by the Valar.★ Quenya shared its ancestry with Sindarin★ Elvish. Both diverged in grammar, vocabulary and sound, but Quenya was less dynamic, not being exposed to the same extent to geographical and historical influences. Quenya owes its inspiration to Tolkien's love of Finnish. An example revealing the great beauty of Quenya is the song *Namárië*, set to music by Donald Swann (*see THE ROAD GOES EVER ON*). Tolkien's use of Quenya throughout his stories of Middle-earth★ in names, quotations and fragments of song, helps to give a numinous★ quality that achieves great beauty.

**The quest**   The quest often takes the form of a journey in symbolic literature (*see* SYMBOLISM) in fiction such as Tolkien's. Life and experience have the character of a journey, and this character can be intensified by art. The Christian possibilities of the quest have been explored by Thomas Malory (in *Morte d'Arthur*), by John Bunyan (in *The Pilgrim's Progress*) and by Tolkien—to name a few writers.

   The greatest quests in Tolkien's fiction are Beren's★ for the Silmaril (but really for the hand of his beloved

Lúthien★), and Frodo and Sam's for the destruction of the One Ring.★ In Tolkien's profound little tale, *Leaf by Niggle*,★ there is both a quest (to complete the painting of the tree) and a journey—from Niggle's call by the Inspector to his arrival at the beginning of the mountains.

The tales of Middle-earth★ abound with quest heroes: Beren, Lúthien, Tuor,★ Eärendil,★ Bilbo,★ Frodo, Sam, Aragorn, to instance a few. For Tolkien, the ultimate model of the quest hero is Christ, with his mission to die and then to turn the cosmic table by rising again (*see* HERO).

The main quest heroes of Middle-earth follow the traditional theme. Each has a specific task or tasks to undertake, sometimes taking up much of his or her life. Some of them marry into the Elvish★ race, like Beren and Eärendil, creating a pattern of relationships. Beren marries the Elven Lúthien. Their child, Dior,★ is father of Elwing,★ who becomes the wife of Eärendil. The children of Eärendil are Elros and Elrond.★ Aragorn is a descendent of Elros, who became the first King of Númenor. Aragorn's wife, Arwen,★ is the daughter of Elrond.

Each of the quests is different. Beren seeks marriage with Lúthien; his motivation is romantic love, and the quest of the Silmarils arises out of this. Eärendil seeks the blessed realm of Valinor★ in order to intercede for the threatened people of Beleriand.★ Aragorn seeks the return of kingship in the Númenórean tradition, to uphold civilisation in a reunited Middle-earth. Also there is the quest of Arwen, and its romantic theme.

As these quests are conducted, all aspects of Christ (love, resurrection, mediation, sacrifice, kingship, conquering of death, healing) are illuminated (*see* CHRISTIANITY, TOLKIEN AND).

The fiction of Middle-earth essentially begins and ends with a quest. After the awakening of the Elves at Cuiviénen★ they are called on a Great Journey to the Uttermost West, Aman,★ by the Valar,★ their guardians. At the end of

214

the Third Age,★ after the War of the Ring,★ the Ring-
bearers Bilbo★ and Frodo,★ and many of the Elves, pass
from Grey Havens★ over the great sea by the Straight
Road★ to seek the Undying Lands beyond the world.

# R

**Radagast**  One of the wizards,★ and called Radagast the Brown. His responsibilities included the welfare of animals. He was particularly friendly with birds. He lived in the Anduin★ region, near Mirkwood.★

**Rangers of the North**  The name given to the Dúnedain of the North, of the lost kingdom of Arnor,★ who guarded the Shire★ and the larger region of Eriador.★ They were led by the Chieftains of the Dúnedain,★ heirs of Isildur.★ In the time of *The Lord of the Rings*,★ this was Aragorn.★

**Recovery**  In the fiction of Tolkien, recovery is related to escape and consolation (*see* 'ON FAIRY-STORIES'). Tolkien, like C.S. Lewis,★ believed that through story the real world becomes a more magical place, full of meaning. We see its pattern and colour in a fresh way. The recovery of a true view of things applies both to individual things like hills and stones, and to the cosmic—the depths of space and time itself. For in sub-creation,★ Tolkien believed, there is a survey of space and time. Reality is captured in miniature. Through sub-creative stories—the type to which *The Lord of the Rings*★ and 'The tale of Beren and Lúthien the Elf-maiden'★ belong—a renewed view of reality in all its dimensions is given: the homely, the spiritual, the physical, the moral.

Tolkien, like Lewis, rejected what they saw as the restless

quest of the modern world to be original. Meaning was to be discovered in God's created world, not somehow to be created by mankind (*see* IMAGINATION). G.K. Chesterton somewhere speaks of the way that children normally are not tired of familiar experience. In this sense they share in God's energy and vitality; he never tires of telling the sun to rise each morning. The child's attitude is a true view of things, and dipping into the world of story can restore such a sense of freshness.

For Tolkien, fairy-stories help us to make such a recovery—they bring healing*—and 'in that sense only a taste for them may make us, or keep us, childish'.

**Red Book of Westmarch** This book was so named because of its red leather covers, and because it was preserved in the Shire* in Westmarch after the War of the Ring.* It was written in by Bilbo* and Frodo* Baggins, and Sam Gamgee,* as well as others. Its subject was the events recorded in *The Hobbit** and *The Lord of the Rings*,* and was Tolkien's supposed source.

With the Red Book were the three volumes of *Translations from the Elvish* by Bilbo, the supposed source of *The Silmarillion*.* Many copies of the Red Book, and presumably the Translations, were made.

**The Return of the King (1955)** The third volume of *The Lord of the Rings** comprising Books Five and Six and extensive appendices.

Book Five tells of the arrival of Pippin and Gandalf* at Minas Tirith;* the passing of the Grey Company (those led by Aragorn* on the Paths of the Dead); the muster of Rohan;* the siege of Gondor;* the ride of the Rohirrim; the Battle of the Pelennor Fields (*see* WAR OF THE RING); the suicide of Denethor;* the restoration of Éowyn and Faramir at the Houses of Healing; the last debate of the western allies; and the opening of the Black Gate of Mordor* when all seems lost.

Book Six is parallel for much of its narration to Book

Five. It tells of Sam searching for Frodo★ at the Tower of Cirith Ungol;★ their perilous journey into Mordor's land of shadow; their arrival at Mount Doom★ and the end of the quest★ to destroy the Ring;★ the reunion at the Field of Cormallen; the crowning of Aragorn; the various partings; the hobbits' journey back to the Shire;★ the scouring of the Shire and the death of Saruman;★ and the passing of the Ring-bearers from Grey Havens.★

The appendices provided a major source of information about the earlier Ages of Middle-earth★ until the publication of *The Silmarillion*★ in 1977.

**The Return of the Shadow (1988)**   This is Volume 6 of *The History of Middle-earth.*★ It is also Part One of *The History of The Lord of the Rings.*★ The book is made up of Tolkien's early drafts of what was to become the first volume of *The Lord of the Rings,*★ *The Fellowship of the Ring.*★ Frodo Baggins★ is here called Bingo, and Strider (Aragorn) has the name of Trotter. The collection provides fascinating insights into Tolkien's manner of composition.

**Ring**   *See* RINGS OF POWER.

**Ring of Barahir**   An Elven-ring given by King Finrod Felagund to Barahir, father of Beren,★ in gratitude. It was a pledge of help in time of need, taken up by Beren, who bore the ring after his father's death.

The ring was treasured and passed on through the ages, until it became one of the heirlooms of the North-kingdom, inherited by Aragorn.★

**Rings of Power**   Also called the Rings or the Great Rings, these were fashioned by Noldorin★ Elves★ in Eregion★ and by Sauron★ in the Second Age★ of Middle-earth.★ They made Three Rings★ for the Elves, Seven Rings★ for the Dwarves and Nine Rings★ for mankind. In characteristic treachery, Sauron later created the One Ring★ to rule the others.

Just as the tales of the First Age★ of Middle-earth are dominated by the motif of the Silmarils, the events of the

Third Age,* particularly as it reached its climax with the War of the Rings,* are dominated by the motif of the Rings. The significance of the Rings is interpreted vividly by Gandalf* at the last debate in Gondor. The wizard* warns the leaders of the triumphant armies of the West that they have not won the final victory over Sauron; such a victory could not be won by military might. He tells them:

> I still hope for victory, but not by arms. For into the midst of all these policies comes the Ring of Power, the foundation of Barad-dûr, and the hope of Sauron . . . If he regains it, your valour is vain, and his victory will be swift and complete: so complete that none can foresee the end of it while this world lasts. If it is destroyed, then he will fall; and his fall will be so low that none can foresee his arising ever again. For he will lose the best part of the strength that was native to him in his beginning, and all that was made or begun with that power will crumble, and he will be maimed for ever, becoming a mere spirit of malice that gnaws itself in the shadows, but cannot again grow or take shape. And so a great evil of this world will be removed (*The Return of the King*, Bk 5, Ch. 9).

**Rivendell** An Elven dwelling, remnant of the great, protected Elven kingdoms of Nargothrond* and Doriath* in the First Age* of Middle-earth.* It was founded in the Second Age* by Elrond* in the foothills of the Misty Mountains,* in a hidden, deep-cloven valley. Rivendell lay between the rivers Hoarwell and Loudwater. Its Elvish name was Imladris.

In *The Hobbit*,* Rivendell is described as 'the Last Homely House East of the Sea', a place of refuge for any of the faithful, not just Elves.* Bilbo* spent many years here translating the Elvish tales of The Silmarillion.*

*The Hobbit* tries to capture the special essence of Elrond's Rivendell: 'His house was perfect, whether you liked food, or sleep, or work, or story-telling, or singing, or just sitting and thinking best, or a pleasant mixture of them all. Evil things did not come into that valley.'

**Roäc** The chief of the friendly ravens of Erebor,★ like the eagles,★ agents of providence.★ Roäc informed Thorin★ of the death of Smaug.

***The Road Goes Ever On: A Song Cycle* (1968, 1978)** Poems by Tolkien on the theme of The Road,★ set to music by Donald Swann. The musical scores are included, along with notes on, and translations of, the Elvish★ poems by Tolkien. The first edition included 'The road goes ever on', 'Upon the hearth the fire is red', 'In the Willow-Meads of Tasarinan', 'In western lands', 'Namárië (Farewell)', 'I sit beside the fire' and 'Errantry'. In the second edition, 'Bilbo's last song' was added. A recording of the poems, sung by William Elvin and accompanied at the piano by the composer, is available. The recording, *Poems and Songs of Middle-earth*, also contains recordings of Tolkien reading the poems.

**The Road** The Road, which 'goes ever on', is a potent and central image in Tolkien, particularly in *The Hobbit*★ and *The Lord of the Rings*.★ As in John Bunyan's *The Pilgrim's Progress*, there is the path to be taken by choice leading to perils and adventures. As Frodo★ and Sam set off with the Ring,★ at first 'the road wound away before them like a piece of string'. This road, which leads across rivers, through the underworld, over the dreadful bridge in Khazad-dûm, and finally into Mordor★ itself through She-lob's Lair, is charted in Barbara Strachey's *Journeys of Frodo*.

The link between the Road and the theme of quest★ is brought out by Elrond★ at his Council in Rivendell,★ speaking of the need to go into Mordor★ to destroy the Ring:

Now at this last we must take a hard road, a road unforeseen. There lies our hope, if hope it be. To walk into peril—to Mordor . . . The road must be trod, but it will be very hard. And neither strength nor wisdom will carry us far upon it. This quest may be attempted by the weak with as much hope as the strong. Yet such is oft the course of deeds that move the wheels of the world: small hands do them because they must, while the eyes of the great are elsewhere (*The Fellowship of the Ring*, Bk 2, Ch. 2).

*See also* THE STRAIGHT ROAD.

**Rohan** Kingdom of the horsemen—the Rohirrim—in southern Middle-earth.★ Its people raised horses on the country's large plains. The capital was Edoras★ below ancient Dunharrow. Rohan was originally a province of Gondor★ and traditionally had close links with it. At the time of the events recorded in *The Lord of the Rings*,★ Théoden★ was King of Rohan

**Rohirric** In *The Lord of the Rings*,★ the language used by the people of Rohan.★ It is related to the languages belonging to the Men of the Anduin★ region. Like Westron★ Rohirric was descended from Adûnaic★ and in fact is an archaic form of Westron. There are similarities with the dialect of Westron used in the Shire★ by hobbits.★ In representing Rohirric in English translation it was natural for Tolkien to draw on Old English or archaic English.

**Romanticism** C.S. Lewis wished for the word 'romantic' to be banned as it now had so many usages as to be virtually useless. He and his friends in The Inklings,★ including Tolkien, failed to find another term however to characterise the central preoccupation they shared or they found in kindred spirits like G.K. Chesterton and George MacDonald.★

When C.S. Lewis wrote *The Pilgrim's Regress* he meant 'romanticism' to mean the special experience of inconsolable longing or joy.★ Although joy was also important to Tolkien, he was more concerned with central qualities of fairy-story or fantasy such as recovery,★ escape★ or

221

consolation.★ He anatomised these in his essay 'On Fairy-Stories'.★ He, like Lewis, was certainly not in revolt against reason or classicism, which romanticism is sometimes assumed to mean. He was not a subjectivist, seeing art as the expression of its maker's soul.

In English literature, the Romantic Movement is often taken to begin with the publication of *Lyrical Ballads* in 1798 by Wordsworth and Coleridge. This was part of a wide reaction against deism and a mechanistic view of nature and mankind. Romanticism gave rise to the Gothic genre, and its offspring, Mary Shelley's remarkable *Frankenstein* (1818) and the rise of science fiction. It also created a vogue for historical romance, as in the novels of Sir Walter Scott. In Germany, romanticism was connected with the rise of modernist theology in reaction to rationalism. George MacDonald's rejection of his native Calvinism was part of the same trend.

The subjective link between different aspects of romanticism, as far as Tolkien and his friend C.S. Lewis were concerned, is a preoccupation with the imagination★ and creative fantasy. This linking thread can be seen in all the main influences upon The Inklings. Indeed, a brief outline of these influences is the best way of characterising the romanticism of Tolkien, C.S. Lewis and their friends.

'Romantic' influences upon The Inklings can for convenience be divided into four areas: (1) ancient mythology; (2) older writers; (3) nineteenth- and early twentieth-century writers; and (4) contemporary sources. These influences are mentioned by C.S. Lewis or come through The Inklings themselves.

*(1) Ancient mythology.* Old Norse mythology deeply influenced Tolkien's fantasies, and affects some features of Lewis' Narnia stories. Tolkien and Lewis believed that scattered among pagan myths there are certain 'good stories' which prefigure Christian truth. They anticipate and give form to adequate vehicles of truth.

*(2) Older writers.* The main sources seem to be the author of *Beowulf* (especially with Tolkien), Dante (particularly with Williams) and Milton, whose influence on Lewis' *Perelandra* is marked. Milton is probably an important root of the science-fiction genre, of which, according to Brian Aldiss, C.S. Lewis is an important part. John Bunyan and earlier medieval allegorists deeply influenced C.S. Lewis also. Edmund Spenser was one of Lewis' favourite authors. Tolkien made clear his dislike of the same author, but nevertheless he and Spenser bear comparison.

*(3) Nineteenth- and early twentieth-century writers.* Most important of writers from this period was George Mac-Donald, influencing in different ways both Tolkien and Lewis, though Tolkien later in life expressed a dislike for MacDonald's fantasies. MacDonald in turn confesses a debt to the German romanticism of Novalis and others. C.S. Lewis' concept of joy or *sehnsucht* is found in German romanticism. He also discusses the ideas of Rudolf Otto (1869–1937) on the numinous★ in his *The Problem of Pain*. He sought to embody that quality in his fantasies. The numinous is also an important quality throughout Tolkien's fiction.

C.S. Lewis points out that William Morris (1834–1896) influenced his work. Tolkien valued Morris as well. There seem to be affinities. While an undergraduate at Oxford,★ C.S. Lewis gave a paper on Morris To The Martlets, a university society. Lewis later wrote that Morris 'seems to retire far from the real world and to build a world out of his wishes; but when he has finished the result stands out as a picture of experience ineluctably true'. The same could be said of Tolkien's work.

*(4) Contemporary sources.* A number of influences on his work are mentioned by C.S. Lewis, including James Stephens, G.K. Chesterton (his thought, not so much his fiction), E.R. Eddison and David Lindsay. These sorts of writers were discussed by The Inklings. Both C.S.

Lewis and J.R.R. Tolkien considered E.R. Eddison (1882–1945) an important writer, and he was much spoken of by The Inklings. Tolkien disliked his invented names; he felt that they lacked colour and conviction. Eddison's geography of his imaginary three kingdoms—Rerek, Meszria and Fingiswold—bears a superficial resemblance to the geography* of Middle-earth.* Eddison was appreciated for his attempts at sub-creation.*

The Inklings influenced each other. Lewis knew versions of Tolkien's *The Silmarillion** and tales of Númenor.* Tolkien believes some names in *Perelandra* were based on his creations. Many of The Inklings were Christians, and Christian meanings are embodied in their work. Even the anthroposophist, Owen Barfield,* deliberately retained Christian elements in his thinking, and belonged to the Church of England.

In his book *The Road to Middle-earth*, T.A. Shippey provides informed speculation as to Tolkien's sources. He refers to Old English texts, including *Beowulf,* as well as Old Norse works. Usefully, he points out the effect of the folk-tales of North-West Europe. He feels also that the ballad tradition is significant. Middle English texts such as *Pearl, Sir Gawain* and *Sir Orfeo* are mentioned, as well as modern authors of Tolkien's youth.

More eccentric, but stimulating, is the study *J.R.R. Tolkien: The Shores of Middle-earth* by Robert Giddings and Elizabeth Holland. This argues for sources for Tolkien's fiction in familiar texts of romance and fantasy such as *The Thirty-Nine Steps, King Solomon's Mines, Lorna Doone, The Lost Horizon* and *The Wind in the Willows.* Though the case is dubious, the book draws attention to the fact that Tolkien and Lewis consciously worked on narrative technique, and the skills of story-telling were appreciated by The Inklings.

*See also* STORY, THEOLOGY OF; MYTH; IMAGINATION; PHILOLOGIST, TOLKIEN AS A; CHRISTIANITY, TOLKIEN AND.

**Further reading**

C.S. Lewis, *The Letters of C.S. Lewis* (1966, 1988); C.S. Lewis, *Of This and Other Worlds* (1982); J.R.R. Tolkien, *The Letters of J.R.R. Tolkien* (1981); Robert Giddings and Elizabeth Holland, *J.R.R. Tolkien: The Shores of Middle-earth* (1981); T.A. Shippey, *The Road to Middle-earth* (1982).

**Rosie Gamgee (née Cotton)**  Rose, from the Shire,★ married Sam Gamgee★ in *The Lord of the Rings*.★ Tolkien was enjoying a joke here, as 'Gamgee' in the West Midlands of his childhood was a household term for cotton wool, after a certain Dr Gamgee from Birmingham who had invented 'gamgee-tissue', a surgical dressing made from cotton wool.

Rosie and Sam had thirteen children, including Elanor the Fair.

**Rúmil**  In the First Age★ of Middle-earth,★ a wise scholar of Tirion★ who, it is said, wrote the *Ainulindalë*.★ He also invented the first writing system. He plays an important part in the earliest versions of *The Silmarillion*.

# S

**Sacrifice**   In the tales of Middle-earth★ there are many examples of sacrifice, a constant theme. In *The Silmarillion*★ we read of Lúthien★ abandoning her immortality for love of Beren,★ and of first Eärendil★ and then Amandil★ sailing to the Undying Lands of the West to intercede on behalf of mankind before the Valar,★ knowing they could not return. In *The Lord of the Rings*★ we learn of the sacrifice of Frodo★ and Sam in their quest★ to destroy the Ring. The burden of the sacrifice falls mostly on Frodo, revealed in his words to Sam as he prepares to leave Middle-earth:

> 'But,' said Sam, and tears started in his eyes, 'I thought you were going to enjoy the Shire, too, for years and years, after all you have done.'
>
> 'So I thought too, once. But I have been too deeply hurt, Sam. I tried to save the Shire, and it has been saved, but not for me. It must often be so, Sam, when things are in danger: some one has to give them up, lose them, so that others may keep them. . .'

One supreme example of sacrifice in the story of *The Lord of the Rings* is that of Gandalf★ on the dreadful bridge of Khazad-dûm,★ fighting a Balrog.★ In Middle-earth, Tolkien points out (*Letters*,★ Letter 156), 'angelic' powers such as wizards★ are capable of error, or worse, especially as they are incarnate. Of the wizards, writes Tolkien,

> Gandalf alone fully passes the tests, on a moral plain anyway (he makes mistakes of judgement). For in his condition it was for him a *sacrifice* to perish on the Bridge in defence of his companions, less perhaps than for a mortal Man or Hobbit, since he had a far greater inner power than they; but also more, since it was a humbling and abnegation of himself in conformity to 'the rules': for all he could know at that moment he was the *only* person who could direct the resistance to Sauron successfully, and all *his* mission was vain. He was handing over to the Authority that ordained the Rules, and giving up personal hope of success.

*See also* PROVIDENCE; CHRISTIANITY, TOLKIEN AND; THE HERO.

**Sarehole Mill** In 1896, Mabel Tolkien★ took her two young sons to live in a rented house in Sarehole, Warwickshire, then in the countryside outside Birmingham city limits. Here an old brick mill stood, with a tall chimney. Though now powered by a steam engine, a stream still ran under its great wheel. The mill, with its frightening miller's son, made a deep impression on Tolkien's imagination. In Hobbiton,★ located on the water, stood a Mill which was torn down and replaced by a brick building which polluted both the air and water.

**Saruman** One of the wizards★ sent to Middle-earth★ to aid the faithful resisting Sauron.★ He was originally the chief of the Order, until desire for possession★ of the One Ring★ brought about his downfall. Centuries before the events recorded in *The Lord of the Rings*, he had taken over the ancient stronghold of Isengard. Among his many evils were his misleading of the White Council,★ his employment of Orcs,★ his manipulation of King Théoden of Rohan,★ and his control of the Shire.★ He brought about his own destruction by trying to capture Frodo★ the Ring-bearer with an Orc band. They captured only Merry and Pippin, who escaped into Fangorn Forest★ and won the help of Treebeard and his Ents.★

**Sauron** The greatest of Morgoth's servants, his deeds encompass three Ages of Middle-earth,★ until his final downfall with the War of the Ring.★ In origin he is one of the Maiar,★ the lesser Ainur,★ the same order of being as Gandalf.★

He appears in the tale of Beren★ and Lúthien,★ figures strongly in the fall★ of Númenor★ and creates the One Ring★ to rule the Rings of Power.★ He lost the Ring to the ill-fated Isildur★ but, by near the end of the Third Age,★ had consolidated his power enough to attempt to dominate Middle-earth,★ as Morgoth his master had attempted long before to enslave Beleriand.★

Sauron is a more subtle image of incarnate evil★ than Morgoth. Before being caught in the destruction of Númenor, he was able to assume a fair appearance, helping him to win over the minds of Elves★ and Men.

***Sauron Defeated*** This is volume 9 of *The History of Middle-earth*.★ It is also Part Four of *The History of the Lord of the Rings*.★ The book shows Tolkien's developing conception of the final part of the story. It also includes 'The Notion Club Papers'★ and 'The Drowning of Anadûnê'. Anadûnê is the Adûnaic★ form of Númenor.

**Sea-elves** *See* TELERI.

**Second Age** In the history of Middle-earth,★ this is the period of Númenor★ and the exile of Elves to Tol Eressëa from the devastation of Beleriand.★ Here they built Avallónë and planted Celeborn,★ a seedling of Galathilion. Tolkien describes it as a dark age of the world.

The themes of the Second Age, according to Tolkien, are:

1. The delaying Elves who lingered in Middle-earth;
2. Sauron's★ growth into a new Dark Lord, master and

god of mankind, replacing the banished Morgoth;★
3.    The civilisation of Númenor (Atlantis).

The period is mainly dealt with annalistically or historically, as in the *Akallabeth*, published in *The Silmarillion*.
There are very few tales and none comparing with stories
like Beren and Lúthien the Elf-maiden.★
    In *Unfinished Tales* is an incomplete tale, 'Aldarion and
Erendis: The Mariner's Wife', as well as a description of the
island of Númenor. Had Tolkien persisted with 'The Lost
Road' or 'The Notion Club Papers' many tales may have
opened up.

**Second Music of Ilúvatar**    This is the theme which is to be
sung after the end of the world by the Ainur★ and mankind.
The Valar★ do not know what this music will be, or what
role will be played by Elves and Dwarves.★
    *See also* APOCALYPTIC, TOLKIEN AND.

**Seven Rings**    The Rings of Power of the Dwarves,★
referred to in the rhyme on the One Ring★ revealed in *The
Lord of the Rings*.★ They had metal bands set with single
gems.

**The Shaping of Middle-earth (1986)**    This is the fourth
volume of the series *The History of Middle-earth*, edited by
Christopher Tolkien★ from his father's unfinished material.
The book is sub-titled *The Quenta, The Ambarkanta and The
Annals*. Christopher Tolkien provides an exhaustive
commentary on the development of his father's invention.

    'The Quenta' is sometimes given the fuller name 'The
Quenta Silmarillion', another name for 'The Silmarillion'
(meaning 'The history of the Silmarils'). The book includes
the original 'Silmarillion', written by Tolkien in 1926, and
also the 'Quenta Noldorinwa' of 1930 (the largest section of
the book). The latter was the only form of the mythology
of the First Age★ that Tolkien ever completed. To it is
appended a fragment translated into Old English,
supposedly by Aelfwine.★

'The Ambarkanta' (or 'The Shape of the World') is the only account found of the nature of Tolkien's imagined universe. Though a short work, it throws valuable light on his cosmology and the effect of the change of the world at the time of the destruction of Númenor.*

'The Annals' are in effect annotated chronologies reflecting Tolkien's preoccupation with chronology. This book gives the earliest 'Annals of Valinor' (there were three versions in all), and also the earliest version of the 'Annals of Beleriand' (other versions followed).

*The Shaping of Middle-earth* shows the development of Tolkien's mythology up to some time in the 1930s. He continued to work on and modify 'The Silmarillion' up to his death in 1973.

See also *THE SILMARILLION*.

**Shelob**   A monstrous spider, possibly bred by Ungoliant* in Nan Dungortheb* in the First Age.* She escaped the destruction of Beleriand* and made her way south. Making a den in Cirith Ungol, she preyed on Men, Elves and Orcs, providing a guard for that route into Mordor.* Gollum* treacherously led Frodo* and Sam into her Lair, but Shelob was blinded by the courageous Sam.

**The Shire**   A region of Eriador* in Middle-earth* and the home of hobbits,* settled in the Third Age.* Hobbits lived comfortably in its four Farthings. Its chief town was Michel Delving,* Bilbo Baggins* lived in Bag End, Hobbiton,* where he was joined by Frodo* when Bilbo adopted him after the adventures chronicled in *The Hobbit*.* Frodo had grown up in Buckland.*

Tolkien was attached to the West Midlands, and tried to convey the quality of life in turn-of-the-century Worcestershire and Warwickshire in his creation of the Shire.

See also SAREHOLE MILL; GEOGRAPHY OF MIDDLE-EARTH.

**The Silmarillion (1977)**   This was published posthumously and edited by Tolkien's son, Christopher, who is the person closest to his thinking. *The Silmarillion* is based on Tolkien's unfinished work, and is not intended to suggest a finished work, though Christopher Tolkien's editorial work is highly skilled and faithful to his father's intentions. The unfinished nature of the book is most apparent in several independent tales that are contained therein, such as 'Beren and Lúthien the Elf-maiden',★ 'Túrin★ Turambar' and 'Tuor and the Fall of Gondolin'.★ These are in fact summaries of tales intended to be on a larger, more detailed, scale and never completed. The condensed, summary nature of much of the published *The Silmarillion* presents difficulties for many readers. This difficulty is compounded by the plethora of unfamiliar names. When J.E.A. Tyler updated his *Tolkien Companion* to include *The Silmarillion* he had to add about 1,800 new entries!

To help Tolkien readers, this handbook has concentrated on the two independent tales for which most detailed story-telling exists— those of Beren and Lúthien, and Túrin Turambar. The mythology and earlier history of Middle-earth exists as background to these stories. Speaking of the Tale of Beren and Lúthien, Tolkien commented: 'There are other stories almost equally full in treatment, and equally independent and yet linked to the general history.'

The Silmarillion evolved through all the years of Tolkien's adulthood, and strictly is only a part of the published *The Silmarillion*. It chronicles the ancient days that include the First Age★ of Middle-earth. It begins with the creation of the Two Lamps (*see* LIGHT) and concludes with the Great Battle in which Morgoth★ is overthrown (*see* BATTLES OF BELERIAND). The unifying thread of the annals and tales of The Silmarillion is, as its title suggests, the fate of the Silmarils.

The published *The Silmarillion* is divided into several sections. The first is the *Ainulindalë*★—the account of the creation of the world. This is one of Tolkien's finest pieces of writing, perfectly taking philosophical and theological matter into artistic form. The second section is the *Vala-quenta*—the history of the Valar.★ Then follows the main and largest section, the *Quenta Silmarillion*—The Silmarillion proper (the 'history of the Silmarils'). The next section is the *Akallabêth*,★ the account of the downfall of Númenor. The final section concerns the history of the Rings of Power★ and the Third Age.★ Tolkien intended all these sections to appear in one book, giving a comprehensive history of Middle-earth.★ He comments at length on the development of the history of Middle-earth through the Three Ages in the important and lengthy Letter 131 in his *Letters*.★

The mythology, history and tales of Middle-earth are, in fact, found in unfinished drafts dating over half a century, with considerable developments and changes in narrative structure. Not least, some of the great tales have poetic and prose versions. The published *The Silmarillion* provides a stable point of reference by which to read the unfinished publications (collected by Christopher Tolkien in *Unfinished Tales* and *The History of Middle-earth*★). Further stability is provided by Tolkien's own often lengthy commentaries on The Silmarillion in his *Letters*.

To illustrate the spread of material in different publications, there are several versions of the creation of the world (Arda★): 'The Music of the Ainur' (*The Book of Lost Tales, 1*, ch. 2); 'The Ambarkanta' ('The Shape of the World') (*The Shaping of Middle-earth*, ch. 5); and the 'Ainulindalë' (*The Lost Road*, part 2, ch. 4). Earlier versions of The Silmarillion can be found as follows: *The Book of Lost Tales 1 and 2*★ (the beginning of the tales that eventually became The Silmarillion); 'The earliest "Silmarillion"' (*The Shaping of Middle-earth*,★ ch. 2; 'The Quenta' (*The Shaping of Middle-earth*, ch. 3); and The 'Quenta Silmarillion' (*The Lost Road*, part 2, ch. 6).

Much of The Silmarillion was cast by Tolkien into annalistic form, in his concern for astonishing consistency and detail in dates and history. (Such consistency was part of his theory of sub-creation.★) There are therefore a number of summaries of the key events of the First Age and before, as follows: 'The earliest annals of Valinor' (*The Shaping of Middle-earth*, ch. 6); 'The earliest annals of Beleriand' (*The Shaping of Middle-earth*, ch. 7); 'The later annals of Valinor' (*The Lost Road*, part 2, ch. 2); and 'The later annals of Beleriand' (*The Lost Road*, part 2, ch. 3).

**Further reading**

Paul H. Kocher, *A Reader's Guide to The Silmarillion* (1980); Karen Wynn Fonstad, *The Atlas of Middle-earth* (1981).

**Silvan Elves** These were Elves other than the Eldar,★ who were not enriched by the westward journey to Aman.★ They lived in forests or mountains. At the time of the events of *The Hobbit*★ and *The Lord of the Rings*★ they lived in places such as the Woodland Realm (whence came Legolas★) or Lórien★ which were ruled by Eldar such as Galadriel★ and Celeborn,★ or Thranduil.★ They were also know as the Wood-elves, or the woodland Elves.

**Sindar** Also called Grey-elves, these lived in Beleriand,★ and did not complete the Great Journey to the Uttermost West. Their chief habitation was the kindgom of Doriath,★ ruled by Thingol★ and Melian.★ They spoke Sindarin, a major variant of Elvish.★

**Sindarin** A major form of Elvish★ used by Sindarin or Grey-elves. It had a common ancestry with Quenya★ Elvish, but both diverged in grammar, vocabulary and sound. Sindarin owes its inspiration to Tolkien's love of Welsh, which it structurally resembles. The changes in Elvish which resulted in Sindarin are accounted for in terms of geography and history by Tolkien. The main factor was that the Sindarin Elves remained in Beleriand★ rather than

completing the Great Journey to Aman.★ Historically,
Fëanor's★ rebellion against the Valar,★ and the Kinslaying,★
alienated Thingol★ of Doriath★ from the Quenya-speaking
Elves of Valinor.★ Sindarin enriched the Mannish language
which became Westron.★

## Further reading

Ruth S. Noel, *The Languages of Tolkien's Middle-earth* (1980);
Jim Allan, *An Introduction to Elvish* (1978).

*Sir Gawain and the Green Knight* (1925)  Edited by J.R.R.
  Tolkien and E.V. Gordon.★ This presentation of the text of
  the finest of all the English medieval romances helped to
  stimulate study of this work, much loved by Tolkien. It
  contains a major glossary. His own translation of it was
  published in 1975. A new edition of Tolkien's and Gordon's
  book came out in 1967, edited by Norman Davis.
*Sir Gawain and the Green Knight, Pearl and Sir Orfeo*
  (1975)  These are Tolkien's own translations of three major
  medieval English poems. His verse translations skilfully
  represent the poetic structures of the original poems. The *Sir
  Gawain* and *Pearl*★ poems are by the same unknown author
  from the West Midlands, an area of England with which
  Tolkien identified, basing the Shire★ upon it.
**Sirion**  The major river of Beleriand★ in *The Silmarillion*.★ Its
  name means 'river' in Sindarin★ Elvish.★ The Sirion's main
  tributaries were the Teiglin, Esgalduin, Aros and Narog.
**Sisam, Kenneth**  Tolkien's tutor in the English School at
  Exeter College, Oxford,★ when he was an undergraduate.
  Sisam was a young New Zealander who greatly inspired
  Tolkien in the area of Medieval Literature. Later the two men
  collaborated on a book of extracts from Middle-English,
  Tolkien painstakingly supplying the glossary. Sisam eventu-
  ally joined the Clarendon Press (Oxford University Press).

**Smaug**   A winged dragon★ who appears in *The Hobbit*.★ Smaug hoarded treasure stolen from the Dwarves★ and the people of Dale,★ including the Arkenstone.★ Bilbo Baggins★ is indirectly responsible for his death by discovering the weak point in his scaly armour.

**Smith, G.B.**   A close friend of Tolkien's from school-days and a member of the society, the T.C.B.S.★ He commented on a number of Tolkien's early poems, including his original verses about Eärendil★ (then written 'Eärendel'). Smith was killed on active service in the winter of 1916. He wrote to Tolkien shortly before his death, speaking of how the T.C.B.S.—the 'immortal four'—would live on, even if he died that night. He concluded: 'May God bless you, my dear John Ronald, and may you say the things I have tried to say long after I am not there to say them, if such be my lot.'

***Smith of Wootton Major* (1967)**   This short story was Tolkien's last, and complements his essay 'On Fairy-Stories'★ in tracing the relationship between the world of faery and the primary world. The story seems simple at first, but, though children can enjoy it, it is not a children's story. Tolkien described it as 'an old man's book, already weighted with the presage of "bereavement"'. It was as if, like Smith in the story with his Elven star, Tolkien expected his imagination to come to an end. In a review, Tolkien's friend and one of The Inklings,★ Roger Lancelyn Green, wrote of the book: 'To seek for the meaning is to cut open the ball in search of its bounce.'

Like *Farmer Giles of Ham*,★ the story has an undefined medieval setting. The villages of Wootton Major and Minor could have come out of the Shire.★ As in Middle-earth,★ it is possible to walk in and out of the world of faery (the realm of Elves★). The story contains an Elven-king in disguise, Alf, apprentice to the bungling cake-maker Nokes. Nokes has no concept of the reality of faery, but his sugary cake for the village children, with its crude Fairy

Queen doll, can stir the imagination of the humble. A magic Elven star in the cake is swallowed by Smith, giving him access to faery. In the village it is the children who can be susceptible to the 'other', the numinous,★ where their elders are only concerned with eating and drinking.

As in *Leaf by Niggle*★ glimpses of other worlds transform art and craft in human life (*see* ELVEN QUALITY). The humble work of the village smith is transformed into the sacramental.

The writing of the story was inspired by a growing dislike of some of the fantasy of George MacDonald,★ particularly his short story *The Golden Key*. That story however is one of MacDonald's great achievements, as *Smith of Wootton Major* is one of Tolkien's, in its deceptive simplicity.

**Song**  *See* MUSIC.

**Stoors**  One of three varieties of hobbit;★ the one that stayed longest in the Anduin★ region before crossing the Misty Mountains.★ At the time of the events of *The Lord of the Rings*★ Stoors were to be found in the Marish and Buckland.★ They liked flat lands and riversides and were the only hobbits to enjoy watery pursuits like swimming, boating and fishing.

**Story, Theology of**  Like his friends, C.S. Lewis★ and Charles Williams,★ Tolkien worked in his fiction according to a theology of romanticism★ which owed much to the nineteenth-century writer who was Lewis' mentor, George MacDonald.★ The term 'romantic theologian', Lewis tells us, was invented by Charles Williams. What Lewis says about Williams in his introduction to *Essays Presented to Charles Williams* applies also to Tolkien and himself.

A romantic theologian [C.S. Lewis points out] does not mean one who is romantic about theology but one who is theological about romance, one who considers the theological implications of those experiences which are called romantic. The belief that the most serious and ecstatic experiences either of human love or of imaginative literature have such theological implications and that they can be healthy and fruitful only if the implications are diligently thought out and severely lived, is the root principle of all his [Williams'] work.

Whereas a key preoccupation of Charles Williams was romantic love, C.S. Lewis was 'theological' about romantic longing or joy,★ and Tolkien reflected deeply on the theological implications of fairy-tale and myth,★ particularly the aspect of sub-creation★ (*see* IMAGINATION).

In a doctorial thesis, *Romantic religion in the works of Owen Barfield, C.S. Lewis, Charles Williams and J.R.R. Tolkien*, R.J. Reilly saw C.S. Lewis as an advocate of 'romantic religion'. This was the 'attempt to reach religious truths by means and techniques traditionally called romantic, and . . . to defend and justify these techniques and attitudes of romanticism by holding that they have religious sanction'.

In his autobiography *Surprised by Joy*, C.S. Lewis reported some of his sensations—responses to natural beauty, and literary and artistic responses—in the belief that others would recognise similar experiences of their own.

J.R.R. Tolkien was fascinated by several structural features of fairy-tales and other stories that embodied myths. These features are all related to a sense of imaginative decorum; a sense that imagining can, in itself, be good or bad, as rules or norms apply strictly in fantasy, as they do in thought. Meaning can only be created by skill or art, and play an essential part in human thought and language. As Tolkien said, 'The incarnate mind, the tongue, and the tale are in our world coeval.' As Barfield has shown in his introduction to the new edition of *Poetic Diction*, the ideal in logical positivism and related types of modern linguistic philosophy is, strictly, absurd; it systematically eliminates meanings from the framing of truths, expecting thereby to guarantee their validity. In Tolkien's view, the opposite is the case. The richer the meanings involved in the framing of truths, the more guarantee there is of their validity.

G.K. Chesterton once wrote that we should sometimes take our tea at the top of a tree, as our perceptions tend to get dulled. One of the essential features of the fairy-tale or mythopoeic fantasy is the sense of 'recovery'*—the regaining of health or a clear view of things. Tolkien pointed out that we too often get caught in the specific corridor of daily, mundane life, and lose a view of 'things as we are (or were) meant to see them'. Entry into an imaginary world 'shocks us more fully awake than we are for most of our lives'. C.S. Lewis said the latter of myth, but it applies to this feature of recovery. Part of this recovery is a sense of imaginative unity, a survey of the depths of space and time. The essential patterns of reality are seen in a fresh way.

Charles Williams' 'romantic religion', though concerned with romantic love, took the form of what he characteristically called the Way of the Affirmation of Images. He developed a distinctive doctrine of the two-fold Way of the Affirmation and Rejection of Images. Here we say of any created person or thing in reference to the Creator: 'This also is Thou; neither is this Thou.' In his *The Descent of the Dove*, Williams described the principle like this:

> The one Way was to affirm all things orderly until the universe throbbed with vitality; the other to reject all things until there was nothing anywhere but He. The Way of Affirmation was to develop great art and romantic love and marriage and philosophy and social justice; the Way of Rejection was to break out continually in the profound mystical documents of the soul, the records of the great psychological masters of Christendom. All was involved in Christendom . . .

The validity of both aspects of the two-fold Way was

connected in Williams' thinking with another key doctrine of Christianity—co-inherence. This doctrine was captured for him, characteristically, in the beautiful Image of the City. This social image brings out, for Williams, the dependence of each of us upon others' labours and gifts, and the necessity of bearing one another's burdens.

Of the friends, Tolkien and Lewis were particularly influenced by Barfield.* He believed that mankind has moved away from a unitary consciousness into a division of subject and object. Lewis came to believe that theoretical reasoning abstracts from real things, real emotions, real events. Tolkien and Lewis saw this desirable unity, for example, in the gospel story, where the quality of myth is not lost in the historical facticity of the events. There is no separation of story and history. Lewis wrote:

> There is . . . in the history of thought, as elsewhere, a pattern of death and rebirth. The old, richly imaginative thought which still survives in Plato has to submit to the deathlike, but indispensable, process of logical analysis: nature and spirit, matter and mind, fact and myth, the literal and metaphorical, have to be more and more sharply separated, till at last a purely mathematical universe and a purely subjective mind confront one another across an unbridgeable chasm. But from this descent, also, if thought itself is to survive, there must be re-ascent and the Christian conception provides for this. Those who attain the glorious resurrection will see the dry bones clothed again with flesh, the fact and the myth remarried, the literal and the metaphorical rushing together (*Miracles*, ch. XVI).

**Straight Road**    Also called the Lost Road. Even before the changing of the world, it was difficult to sail from Middle-earth* to Aman,* the Uttermost West. After the change, when the world became a sphere and the Sea bent, some Elven ships were allowed to pass beyond the world to the

Undying Lands. They used the Straight Road. Tolkien employed the idea of a Lost Road in early formulations of his mythology, involving the voyage of the mariner Aelfwine★ to Tol Eressëa, where he hears the tales of the First Age.★ *See also The Lost Road and Other Writings.*

**Sub-creation** J.R.R. Tolkien believed that the art of true fantasy or fairy-story writing is sub-creation: creating another or secondary world with such skill that it has an 'inner consistency of reality'. This inner consistency is so potent that it compels secondary belief or primary belief (the belief we give to the primary or real world) on the part of the reader. Tolkien calls the skills to compel these two degrees of belief 'fantasy' and 'enchantment' respectively. A clue to the concept of sub-creation lies in the fact that the word 'fairy', or more properly 'faery', etymologically means 'the realm or state where faeries have their being'. A faery-story is not thus a story which simply concerns faery beings. They are in some sense other-worldly, having a geography and history surrounding them.

Tolkien's key idea is that faery, the realm or state where faeries have their being, contains a whole cosmos. It contains the moon, the sun, the sky, trees and mountains, rivers, water and stones, as well as dragons, trolls, Elves, Dwarves, goblins, talking animals, and even a moral person when he or she is enchanted (through giving primary belief to that other world). Faery is sub-creation rather than either representation or allegorical interpretation of the 'beauties and terrors of the world'. Sub-creation comes, says Tolkien, as a result of a two-fold urge in human beings: (1) the wish to survey the depths of space and time, and (2) the urge to communicate with living beasts other than mankind, to escape from hunger, poverty, death, and to end the separation between mankind and nature. Just as the reason wishes for a unified theory to cover all phenomena in the universe, the imagination★ also constantly seeks a unity of meaning appropriate to itself.

*See also* 'ON FAIRY-STORIES'.

**Symbolism**   Tolkien belongs to the tradition of romanticism, but with important differences (*see* ROMANTICISM); one being that the imagination★ is not the organ of truth. As with the romantics, symbols play an integrating part in his fiction. His symbolism helps to make his work a lamp as well as a mirror; depicting reality, but also illuminating it. In this handbook a number of his characteristic symbols or symbolic themes are included, such as death,★ angels,★ dragons,★ eagles,★ an Elven quality,★ healing,★ light,★ music,★ the numinous,★ the quest,★ the Rings of Power,★ the Road,★ the tree★ and underground places and journeys.★

On a greater scale, the geography★ and history★ of Middle-earth★ is symbolic, enriching the stories that come from the various Ages. Further enrichment is obtained from invented beings such as the Valar,★ the Maiar,★ Balrogs,★ Elves,★ Dwarves★ and hobbits.★

The process of invention that Tolkien calls sub-creation★ allows the imagination to employ both unconscious and conscious resources of the mind. This is particularly so with regard to language, which is intimately connected to the whole self, and not just theoretical thought. Sub-creation allows powerful archetypes to become an effective part of an art-work. This accounts for the universal appeal of deeply imaginative writing like Tolkien's. The chart following outlines some central archetypes in imaginative literature, many of which are found in Tolkien, strengthening the moral purpose of his work (*see* EVIL). It is taken, with the author's permission, from Leland Ryken's *Triumphs of the Imagination*. Mr Ryken in turn adapted the material from the literary criticism of Northrop Frye. Archetypes are recurrent symbols, plot structures and character types that make up much of the material of literature. In symbolic literature like Tolkien's the archetypes are focused and definite, but so-called realistic fiction

241

is also replete with hidden archetypes. Tolkien takes many archetypes from the Bible (*see* CHRISTIANITY, TOLKIEN AND), which Northrop Frye called 'a grammar of literary archetypes', and Leland Ryken described as '*the* great repository of archetypes in Western literature'.

| Category of Experience | The Archetypes of Ideal Experience | The Archetypes of Unideal Experience |
|---|---|---|
| *The supernatural* | Any beneficent deity; angels; the heavenly society | Demons (including Satan), or malicious deities; hobgoblins, ogres; blind fate. |
| *Human characters* | The hero or heroine; the good mother or father; the innocent child; the benevolent king or ruler; the wiseman; the shepherd. | The villain; the tempter or temptress; the harlot (prostitute); the witch; the idiot; the taskmaster or tyrant; the wicked father or step-mother; the malicious parent; the outcast or wanderer; the traitor; the malicious giant; the shrewish or domineering woman; the sluggard or lazy person; any 'blocking character' who stands in the way of happiness, the churl or refuser of festivities. |
| *Human relationships* | The community or city; images of symposium, communion, order, unity, friendship, love; the wedding, or marriage; the feast, meal or supper; the family; freedom. | Tyranny or anarchy; isolation among people; images of torture, mutilation (the cross, stake, scaffold, gallows, stocks), slavery or bondage; images of war, riot, feud or family discord. |

243

| Category of Experience | The Archetypes of Ideal Experience | The Archetypes of Unideal Experience |
|---|---|---|
| *Clothing* | Any stately garment symbolizing legitimate position or success; festal garments such as wedding clothes; fine clothing given as gifts of hospitality; white or light coloured clothing; clothing or adornment (such as jewels); protective clothing, such as a warrior's armour. | Ill-fitting garments (often symbolic of a position that is usurped and not held legitimately); garments symbolising mourning (the shroud, dark mourning garments, sackcloth, mourning bands); dark clothes; tattered, dirty or coarse clothing; any clothing that suggests poverty or bondage; a conspicuous excess of clothing (the overdressed person). |
| *The human body* | Images of health, strength, vitality, potency; feats of strength and dexterity; images of sleep and rest; wish-fulfilment dreams; birth. | Images of disease, deformity, barrenness, injury or mutilation; sleeplessness or nightmare, often related to guilt of conscience; death. |
| *Food* | Staples, such as bread, milk and meat; luxuries, such as wine and honey; the harvest. | Hunger, drought, starvation, cannibalism; poison or magic potions. |

| | | |
|---|---|---|
| *Animals* | A community of domesticated animals, usually a flock of sheep; a lamb; a gentle bird, often a dove; a faithful domesticated animal, such as a dog; a group of singing birds; the beneficent talking animals of folktales; animals or birds noted for their strength, such as the lion or eagle. | Monsters or beasts of prey; the wolf (enemy of sheep), the tiger, the dragon, the vulture, the cold and earthbound snake, the owl (associated with darkness), the hawk; any wild animal harmful to people; the scapegoat. |
| *Landscape* | A garden, grove, or park; the mountaintop or hill; the fertile and secure valley; pastoral settings or farms; the pathway. | The sinister or dark forest, often enchanted and in the control of demonic forces; the heath or wilderness or wasteland, which is always barren and may be either a tropical place of intense heat or a place of ice and intense cold; the dark and dangerous valley; the underground cave or tomb; the graveyard; the labyrinth. |
| *Plants* | Green grass; the rose; the vineyard; the tree of life; the lily; evergreen plants (symbolic of immortality); herbs or plants of healing. | The thorn or thistle; weeds; dead or dying plants; the willow tree (symbolic of mourning). |
| *Buildings* | The city or palace or castle; the temple or church; the house or home; the tower of contemplation; the capital city, symbol of the nation; the rustic cottage. | The prison or dungeon; the wicked city of violence, sexual perversion and crime; the tower of imprisonment or wicked aspiration (the tower of Babel). |

| Category of Experience | The Archetypes of Ideal Experience | The Archetypes of Unideal Experience |
| --- | --- | --- |
| *The inorganic world* | Images of jewels and precious stones, often glowing and fiery; fire and brilliant light; burning that purifies and refines; rocks of refuge. | The inorganic world in its unworked form of deserts, rocks and wilderness; dry dust or ashes; fire that destroys and tortures instead of purifying; rust and decay. |
| *Water* | A river or stream; a spring or fountain of water; showers of rain; dew; flowing water of any type; tranquil pools in a formal garden. | The sea and all that it contains (sea beats and water monsters); stagnant pools. |
| *Forces of nature* | The breeze or wind; the spring and summer seasons; calm after storm; the sun or the lesser light of the moon and stars; light, sunrise, day. | The storm or tempest; the autumn and winter seasons; sunset, darkness, night. |
| *Sounds* | Musical harmony; singing; laughter. | Discordant sounds, cacophony, weeping, wailing. |
| *Direction and motion* | Images of ascent, rising, height (especially the mountaintop and tower), motion (as opposed to stagnation). | Images of descent, lowness, stagnation or immobility, suffocation, confinement. |

# T

**Taniquetil** In *The Silmarillion*,★ the highest mountain in the world, located in Aman★ on the borders of the Sea. The Valar★ Manwë★ and Varda★ have their halls on its summit. Some of the Elves★ the Vanyar★—lived on its slopes.

**Tar-** A prefix added to names to denote kings and queens who ruled and who took Quenya★ names in Númenor★ in the Second Age★ of Middle-earth.★

**Taur-nu-Fuin** The name given to the forested region of Dorthonian★ after Morgoth★ brought evil and terror to it. Beren★ and his father Barahir were among the last Men to remain here. Beleg found Gwindor here, resulting in Túrin's★ rescue from the Orcs.★ Taur-nu-Fuin in some ways resembled Mirkwood.★

**T.C.B.S.** A club of four friends formed while Tolkien was a schoolboy in King Edward VI Grammar School. The other three members were G.B. Smith,★ R.Q. 'Rob' Gilson★ and Christopher Wiseman.★ Only Wiseman and Tolkien survived World War I. At first the original group was called the Tea Club (T.C.), and then later the Barrovian Society (B.S.), as the tea room in Barrow's Stores in Corporation Street, Birmingham,★ became a favourite place to meet. T.C.B.S. members combined the two groups. Constant members were Tolkien, Gilson and Wiseman, and later Smith. Tolkien's friends enjoyed his interest in Norse Sagas and medieval English literature. After leaving school, the four core members of the T.C.B.S. continued to meet up occasionally, and to write to each other, until the war destroyed their association. The T.C.B.S. left a permanent mark on Tolkien's character, which he captured in the idea of 'fellowship', as in the fellowship of the Ring. Friendship with C.S. Lewis★ helped to satisfy this important side of his nature.

**Teleri** In *The Silmarillion*,★ the third and largest group of Elves★ known as the Eldar.★ In Quenya★ Elvish★ 'teleri' means 'last' or 'hindmost'. They trailed behind during the Great Journey to the Uttermost West, Aman,★ and only reluctantly left the shores of Middle-earth.★ The Teleri had a great love of the Sea, and eventually settled in the beautiful city of Alqualondë. Fëanor★ turned against them for refusing to help him in his rebellion against the wishes of the Valar,★ and the dreadful Kinslaying took place.

The Teleri were taught the art of ship-building by the Vala, Ossë.

**Thangorodrim** In *The Silmarillion*,★ a great mountain with three peaks made by Morgoth★ above Angband.★ He made the mountain out of the slag from his mines. Like Mount Doom, it was a volcano, its smoke visible from a great distance. The mountain was destroyed when the dragon,★ Ancalagon,★ fell upon it.

Húrin,★ father of Túrin,★ was set high on the slopes of Thangorodrim by Morgoth for twenty-eight years, so that he could see the outworkings of Morgoth's curse against him on his family.

**Théoden** In *The Lord of the Rings*,★ the seventeenth King of Rohan.★ He had been deceived by Saruman★ for many years through his counsellor, Gríma (Wormtongue★). The spell was broken by Gandalf★ and Théoden found healing★ through him. Théoden then joined his forces with Gondor against Sauron.★ He was killed by the Lord of the Nazgûl★ in the Battle of Pelennor Fields (*see* WAR OF THE RING).

**Third Age**   This Age of Middle-earth★ was reckoned from the first defeat of Sauron,★ when Gil-galad★ died, to the War of the Ring,★ when Sauron was defeated for a second and seemingly final time. At the end of the Age the Ring-bearers and the greatest of the Elves★ passed over the Sea to the Uttermost West. The period was called by Elves the Fading Years, as it marked the end of their dominance and the beginning of the dominance of mankind. Much of the history of the Age concerns the Mannish kingdoms of Arnor and Gondor, and, unexpectedly, the Shire★ of the hobbits★ (distant relations of Men).

**Third House of the Edain**   In *The Silmarillion*,★ the last and probably the largest group of the Edain★ to enter Beleriand.★ Eventually, they consolidated under Hador★ in Dor-lómin.★ They were renowned for their courage in resisting Morgoth,★ and heroes★ such as Túrin,★ Tuor★ and Eärendil★ belonged to the Third House. In Dor-lómin both Sindarin★ and an early form of Adûnaic★ were spoken.

**Thorin and Company**   The Company, in *The Hobbit*,★ led by Thorin Oakenshield★ to recover treasure from Smaug★ the dragon★ in Erebor.★ Bilbo Baggins★ was employed as their burglar. The remainder of the Company were Dwarves:★ Thorin, Balin, Dwalin, Fíli, Kíli, Dori, Ori, Nori, Óin, Glóin, Bifur, Bofur and Bombur. Gandalf★ was with them for some of their journey.

**Thorin Oakenshield**   In *The Hobbit*,★ the Dwarf★ king who led the party, Thorin and Company, to recover the treasure hoarded by Smaug★ the dragon.★ He grew to respect the hobbit Bilbo Baggins.★ The king died in the Battle of Five Armies. He was called Oakenshield because, in his youth, he had fought bravely in the Battle of Azanulbizar, the greatest battle between Dwarves and Orcs,★ and had used an oak-branch as a shield and club.

**Thorondor**   In *The Silmarillion*,★ the Lord of the Eagles★ helping to protect Elves★ and Men. Part of his role was the guarding of Gondolin.★ Among his many great deeds was the rescue of Beren★ and Lúthien★ as they fled from Morgoth★ after stealing back a Silmaril.

**Thráin II**   A Dwarf★ king captured by Sauron★ and imprisoned in Dol Guldur.★ One of the Seven Rings★ was extracted from him after long torture. Gandalf★ found him before he died, and the king gave him the key to the Side-door of Erebor,★ the Lonely Mountain. This key allowed Thorin and Company★ access to Smaug's★ hoard in *The Hobbit.*★

**Thranduil**   In *The Hobbit,*★ the Elvenking of the Woodland Realm. He captured Thorin Oakenshield★ and his Dwarves,★ but Bilbo★ rescued them. In the Battle of the Five Armies he led the Elven army. He also fought in the War of the Ring★ against Sauron's forces. Legolas,★ of the Company of the Ring, was his son.

**Three Rings**   These were the Rings of Power belonging to the Elves.★ Though they were made without Sauron's★ help, they could be controlled by the One Ring.★ When the Ring was destroyed, they lost their power.

Unlike the other Rings, their power did not lie in control and domination. Rather, their power lay in building, understanding and healing.★ The Three Rings were called Vilya, Nenya and Narya.★ Nenya was worn by Galadriel,★ and Narya by Gandalf.★

**Thrimidge**   In the Reckoning of the Shire★ this was the fifth month, approximating our May.

**Tinúviel**   Sindarin★ Elvish★ for 'twilight-maiden', a poetic name for the nightingale. Beren★ gave Lúthien★ this name when he first heard her singing in Doriath.★

**Tirion**   In *The Silmarillion,*★ the first habitation of Elves★ in Eldamar and its main city. It was built on the hill of Túna, having white walls and crystal stairs. It was set in the great ravine in the great mountains of the Pelóri through which passed the light of the Two Trees.★

**Tol Eressëa**   In *The Silmarillion,*★ a large island in the Bay of

Eldamar, off Valinor.★ Its western shore received the light of the Two Trees.★ The Teleri★ lived here for a long time. At the end of the First Age★ many Elves★ settled on the island, building Avallónë. In the Second Age★ there was communion between the Elves of Tol Eressëa and the Men of Númenor.★

**Tol Sirion**  In *The Silmarillion*,★ a beautiful green island of the River Sirion,★ where the river flows through the Pass of Sirion. Finrod Felagund built a fortress here which was eventually captured by Sauron and renamed Tol-in-Gaurhoth. When Finrod and Beren★ were imprisoned here, Finrod was murdered by Sauron's wolf. Lúthien★ cast out Sauron and broke the tower.

***The Tolkien Reader* (1966)**  Published only in the United States, this collection contains an introduction by Peter S. Beagle and the following pieces by Tolkien:

'The Homecoming of Beorhtnoth Beorhthelm's Son' (a short play);

'On Fairy-Stories'★ (an essay);

'Leaf by Niggle'★ (an allegorical short story);

'Farmer Giles of Ham'★ (a comic short story);

'The Adventures of Tom Bombadil'★ (a collection of hobbit★ verses).

The collection was important for introducing devotees of *The Lord of the Rings*★ to the wider range of Tolkien's writings.

**Tolkien, Arthur (1857–1896)**  The father of J.R.R. Tolkien, and a manager of Lloyds Bank. He moved to South Africa to improve his prospects, and Mabel Suffield (*see* TOLKIEN, MABEL) left Birmingham to marry him there. They married in April 1891. Arthur died quickly from rheumatic fever. He contracted the illness while the rest of the young family were visiting England to improve the young J.R.R. Tolkien's health. The child was just four.

**Tolkien, Christopher**  The third son of J.R.R. Tolkien,

born in 1924. He was called Christopher in honour of Christopher Wiseman,* one of the T.C.B.S.* The father was especially fond of Christopher, finding a great affinity with him (perhaps captured in the unfinished story 'The Lost Road'*). During the war years, when Christopher was posted to South Africa with the RAF, Tolkien sent him instalments of his work in progress, *The Lord of the Rings.** In a sense, he was the original audience for the work. In earlier years, he had listened intently as his father read to him from the material making up The Silmarillion.* Christopher also prepared maps for the publication of that work. After his father's death he devoted himself to editing his unfinished work, such as the published *The Silmarillion* (1977), as was Tolkien's wish.

Christopher Tolkien was a member of the informal literary group, The Inklings.* He studied at Trinity College, Oxford* and became a Fellow at New College. He eventually resigned his academic duties to devote himself to editing his father's work.

**Tolkien, Edith**    *See* TOLKIEN, J.R.R.

**Tolkien, Hilary**    The younger brother of J.R.R. Tolkien, born in South Africa, February 1894. After leaving school, he helped run a farm with his Aunt before enlisting as a bugler in 1914. After the war he bought a small orchard and market garden near Evesham in Worcestershire, the ancestral home of his mother's family. Worcestershire was one of the inspirations for the Shire* in his brother's fiction.

**Tolkien, J.R.R. (1892–1973)**

> I was born in 1892 and lived for my early years in 'The Shire' in a premechanical age. Or more important, I am a Christian (which can be deduced from my stories), and in fact a Roman Catholic. The latter 'fact' perhaps cannot be deduced . . . I am in fact a *Hobbit* (in all but size). I like gardens, trees and unmechanized farmlands; I smoke a pipe and like good plain food . . . I like, and even dare to

wear in these dull days, ornamental waistcoats. I am fond of mushrooms (out of a field); have a very simple sense of humour (which even my appreciative critics find tiresome); I go to bed late and get up late (when possible). I do not travel much (Letter, 25th October 1958).

John Ronald Reuel Tolkien, whose name and distant origins are Germanic, was born in Bloemfontein, South Africa, of English parents in 1892. He told his son Christopher that his earliest memory of Christmas was 'of a blazing hot day'. After his father's death his family moved to the West Midlands, living in countryside like the Shire★ near Birmingham,★ which he described as his 'home town'. As a child, reading Welsh place names on coal trucks gave him a love for that language. He attended Birmingham's King Edward VI Grammar School, then located near the city centre, and was familiar with Worcestershire and the Vale of Evesham. It is suggested that the Malvern Hills helped to inspire the mountains of Gondor in Middle-earth.

His mother, he remembered as 'a gifted lady of great beauty and wit, greatly stricken by God with grief and suffering, who died in youth (at 34) of a disease hastened by persecution of her faith'. Her non-conformist family were opposed to her move to Roman Catholicism. In her will, she requested that Father Francis Morgan★ became the guardian of Tolkien and his younger brother Hilary. 'It is to my mother,' wrote Tolkien, 'who taught me (until I obtained a scholarship . . . ) that I owe my tastes for philology, especially of Germanic languages, and for romance.'

In 1908, Father Morgan found better lodgings for the orphaned brothers at Duchess Road in Birmingham. Here Tolkien fell in love with another, older lodger, Edith Bratt. She was attractive, small and slender, with grey eyes like Lúthien Tinúviel.★ Concerned that Tolkien kept his mind on his education, Father Morgan eventually forbade

Tolkien to see her until he reached the age of twenty-one. They were formally engaged when he was twenty-two, after she had been received into the Roman Catholic Church. His Roman Catholicism was to be a source of tension in their marriage.

After graduating from Exeter College, Oxford, in 1915, and marrying Edith in the next year, he saw bitter action in World War I, losing all but one of his best friends. With several of these friends he had formed a club, the T.C.B.S.* It was during the Great War years that Tolkien began working on The Silmarillion,* writing 'The Fall of Gondolin' in 1917 while convalescent. In fact, in general plot, and in several major episodes, most of the legendary cycle of The Silmarillion was already constructed before 1930— before the writing and publication of *The Hobbit*,* the forerunner of *The Lord of the Rings*.* In the latter books there are numerous references to matters covered by The Silmarillion; ruins of once-great places, sites of battles long ago, strange and beautiful names from the deep past, and Elvish swords made in Gondolin, before its fall, for the Goblin Wars.

In a letter written many years later, Tolkien outlined to an interested publisher the relationship between his life and his imaginary world. He emphasises that the origin of his fiction was in language.

I do not remember a time [he recalls] when I was not building it. Many children make up, or begin to make up, imaginary languages. I have been at it since I could write. But I have never stopped, and of course, as a professional philologist (especially interested in linguistic aesthetics), I have changed in taste, improved in theory, and probably in craft. Behind my stories is now a nexus of languages (mostly only structurally sketched) . . . Out of these languages are made nearly all the *names* that appear in my legends. This gives them a certain character

(a cohesion, a consistency of linguistic style, and an
illusion of historicity) to the nomenclature . . .

Tolkien's life-long study and teaching of languages was the
spring and nourishment of his imaginative creations. Just as
science-fiction writers generally make use of plausible
technological inventions and possibilities, Tolkien has used
his deep and expert knowledge of language in his fantasies.
He created in his youth two forms of the Elvish tongue,
inspired by his discovery of Welsh and Finnish, starting a
process which led to a history and geography to surround
these languages, and peoples to speak them (and other
tongues). He explains: 'I had to posit a basic and phonetic
structure of Primitive Elvish, and then modify this by series
of changes (such as actually do occur in known languages)
so that the two end results would have a consistent structure
and character, but be quite different.' In a letter to W.H.
Auden,★ Tolkien confessed that he always had had a
'sensibility to linguistic pattern which affects me emo-
tionally like colour or music'.

Equally basic to language in Tolkien's complicated make-
up from a very early age was a passion for myth★ and for
fairy-story, particularly, he says, for 'heroic legend on the
brink of fairy-tale and history'.

Tolkien reveals that he was an undergraduate before
'thought and experience' made it dawn on him that story
and language were 'integrally related'. His imaginative and
scientific interests were not on opposite poles. Myth and
fairy-story, he saw, must contain moral and religious truth,
but implicitly, not explicitly or allegorically★ (see
CHRISTIANITY, TOLKIEN AND). Both in his linguistic and in his imaginative interests he was seeking constantly
'material, things of a certain tone and air'. Myths, fairy-
stories and ancient words constantly inspired and sustained
the unfolding creations of his mind and imagination★—his
Elvish★ languages and the early seeds of *The Silmarillion.*

255

The tone and quality that he ever sought he identified with North-Western Europe, particularly England. It could perhaps be called 'northernness'. He sought to embody this quality in his fiction and invented languages.

The stories he invented in his youth—such as The Fall of Gondolin*—came to him as something given, rather than as conscious creation. This sense of givenness and discovery remained with him throughout his life; a spring that never dried up, stopped only by death.

After the Great War, Tolkien began university teaching in Leeds, after a period of working on the new edition of the Oxford English Dictionary. After a few years he moved to Oxford* to become Rawlinson and Bosworth Professor of Anglo-Saxon; this was in 1926. It was in this year that he met C.S. Lewis.* Their long friendship was soon to begin. Lewis had then been an English Don at Magdalen College for one year. They met at the English Faculty Meeting on 11th May 1926, and Lewis was not amused, recording in his diary:

> He is a smooth, pale, fluent little chap. Can't read Spenser because of the forms—thinks language is the real thing in the English School—thinks all literature is written for the amusement of men between thirty and forty—we ought to vote ourselves out of existence if we are honest . . . No harm in him: only needs a smack or two.

Any initial antipathy, however, was soon forgotten. Within a year or so they were meeting in each other's rooms and talking far into the night.

These conversations proved crucial both for the two men's writings, and for Lewis' conversion to Christianity. As the Ulsterman Lewis remarked in Surprised by Joy: 'Friendship with Tolkien . . . marked the breakdown of two old prejudices. At my first coming into the world I had been (implicitly) warned never to trust a Papist, and at my first coming into the English Faculty (explicitly) never to trust a philologist. Tolkien was both.'

A typical note of the time occurs in a letter from C.S. Lewis to his Ulster friend Arthur Greeves in December 1929: 'Tolkien came back with me to college and sat discoursing of the gods and giants of Asgard for three hours.'

Tolkien himself recalled sharing with Lewis his work on *The Silmarillion*, influencing his science-fiction trilogy. The pattern of their future lives, including the later Inklings,★ was being formed. Tolkien remembered: 'In the early days of our association Jack used to come to my house and I read aloud to him The Silmarillion so far as it had then gone, including a very long poem: Beren and Lúthien.' Lewis actually was given the unfinished poem to take home and read, and was delighted by it, offering Tolkien suggestions for improvements.

The gist of one of the long conversations between Lewis and Tolkien was fortunately recorded by Lewis in another letter to Arthur Greeves in October 1931. It was a crucial factor in Lewis' conversion to Christianity. Tolkien argued that human stories tend to fall into certain patterns and can embody myth. In the Christian gospels there are all the best elements of good stories, including fairy-stories, with the astounding additional factor that everything is also true in the actual, primary world. It combines mythic and historical, factual truth, with no divorce between the two. C.S. Lewis' conversion deepened the friendship; a friendship only later eclipsed by Lewis' acquaintance with Charles Williams,★ and what Tolkien called his 'strange marriage' to Joy Davidman.

Tolkien's academic writings were sparing and rare. In 1937 he published an article entitled 'Beowulf: the Monsters and the Critics',★ which, according to Donald K. Fry, 'completely altered the course of Beowulf studies'. It was a defence of the artistic unity of that Old English tale.

In 1938 he gave his Andrew Lang lecture at St Andrew's University, 'On Fairy-Stories', which was later published in *Essays Presented to Charles Williams*—The Inklings' tribute to the writer who had a great deal in common with Tolkien and Lewis. It sets out Tolkien's basic ideas concerning imagination,★ fantasy and sub-creation.

The Professor's famous children's story, *The Hobbit*,★ came out in 1937. He continued with its adult sequel, *The Lord of the Rings*,★ more and more leaving aside his first love, The Silmarillion. It was a long, painstaking task, some of it written in instalments to one of his four children, Christopher, on war-time service with the RAF. At one point, he did not touch the manuscript for a whole year. He wrote it in the evenings, for he was fully engaged in his university work and other matters. During World War II years, and afterwards, he read portions to The Inklings, or simply to Lewis alone. He attended almost all The Inklings' meetings.

In 1945 Tolkien was honoured by a new Chair at Oxford, Merton Professor of English Language and Literature, reflecting his by now wider interests. He was not now as cool as he had been previously to the idea of teaching literature at university. Tolkien retained the Chair until his retirement in 1959. The scholarly story-teller's retirement years were spent revising *The Lord of the Rings*, brushing up and publishing some shorter pieces of story and poetry, and intermittently working on various drafts of The Silmarillion. Tolkien also spent much time dodging reporters and youthful Americans, as the 1960s marked the exploding popularity of his fantasies, and his readership went from thousands to millions.

An interviewer at the time of this new popularity, Daphne Castell, tried to capture his personal manner:

He talks very quickly, striding up and down the converted garage which serves as his study, waving his pipe, making little jabs with it to mark important points; and now and then jamming it back in, and talking round it . . . He has the habits of speech of the true story-teller . . . Every sentence is important, and lively, and striking . . .

His voice is captured on several recordings of poems and other extracts from his fiction.

## Brief chronology

1857    Arthur Reuel Tolkien (father) born in Birmingham, England.
1870    Mabel Suffield (mother) born in Birmingham, her family originally from Evesham, Worcestershire, England.
1889    Birth of Edith Bratt.
1892    John Ronald Reuel Tolkien born in Bloemfontein, in South Africa, 3rd January, where his father worked for Lloyd's Bank.
1894    Birth of Hilary Arthur Reuel Tolkien.
1896    Death of Arthur Tolkien. The family moves near to Sarehole Mill, then outside the city of Birmingham.
1900    He enters King Edward VI School, Birmingham.
1904    Death of Mabel (Suffield) Tolkien.
1908    He meets Edith Bratt.
1909    Their romance is discovered by Father Morgan.
1911    Enters Exeter College, Oxford, to read Classics.
1915    First Class in English Language and Literature. He is commissioned in the Lancashire Fusiliers.
1916    Marries Edith Bratt. He serves from July to November in the Battle of the Somme. Returns to England suffering from 'trench fever'.
1917    His son, John, born. Begins writing the tales which will become *The Silmarillion*.
1918    The war finished, he takes up work with the new Oxford English Dictionary.

1920 Appointed Reader in English Literature at Leeds University. His second son, Michael, born.
1924 His third son, Christopher, born.
1925 Elected to the Chair of Anglo-Saxon at Oxford University.
1926 Friendship with C.S. Lewis begins.
1929 His daughter, Priscilla, born.
1930 Begins to write *The Hobbit*.
1936 His lecture, 'Beowulf: The Monsters and the Critics'.
1937 *The Hobbit* is published. He begins a sequel which will become *The Lord of the Rings*.
1939 His lecture, 'On Fairy-Stories'.
1945 Takes up Chair of English Language and Literature at Oxford University. Sudden death of his friend and Inkling Charles Williams.
1954 Publication of first two volumes of *The Lord of the Rings*.
1955 Publication of final volume of *The Lord of the Rings*.
1959 Retires from his work at Oxford.
1965 Increasing popularity on American college campuses after an unauthorised paperback edition of *The Lord of the Rings* is issued.
1968 He and his wife move to Bournemouth.
1963 Death of his friend and Inkling C.S. Lewis.
1971 Death of Edith Tolkien. He returns to Oxford.
1973 Dies on 2nd September.
1977 Publication of *The Silmarillion*, edited by Christopher Tolkien.
1980 Publication of *Unfinished Tales*, edited by Christopher Tolkien, the first of a number of publications of early versions of *The Silmarillion*, and other stories and annals from the first three Ages of Middle-earth. Most notable is *The Lays of Beleriand* (1986).

**Further reading**

Humphrey Carpenter, *J.R.R. Tolkien: A biography* (1977); Humphrey Carpenter, *The Inklings: C.S. Lewis, J.R.R. Tolkien, Charles Williams and their friends* (1978); edited by Humphrey Carpenter with the assistance of Christopher Tolkien, *The Letters of J.R.R. Tolkien* (1981); Daniel Grotta, *The biography of J.R.R. Tolkien: architect of Middle-earth* (1976, 1978); Daphne Castell, 'The Realms of Tolkien', *New Worlds SF.* Vol. 50, No. 168 (1966).

**Tolkien, Mabel (1870–1904)** The mother of J.R.R. Tolkien. Her family, the Suffields, were associated with Evesham, Worcestershire, and Tolkien identified himself with these West Midlands roots of his mother. When twenty-one, Mabel sailed to South Africa to marry Arthur Tolkien,★ who had sought to better himself by being posted there for Lloyd's Bank. Mabel had to adjust to life in Bloemfontein. Arthur Tolkien died in 1896, while Mabel and her two young sons were visiting England. Soon the family moved to Sarehole, in the countryside south of Birmingham. Mabel, a highly talented woman, educated the boys until they entered formal education.

Mabel's religious background was mixed, and she eventually moved from a high church position to Roman Catholicism. Both the Tolkien and Suffield families were non-conformist or Anglican, so her conversion created great tension, especially as the boys were now exposed to Roman Catholicism. Tolkien came to believe that the effect on her health of this opposition eventually proved fatal. She succumbed to diabetes in 1904. She had arranged for the boys to have the guardianship of Father Francis Morgan.★

**Tragedy** Traditionally, in tragedy, the tragic person or hero★ has within him or herself a fatal weakness. Tragedy however also involves a moral fall,★ a before and after. In tragedy, therefore, there is a complex mixture of subjective and objective evil.★ For a Christian writer like Tolkien, there is the additional question: Has tragedy a place in Christian art, or only 'comedy' and triumph? Tolkien shows it has (as does the Bible, with its continual emphasis on the necessity of suffering in a distorted world). Tragedy in the Bible however is subsidiary to what Tolkien calls *eucatastrophe* (*see* CONSOLATION), the denial of ultimate defeat.

In *The Silmarillion*★ tragedy is a major element in the characters of such as Melkor (Morgoth★), Fëanor★ and particularly Túrin★ Turambar. Tolkien (*Letters*,★ Letter 131) remarks that Túrin is 'a figure that might be said (by people who like that sort of thing, though it is not very useful) to be derived from elements in Sigurd the Volsung, Oedipus and the Finnish Kullervo'.

Túrin is flawed in being swift to anger, proud and unteachable. Yet, as Paul Kocher points out, Túrin has freewill, even though cursed by the oath of Morgoth against his father, Húrin★ (whose innocent suffering is Job-like). His mistaken wrath and pride make him an outlaw and cut him off from Thingol★ of Doriath★ (with terrible consequences for Nienor★ and his mother). His arrogance at Nargothrond★ means that he rejects the wisdom of both Ulmo★ and King Orodreth,★ bringing ruin, death and the dragon, Glaurung, to the realm.

The fall of Númenor★ is a tragedy, as seems to be suggested by Tolkien (*Letters*, Letter 131): '*The Downfall* is partly the result of an inner weakness in man . . . Its central theme is (inevitably, I think, in a story of Men) a Ban, or Prohibition.'

*The Lord of the Rings*★ records a number of tragic characters: Gollum,★ Boromir,★ Denethor,★ and Saruman,★ to name a few. David Harvey, in *The Song of Middle-earth*, believes that Frodo is a tragic figure (though other interpretations are possible). Harvey believes that Frodo's tragedy lies in his choice in weakness not to destroy the One Ring★ at the decisive moment. Providence has to intervene in the form of Gollum (who, significantly, is only there because of Frodo's earlier pity—as well as the pity of Sam and Bilbo).

**The Treason of Isengard**   This is Volume 7 of *The History of Middle-earth*,★ and Part 2 of *The History of The Lord of the Rings.*★ It helps to show the development of *The Lord of the Rings*★ by publishing earlier drafts.

**Tree**   This is a key symbol in Tolkien's life and writings. It is characteristic that his illustration of a tree appears on the cover of *Tree and Leaf,*★ a fact that gave Tolkien pleasure. It is a symbol too that has a key integrating role in the biblical message (*see* CHRISTIANITY, TOLKIEN AND). Clyde Kilby pointed out that the image of the tree, in both Tolkien's writings and the Bible, is persistent 'particularly as a symbol of beginnings and endings, of significant people and of highly historical events'.

The Bible opens with a garden that includes the Tree of Life and closes with the same Tree in the New Jerusalem, the heavenly city. In Middle-earth, there are in its early history Two Trees,★ one white and one golden, Telperion and Laurelin, that illuminated Valinor.★ At the end of the Third Age★ a seedling modelled on Telperion flowered. This marked the restoration of the realm of King Elessar (Aragorn★). Isildur★ had brought the seed from Númenor,★ from a tree which went back to Tol Eressëa★ and, before that, to Valinor.

Minas Tirith★ presages the New Jerusalem. Significantly, Gondor's emblem is the White Tree and seven stars on a black field. The seven stars are an apocalyptic★ symbol in the biblical Book of Revelation. The flowering of the White Tree was a reassurance to Aragorn, a sign of permanent and ultimate victory over evil.★ Kilby points out that the sapling of a tree on a barren mountainside is parallel to Isaiah's prophecy of the coming Christ (Isaiah 53:2). In Aragorn's case, the shooting tree looks forward to the

Fourth Age and the arrival of the Christian centuries. Aragorn himself is identified with the sapling, a parallel with a forerunner of Christ in the Old Testament, King David (2 Samuel 11).

Tolkien had a deep sense in his invented mythology of a Final Ending, where the earth would be remade, the trees rekindled into life and the lands under the sea restored.

***Tree and Leaf* (1964, 1988)**   This book by Tolkien includes his famous essay 'On Fairy-Stories',★ explaining his view of fantasy and sub-creation,★ and an allegory with autobiographical elements, 'Leaf by Niggle'.★ The new edition of 1988 adds a poem written to C.S. Lewis,★ *Mythopoeia*, incorporating ideas about the relationship between myth★ and fact which were influencial in Lewis' conversion to Christianity (*see* CHRISTIANITY, TOLKIEN AND).

**Trolls**   A variety of troll, the Stone-troll, figures dramatically in *The Hobbit*.★ There seems to have been four types in all, each large and wicked. Trolls originated in the First Age,★ bred by Morgoth,★ perhaps based on Ents★ as Orcs★ were debased Elves.★

**Tulkas**   One of the Valar,★ noted for his strength. He valiantly opposed Morgoth★ (Melkor).

**Túna**   In *The Silmarillion*,★ the high green hill in the ravine through the high mountains of the Pelóri in Aman.★ The beautiful city of Tirion★ was built on it.

**Tuor**   In *The Silmarillion*,★ it is recorded that the man, Tuor, was fostered by the Grey-elves★ of Mithrim. He was given a message by the Vala★ Ulmo★ for the hidden kingdom of Gondolin.★ There he married the Elf-maiden Idril.★ With her, and their son Eärendil,★ he escaped the fall of Gondolin.

**'Tuor and the Fall of Gondolin'**   Tolkien intended this to be a major tale in *The Silmarillion*,★ standing independently of the history of the ancient days and the First Age.★ It was never completed on a grand scale. *The Silmarillion* contains a summary of the story, while in *Unfinished Tales* there is the first part of a detailed treatment, showing, sadly, the promise of what was never achieved. 'The Fall of Gondolin' is the first of the tales of the First Age to be composed— during sick-leave from the Army in 1917. The most complete form of 'The Fall of Gondolin' is to be found in *The Book of Lost Tales*,★ but unfortunately this was written early in the development of *The Silmarillion*.

**Turgon** In *The Silmarillion*,★ the king of the hidden king-dom of Gondolin.★ Though he opposed Fëanor's★ plan to pursue Morgoth★ when he stole the Silmarils, Turgon became one of the exiles from Aman.★ When in Middle-earth★ he settled at Vinyamar, but was led to the site where he founded Gondolin. Though a wise leader, Turgon ignored the warning sent by Ulmo★ through Tuor,★ leading to the downfall of Gondolin. Turgon was the father of Idril★ and grandfather of Eärendil.★

**'Túrin Turambar, The tale of '** The tragedy of Túrin is one of several stories from The Silmarillion★ (the narrative of the ancient days and First Age★ of Middle-earth★) that, according to Tolkien, stand independently of the history and mythology.★ The tale was conceived early, when Tolkien as a young man wished to make use of elements from the Finnish Kalevala. Tolkien was aware that there is a hint of the story of Oedipus in it. The larger title of the tale is 'The Children of Húrin'.

Húrin,★ the father of Túrin, had been captured by Morgoth★ and bound upon the peak of Thangorodrim★ where he could better see the outworkings of Morgoth's curse or doom upon his family. The curse bedevils the life of Túrin and other relations, including Túrin's sister, Nienor. Yet the sorrow in Túrin's life comes not only from external causes, though compounded by them, but also because of a 'fatal flaw' that is the stuff of tragedy. Túrin's flaw was a mixture of pride and rashness of action. In the tension between internal motive and external malice in Túrin's life, Tolkien explores the problem of evil.★ He says that in the tale of Túrin 'are revealed most evil works of Morgoth', and that it was 'the worst of the works of Morgoth in the ancient world'.

There are several accounts of the tale of Túrin. That in *The Silmarillion* is in fact a summary of a story worked out in great detail by Tolkien. A longer, fuller and more powerful version, sadly incomplete, appears in *Unfinished Tales*,★ and an unfinished poetic version is recorded in *The Lays of Beleriand*.★

Húrin, Túrin's father, was captured by Morgoth during the Battle of Tears Unnumbered (*see* BATTLES OF BELERIAND). Húrin's brother, Huor, was killed. Huor had only been married two months before he went to battle. His son, Tuor,★ was brought up by Elves★ of Mithrim, his mother, Rían, having died of sorrow. Húrin also left behind an unborn child, Nienor★ (which means mourning), sister to Túrin.

Because of her hardship, living in the northerly Dor-lómin,★ and afraid that the eight-year-old Túrin would be taken into slavery, his mother sent him to Doriath★ with two old servants. Beren★ was a relation of her father's, so she had a basis for begging King Thingol★ to harbour her son.

Thingol gladly fostered the boy and urged his mother to join him in Doriath. Morwen refused, loath to leave the home she had shared with Húrin, but sent the great heirloom, the Dragon-helm of Dor-lómin.

For the next nine years the boy grew, and every now and then Thingol would send messengers north-west to Dor-lómin to obtain news of Morwen, and Túrin's sister, Nienor. But then no more news came; the messengers failed to return. Afraid for his mother and sister, Túrin asked the Elvenking for arms, including the Dragon-helm of Dor-lómin. For three years he battled on the borders of Doriath against Morgoth's forces, a companion in arms with Beleg, a renowned bowman.

Túrin returned to Menegroth,★ his appearance reflecting

266

his wild existence. Mocked in court by Saeros, a sharp-tongued counsellor of Thingol, Túrin responded in quick anger and was unintentionally responsible for Saeros' death. Here the curse of Morgoth against Húrin's family begins to bite. Túrin ignored good advice to return to Menegroth to ask Thingol's pardon, and became an outlaw, joining a criminal band of brigands.

Thingol had pardoned Túrin and sent Beleg to find him to try to get him to return. He searched long and hard, and after many perils he was captured by the outlaws when Túrin happened to be out of the camp. Túrin returned, and seeing the cruel way his friend was being treated, he was stricken with deep remorse about the activities of the outlaws. He vowed from now on to fight only against Morgoth, and Beleg and Túrin renewed their friendship.

Túrin was too proud to accept the pardon of the king, and refused Beleg's request to fight the incursion of Orcs into Dimbar, close by Doriath. When he asked Beleg to remain with him west of the River Sirion,★ Beleg in turn refused, saying that if he wished for his companionship, he would have to find him in Dimbar. As they parted, Túrin looked westwards and saw the great height of Amon Rûdh,★ and told Beleg to seek him there. Beleg reported back to King Thingol, and asked leave to guard and guide Túrin as far as he could. Thingol granted this wish to him, and gave him the sword Anglachel, made by Eöl the Dark Elf from iron from a meteorite. Queen Melian,★ looking at the sword, sensed the malice of Eöl in it, and warned Beleg. Melian, in turn, gave him a supply of lembas,★ the waybread of the Elves, showing unusual favour to Túrin. The Elves had never before given such a grace to a Man.

After clearing the Orcs from Dimbar, Beleg parted from his companions and went after Túrin. In the meantime, Túrin and his outlaws had come across three Dwarves.★ One they captured, called Mîm, offered to lead them to his hidden halls as a ransom. These were in Amon Rûdh. This is how Túrin came to have his hideout in the high hill. Túrin learned much about Dwarves, and about Mîm's own kind.

In midwinter of that year, during heavy snow, Beleg appeared at Amon Rûdh, much to Túrin's delight. He brought with him the Dragon-helm of Dor-lómin. Túrin still would not return to Doriath, so Beleg remained with the company, tending the hurt and sick. The lembas helped in their healing.* He gained high honour among the Men, but Mîm hated the Elf.

Morgoth's incursions into the central highlands and Beleriand* increased. His motives of evil against mankind and Elf had been worked out before the making of Middle-earth (*see AINULINDALË*). Dimbar and the north marches of Doriath were taken. To the west of Doriath, however, the Orcs became increasingly afraid of a great warrior wearing the Dragon-helm of Dor-lómin, and his companion with a bow. This was Túrin and Beleg. Morgoth heard of this and laughed, for he knew the identity of Túrin from the helm. Before long there was a ring of spies around Amon Rûdh.

The Dwarf Mîm and his son were captured by Orcs, and led them to the hideout. Túrin's company was virtually destroyed as it slept. Túrin was taken prisoner and Beleg lay badly wounded. The master of healing slowly recovered, and then started after the Orcs in the direction of Angband* (Morgoth's stronghold) seeking Túrin.

The Orc party was in no hurry, and Beleg followed them into the darkened forests of Taur-nu-Fuin,* once Dorthonian.* There Beleg came across a sleeping Elf, Gwindor, who had escaped from Morgoth's slavery, and was now lost and bewildered in the haunted forest.

Gwindor had seen the Orc party with their captive. Together, he and Beleg followed the trail until they emerged from the forest onto the high slopes that ran down into the cold, dusty desert of Anfauglith* (originally Ardgalen*). There the Orcs were camped ready for nightfall.

They placed great wolves as sentinels while they slept.

In the darkness Beleg shot the wolves one by one with his bow. Gwindor and Beleg crept into the camp and found Túrin senseless in a weary sleep. They carried him as far as they could out of the camp as a great storm approached. Here the curse of Morgoth worked its way into events again. As Beleg cut the bonds which bound the prisoner he accidently pricked him with the sword made in malice. Túrin woke up in rage and fear, and, believing Beleg to be an Orc come once again to torment him, instantly seized the sword and killed him. Then a great flash of lightning revealed the dead friend's face.

As the wind gusted and great rains fell all around, Túrin sat unmoving beside the body. In the morning the Orcs had gone. Gwindor stirred Túrin to help him bury their friend. Gwindor took the terrible sword, and the lembas given by Queen Melian, to strengthen them in those wild lands.

Túrin took long to recover from Beleg's death. Gwindor, as Beleg had done, guarded and guided Túrin during their long journey. When at last the travellers reached Lake Ivrin at the source of the River Narog, Túrin found healing, and he made a song (*see* MUSIC) for Beleg. Gwindor gave him the fateful sword, Anglachel, and told him he was leading him to his home at Nargothrond* where he would find healing and renewal. By coming to the Elven stronghold of Nargothrond, Túrin brought the curse upon him to them.

The Elvenking's daughter, Finduilas,* loved Gwindor and had never forgotten him. For his sake, Túrin was allowed to dwell with the Elves of Nargothrond, but he kept his name secret from them. He soon grew in favour with them, eventually leading their army—an unpresidented honour for a Man, which fatally reinforced his pride. He was a Man with an Elven quality;* so much so that he seemed like an Elf. Against her will, Finduilas found her heart turning from Gwindor to Túrin. Warning her of

Túrin's likely doom, Gwindor revealed to her his name. He told her of the dreadful curse that Morgoth had put on Túrin's father and his kin.

This is how Túrin's true name was revealed to the Elves, and he was held in even higher honour. He persuaded them to go openly to war. On his advice they built a great bridge over the River Narog to their entrance for speedier movement of their forces. Gwindor spoke against this exposure, believing it unwise, but he was ignored. As the Orcs were pushed back from the surrounding countryside Nargothrond came to the attention of Morgoth. During this stemming of Morgoth's power, Morwen, Túrin's mother, took the opportunity to flee from Dor-lómin with Nienor her daughter, and go to King Thingol in Menegroth.

Elvish messengers came to Nargothrond from the coast. Ulmo★ the Vala★ had come to Círdan★ the shipwright, warning that great peril faced Nargothrond. They must shut their gates and destroy the great bridge they had built.

Túrin now had absolute power over the Elves of Nargothrond. He was stern, and his pride had increased. He ignored the message. Morgoth now unleashed his power, a great army and also the dragon Glaurung. The dragon polluted and defiled Lake Ivrin, and passed southwards into the region of Nargothrond, bringing destruction with him.

Though the Elven army came out bravely to do battle, led by Orodreth★ their king, with Túrin at his right, they were overwhelmed. Orodreth was killed and Gwindor mortally wounded. Túrin came to his aid, and the dying man spoke of the curse upon Túrin. But for Túrin's pride and prowess, said Gwindor, he would have life and love, and Nargothrond would stand a while longer. He urged Túrin to make haste to Nargothrond and save Finduilas. He prophesied: 'She alone stands between thee and thy doom. If thou fail her, it shall not fail to find thee.' With these words he died.

Though Túrin rushed back, Glaurung the dragon and the hordes of Orcs got there before him. Making use of the great bridge over the River Narog Glaurung put his full force against the doors of Nargothrond and shattered them, passing within.

By the time Túrin arrived the people of Nargothrond had been slaughtered, burned, or were herded together to be taken into captivity. As he fought his way towards the caverns, the dragon emerged. Túrin looked at him without fear, but fell under the spell of his lidless eyes, and stood as still as stone. The dragon taunted him over his tragic life, including his slaying of his friend, Beleg, and lied that his mother and sister were hungry slaves in Dor-lómin.

While the eyes of the dragon held him, the Orcs herded away their captives, including Finduilas, who cried out to Túrin. He could do nothing. Her voice was to haunt him.

Glaurung released the still bemused Túrin. The malicious dragon told him to make haste to Dor-lómin to help his mother and sister. If he tarried to rescue Finduilas he would never see his family again.

Túrin, believing the dragon, rushed northwards, while Glaurung destroyed the great bridge and heaped himself a great hoard of the treasure of Nargothrond. As he went north, it seemed to Túrin that Finduilas cried to him from wood and hill. At last he came to the desecrated lake of Ivrin, now a frozen mire. In Dor-lómin he failed to find Morwen and Nienor, and discovered they had long ago gone. His eyes were opened to the deceit of the dragon. His only comfort was that his efforts against the Orcs had made the way open for his mother and sister to travel to Doriath. Knowing they were safe there within the protection of the girdle of Melian,★ Túrin went in search of Finduilas. He discovered from the Men of Brethil that she had been cruelly murdered by the Orcs when they had tried to rescue the prisoners. Her last words were that they should tell Túrin that she was there. There they buried her.

The woodmen took the stricken Túrin into their care, and he took on the name Turambar, 'Master of Doom'. He aided them in fighting the Orcs.

Some survivors of Nargothrond made their way to King Thingol in Doriath. In this way, they knew that Túrin had been there. Morwen was distraught, and went into the wild in search of her son, followed by his sister Nienor. Thingol's chief captain and friend of Túrin, Mablung, travelled with them to protect them. He left them on a hill close to Nargothrond while he went ahead to investigate.

Aware of their approach Glaurung lay down in anger in the river bed, and a great mist and dragon-stench went up. The guards tried to lead Morwen and Nienor away to safety but their horses were maddened by the stench and rushed away. Morwen was never found, but Nienor was thrown from her horse. Making her way back to the hill she climbed out of the mist into sunshine. There she looked into the eyes of the dragon, who had settled his head on the hill.

The dragon put a spell of forgetfulness and terrible darkness on her. Her name was lost to her, as well as the name of all things. Returning to the hill, Mablung and several companions led her towards Doriath and safety.

While camping they were attacked by Orcs, and in the confusion Nienor ran away in terror. Her fear was a kind of madness, and as she ran she tore off her clothes. Mablung and his companions could find no trace of her.

Nienor ran until exhausted, and then, falling, slept. She awoke to the sun, and it was like the first morning, as all seemed new and fresh to her. She could remember nothing of her past. A great storm arose and, in terror, she threw herself down on a mound, the very burial place of Findui-las. Here Túrin came across her, with some Brethil* woodmen, and cast his cloak about her. He had never seen his sister, and did not know who she was. They took her to a safe lodge, and when she opened her eyes and saw Túrin, she felt comforted. He was something she felt she had sought for in her darkness. She wept when asked her name, so Túrin called her Níniel, which means 'tear-maiden'.

By the time they reached Amon Obel★ in the centre of the Forest of Brethil, she had fallen into a fever. She found healing★ through the skill of the lame man, Brandir. Also she was taught language as if she were an infant.

Brandir felt strangely uneasy about the love that arose between Túrin and Níniel. There was a temporary peace in Brethil and, after some hesitation, Níniel joyfully married Túrin and eventually conceived their child.

He promised her he would not go to war against the Orcs unless their homes were threatened. At last, however, Túrin was forced to help the people of Brethil, and his black sword again appeared in battle. Glaurung the dragon heard news of this, and pondered what evil to do to Túrin.

The great dragon emerged from the hills of Nargothrond and made his way to the borders of Brethil. It was plain that he intended to ravage the land. The people sought Turin's advice. His counsel was that the dragon could only be defeated by cunning and good fortune. He bravely offered to seek out the dragon on the borders of the land while the people remained behind and prepared to scatter. In this way, if Glaurung did come many would escape.

Only Dorlas and Hunthor, a relation of the lame and peaceable Brandir, were willing to go with Túrin. Níniel was filled with fear and foreboding as Túrin and his two companions went off. Unwilling to await news, the distraught Níniel, together with many of the people, followed after them. Unable to dissuade them from going Brandir put on a sword and went after them, unable to keep up because of his lameness.

At sundown Túrin arrived near the River Teiglin, where a stream known as the 'Rainy Stair' fell towards the river. Here he discovered that the dragon lay nearby on the edge of a narrow, deep gorge through which the river raced. Túrin planned that he would climb up the gorge underneath where Glaurung lay, and surprise him. It would mean a perilous crossing of the river. On seeing the gorge in the dark of night, Dorlas' heart failed, and only Túrin and Hunthor crossed over. The roaring of the river drowned all sound they made. They started the ascent. Around midnight the dragon stirred, and started to pull his vast bulk across the narrow ravine, leaving his soft underbelly exposed. A dislodged rock struck Hunthor and killed him, but Túrin climbed hastily and struck his sword into the dragon's belly up to its hilt. Glaurung gave a great scream as he felt the death-blow and pulled himself right across the chasm. At last his fire went out and he lay still.

Túrin wished to recover his sword, recrossed the rushing river, and climbed to where the dragon lay. As he retrieved the sword with a shout of victory, Glaurung opened his eyes and looked with malice at his enemy. Túrin passed out like one dead. Meanwhile Níniel and the people with her were by the 'Rainy Stair', and could hear the screams and see the fires of Glaurung. They thought the dragon had been victorious. As the voice of Glaurung reached Níniel, the old darkness crept over her.

Brandir arrived, and when he heard what he thought was the worst he tried to lead Níniel away, but she ran towards the Crossings of Teiglin, near which Túrin had originally found her. In great dread she ran southwards along the river, towards where the dragon lay. Finding Túrin lying beside Glaurung she tried in vain to rouse him. The dragon stirred before he died enough to work more evil. He revealed to her her true name, Nienor; that Túrin was her brother and that 'the worst of all his deeds thou shalt feel in thyself'.

As Glaurung died, her memory was restored. She looked down at the still figure of Túrin. 'Farewell, O twice beloved!' Nienor cried. 'Master of doom by doom mastered!'—referring to his chosen name, Turambar, 'Master

274

of doom'. Then, overcome with horror and anguish, and ignoring Brandir who had heard all that passed, she cast herself into the chasm and disappeared in the rushing waters below.

As the sorrowing Brandir made his way back to the 'Rainy Stair' where the people awaited, he encountered Dorlas and put him to death. Then, when he arrived, he told those gathered there that Níniel, or rather Nienor the sister of Túrin, was dead, and thankfully both the dragon and Túrin were dead.

As he stopped speaking, Túrin came up, weary and sick. He had come out of his swoon when the dragon died, and then out of a deep sleep. The people thought him a ghost, but he told them to rejoice because he lived, and the dragon was dead.

When Túrin asked about Níniel, Brandir said that she was dead. He reported all that had happened, and what the dragon had said, including Glaurung's statement that Túrin was a curse to his kin and to all who sheltered him.

Túrin was convinced that Brandir acted in malice towards him, and cursed and killed him. He had led Nienor to her death, and proclaimed the lies of the dragon. Then Túrin fled the people, but his madness left him as he approached Finduilas' burial place near the Crossings of Teiglin.

As he sat there Mablung crossed the river with a company of Elves. Túrin told them of the dragon's death, and Mablung revealed to him what had happened to his mother and sister. Thus Túrin realised that doom had overtaken him, and that his killing of Brandir was unjust.

Crying that now only the night was left, and shouting a curse against Doriath, Túrin fled swiftly from them to where the body of the dragon lay. The leaves there were falling from the trees like winter. Túrin took his black sword and fell upon it. When the people of Brethil arrived at the scene and learned the reasons for Túrin's madness and death they were aghast. After burning the dragon's body they laid Túrin in a high mound. The Elves sang a lament for the Children of Húrin, and a stone was set on the mound, engraved in runes with the names of Nienor Níniel and Túrin Turambar, the dragon-slayer.

**Further reading**

J.R.R. Tolkien, *The Silmarillion*, ch. 21; *Unfinished Tales*, Part One, ch. II; *The Book of Lost Tales, 2*, ch. II; *The Lays of Beleriand*, ch. I; *The Shaping of Middle-earth*, 'The Quenta', sections 12–13.

***The Two Towers* (1954)**    The second volume of *The Lord of the Rings*,★ comprising Books Three and Four. It tells the adventures of the members of the Company of the Ring★ after the breakup of their fellowship, up to the beginning of a great darkness from Mordor★ and the start of the War of the Ring.★

Book Three marks a division of the narrative, following the fortunes of the Company other than Frodo★ and Sam, who had set off for Mordor.★ The book tells of the confession and death of Boromir;★ the pursuit of the Orcs★ who had taken Merry and Pippin; the meeting with Éomer and the Riders of Rohan;★ the escape of the hobbits★ from the Orcs;★ the reappearance of Gandalf;★ Merry and Pippin's meeting with the Ent★ Treebeard; the meeting with King Théoden★ and Gandalf's removal of the deception upon him; the Battle of Helm's Deep; the destruction of Isengard★ by the Ents; the reunion of Aragorn,★ Gimli,★ Legolas★ and Gandalf with Merry and Pippin; Pippin's look into the palantír.★

Book Four is chronologically parallel to Book Three, telling how Frodo and Sam fared as they made their dangerous way to Mordor. It recounts how Gollum★ joins the two as their reluctant guide; their passage across the Dead Marshes;★ their arrival at the Black Gate; their journey beyond through Ithilien★ and meeting with Faramir★ of Gondor;★ their parting from Faramir at the Cross Roads as they move towards Cirith Ungol;★ their arrival at Shelob's★ Lair and the treachery of Gollum; Shelob's attack on Frodo and his capture by Orcs of Mordor, and Sam's pursuit into their headquarters, now bearing the Ring.★

**The Two Trees** In *The Silmarillion*,★ the Two Trees of Valinor,★ one white and one golden. The first was called Telperion and the second Laurelin. They illuminated Valinor, Eldamar and as far as Tol Eressëa.★ Their glory was such that the sun and moon were made out of their dying light. Before the destruction of the Two Trees by Morgoth★ and Ungoliant,★ Fëanor★ captured their light in the Silmarils that he made.

*See also* LIGHT; TREES.

# U

**Ulmo**   In *The Silmarillion*,★ one of the Valar,★ called Lord of Waters and King of the Sea. In him, providential★ care for Elves★ and Men is often revealed by dreams, appearances and the very music★ of the waters of Middle-earth.★ This is particularly so with Turgon,★ but also with Tuor,★ Elwing★ and others.

**Umbar**   A coastal area in Harad, Middle-earth,★ that contained a natural harbour. It changed hands many times. At the time of *The Lord of the Rings*★ Umbar was in the hands of enemy Corsairs, but in the Fourth Age★ came under the control of Gondor★ once again.

**Underground places and journeys**   In the descent into the underworld, Ruth Noel points out in her book, *The Mythology of Middle-earth*, extraordinary events take place. Sometimes they have the character of the darker side of the numinous★—a dreadful encounter with the supernatural. It is common for underground places to be protected by magic. Examples of such protection are the magic doors in Thranduil's halls, and Melian's★ spell around Menegroth.

Heroism★ is involved in subterranean descent. There is the courage of Bilbo★ before Smaug,★ and of Frodo★ in the Barrow, when he calls to Tom Bombadil★ for help. There is the courage and sacrifice of Gandalf★ against the Balrog. Lúthien★ displays extraordinary resolve in facing Mandos★

on behalf of Beren. The courage of Sam against Shelob★ in her dark lair is notable. For Tolkien, monstrous spiders and dragons★ symbolise the enemy of mankind, greater than death; Sam faced no ordinary danger.

Examples of underground places and paths abound in Tolkien's world. They include the Gate of the Noldor (found by Tuor★), the Halls of Mandos,★ Nargothrond,★ Menegroth,★ Angband★ (into which Beren★ and Lúthien★ ventured), Orc★ tunnels, Thranduil's★ realm, Smaug's★ lair, the Barrow-wight's Chamber, Khazad-dûm,★ Shelob's Lair, the Paths of the Dead and the Glittering Caves.

**Further reading**

Ruth S. Noel, *The Mythology of Middle-earth* (1977).

**Underworld** *See* UNDERGROUND PLACES AND JOURNEYS.

***Unfinished Tales of Númenor and Middle-earth*** **(1980)** A collection of incomplete or unfinalised tales and narratives supplementing *The Silmarillion*,★ *The Hobbit*★ and *The Lord of the Rings*,★ edited by Christopher Tolkien.★

The book is divided into four parts, three of which are devoted to the First, Second and Third Ages★ of Middle-earth,★ while the fourth concerns the strange Druedain, wizards★ and the palantíri,★ or Seeing Stones. There is a useful glossary index.

Part One begins with a beautiful, but sadly unfinished, tale of Tuor★ and his coming to Gondolin,★ most probably written in 1951. Had it been completed it would have been a major work, concerning as it does one of the four independent stories of the First Age★ (*see* THE FALL OF GONDOLIN). Then follows a long, but also unfinished, account of the life of Túrin★ Turambar, another of the four major stories of 'The Silmarillion'. This too is marked by great beauty, complemented by the unfinished poetic version in *The Lays of Beleriand*.★

Part Two, concerned with the Second Age of Middle-earth, opens with a description of the island of Númenor.★ This helps to give flesh to the often annalistic accounts of Númenórean history. Then follows a reconstructed story, the only one in existence about Númenor, entitled 'Aldarion and Erendis'. It is also called 'The tale of the Mariner's Wife', and gives the first hints of the shadow which is to fall, not least in its tone of sadness. After this is a record of the Line of Elros in Númenor, then an account of the history of Galadriel★ and Celeborn,★ including a piece on the origin of the Elessar, the brooch eventually bequeathed to Aragorn★ by Arwen.★

In Part Three there are several events from the Third Age: 'The Disaster of the Gladden Fields' and 'Cirion and Eorl and the Friendship of Gondor and Rohan' (both from the earlier history of Gondor★ and Rohan★); 'The Quest of Erebor' (setting out more fully the links between *The Hobbit* and *The Lord of the Rings*); 'The Hunt for the Ring'; and 'The Battles of the Fords of Isen'.

**Ungoliant**   In *The Silmarillion*,★ the monstrous spider who, with Morgoth★ (Melkor), destroyed the Two Trees★ of Valinor.★ *The Lord of the Rings*★ records that, Ages later, Shelob★ was 'the last child of Ungoliant to trouble the unhappy world'. Ungoliant may have been one of the fallen Maiar.★

**Uruk-hai**   In *The Lord of the Rings*,★ a stronger kind of Orc★ bred by Sauron★ and used both by him and by the traitor Saruman.★

**Utumno**   In *The Silmarillion*,★ Morgoth's★ first great stronghold in the icy North of Middle-earth,★ and destroyed by the power of the Valar.★

# V

**Vairë**   In *The Silmarillion*,★ one of the Valar.★ She was known as 'the Weaver', because she wove the tapestries that adorned the walls of the Halls of Mandos,★ her husband. The tapestries told the story of all events in the creation of Ilúvatar.★

**Valacirca**   In Middle-earth,★ the name of the constellation of the Great Bear, 'the Sickle of the Valar'. The seven stars were shaped by Varda★ to prepare for the awakening of the Elves★ and as a challenge to Morgoth★ (Melkor), foreboding his end.

**Valar**   In *The Silmarillion*,★ the powers, or 'those with power', who entered the world (Eä) at the beginning of creation, and thus time. They are angelic beings, or Ainur,★ demiurgic agents of Ilúvatar★ (God). They function as guardians and governors of the world (both the world of nature and of Elves and humankind). The Valar have some similarity with gods in mythologies such as those of the North, yet are unique as a mythology in having only created being themselves. (For the reasons for Tolkien's theology, *see* CHRISTIANITY, TOLKIEN AND.) The Valar take on human or Elvish appearance, like a person dressing rather than an incarnation. One of the Valar, Melkor, fell into evil, becoming known as Morgoth.★

Some of the Valar were given titles in Middle-earth:★

Manwë★—Lord of the Air.
Yavanna★—the Giver of Fruits.
Tulkas★—the Valiant.
Aulë★—the Master of Crafts.
Varda★—Queen of the Stars (Elbereth★).
Mandos★ (Námo)—Keeper of the Houses of the Dead.
Vairë★—the Weaver.
Oromë★—Lord of Trees.★
Ulmo★—Lord of Waters.
Vána★—the Ever-young.

**Valimar**    Also known as Valmar. In *The Silmarillion*,★ the city of the Valar★ in Valinor.★ It can also be used to refer to Valinor as a whole.

**Valinor**    In *The Silmarillion*,★ the land of the Valar★ in Aman,★ westwards beyond the great mountains of the Pelóri.★

**Vána**    In *The Silmarillion*,★ one of the Valar,★ sister of Yavanna★ and wife of Oromë.★ She was known as the Ever-young, caring for birds and flowers and having gardens with golden flowers in Valinor.★

**Vanyar**    The foremost group of Elves★ on the westward journey from Cuiviénen★ in *The Silmarillion*.★

**Varda**    The most beloved of the Valar★ in Middle-earth★ and wife of Manwë. Also known as Elbereth and Snow-white, she kindled the stars and dwelt with Manwë on Mount Taniquetil.★ Varda was particularly concerned with light,★ setting the star Eärendil★ in the sky and aiding Sam in Shelob's★ Lair with the Phial of Galadriel.★

**Vingilot**    In *The Silmarillion*,★ the name of the ship of Eärendil,★ meaning 'foam-flower' in Quenya★ Elvish.

**Voronwë**    An Elf of Gondolin★ in *The Silmarillion*.★ He was the only survivor from a ship sent into the West for help, and saved by Ulmo★ to help Tuor find Gondolin.★ His name means 'the steadfast' in Quenya★ Elvish.

# W

***The War of the Ring*** **(1990)**   The eighth volume of *The History of Middle-earth*, and third volume of *The History of The Lord of the Rings*, edited by Christopher Tolkien.★ It is made up of early drafts of what was to become part of *The Lord of the Rings*.★ The book concerns the Battle of Helm's Deep; the destruction of Isengard by the Ents; the journey of Frodo,★ Sam and Gollum★ to the Pass of Cirith Ungol;★ the war in Gondor,★ and the parley between Gandalf★ and the ambassadors of Sauron★ in front of the Black Gate of Mordor.★ Developments unforeseen by Tolkien include the emergence of the palantír★ at Isengard and the appearance in the story of Faramir.★ The book contains illustrations and plans, including Orthanc, Dunharrow, Minas Tirith★ and the tunnels of Shelob's Lair. Faramir speaks of ancient history, and the languages of Gondor and the Common Speech (*see* WESTRON), material not retained in *The Two Towers*.★

**War of the Ring**   The great battle between the forces of Sauron★ and those of the faithful at the end of the Third Age★ of Middle-earth,★ as chronicled in *The Lord of the Rings*.★ The battle was won by the heroism (*see* HERO) of Frodo Baggins★ and Sam Gamgee,★ who slipped into Mordor★ under the dreadful eye of Sauron★ and destroyed the Ring. Key battles in the war included those at Helm's Deep and at the Pelennor Fields by Minas Tirith.★

**Wars**  *See* BATTLES OF BELERIAND; WAR OF THE RING.

**Warwick**  A market town and county town of Warwickshire, and part of Tolkien's early mythology as Kortirion. (*Tirion* means 'a mighty tower, a city on a hill'.) Kortirion was the chief town in a region of elms in Tol Eressëa.★ Warwick is thirty-three kilometres south-east of Birmingham.★ Its history is linked to its great castle, which still stands on a hilly site fortified from Saxon times. The River Avon runs alongside the castle. Edith Bratt lived in Warwick from 1913 until her marriage to Tolkien in 1916, and Tolkien visited her from Oxford.★ Tolkien wrote his poem 'Kortirion among the Trees' in 1915, dedicated to Warwick.

Warwickshire was part of the inspiration for Tolkien's Shire.★

**Welsh**  A language much loved by Tolkien ever since as a child he saw Welsh place names on railway coal trucks near his home. He learned the language, and based one of his main variants of Elvish★—Sindarin★—upon its structure. He writes of Welsh in the collection of essays *The Monsters and the Critics and Other Essays.*★

**Westron**  In Tolkien's mythology of Middle-earth,★ the later language of mankind which, in Númenor,★ was called Adûnaic. It goes back to the ancient world, before human beings migrated to the land north of Middle-earth, Beleriand,★ which sank beneath the waves at the end of the First Age.★

Originally, humans learned much of Elvish★ from the Dark Elves★ who stayed behind east of the Misty Mountains★ when others migrated west★ to Valinor.★ This deeply influenced the development of their language. Then many tribes moved to Beleriand, and there Elves and mankind had much to do with each other. To this period belongs the story of Beren★ and Lúthien,★ and the tragedy of Túrin Turambar.★ At the end of the First Age,★ the island of Númenor★ was given to mankind—at least, the Dúnedain★—to live on, and Westron continued to develop. The Númenóreans were great mariners and colonisers, spreading their at first benign civilisation, and Westron with it, as the language of trade and culture. They continued to use Elvish also, as a language of ceremony and tradition in which the great cosmology and history★ of the Elves and other peoples was recorded (see THE SILMA-RILLION).

As Númenor became corrupt, attempts were made to suppress the use of Elvish, but the faithful continued to use it and remember the great Elvish mythology. After the destruction of Númenor, the faithful remnant established Arnor★ and Gondor★ in the North and South of Middle-earth. Elendil was their leader. The common speech they spoke was enriched with Elvish words, often calling themselves the names of Elvish and human heroes from the First Age. As the use of Westron spread through Middle-earth, it increased in diversity.

Tolkien represents Westron with English in The Lord of the Rings,★ varying his style to match some of its range and diversity. The speech of the hobbits★ is represented quite differently from that of the noble people of Gondor, who were steeped in the traditions of Elves and Númenor. He retains this device in The Silmarillion,★ where the high Elvish style is represented by deliberate archaisms of syntax and vocabulary. He intends to suggest the Elvish source of The Silmarillion, and the hobbitish writing of The Hobbit and The Lord of the Rings (see RED BOOK OF WESTMARCH).

**White Council**  In The Lord of the Rings★ we learn of this Council of the Wise. It was summoned by Galadriel★ to plan a strategy in opposition to Sauron★ as his threat to peace grew.

**Williams, Charles (1886–1945)**   Equally enigmatic as an author and a person, Charles Williams was admitted into The Inklings,★ the literary circle surrounding Lewis, during the war years. He exerted a deep and lasting influence on Lewis but not on Tolkien. Tolkien did respect Williams, however, and appreciated his comments on chapters of the unfinished *The Lord of the Rings* as they were read. He contributed his essay 'On Fairy-Stories'★ to a posthumous tribute, *Essays Presented to Charles Williams*. At one stage, Tolkien wrote an affectionate poem to Williams, complaining of difficulty in understanding his writings, but valuing his person nonetheless:

> When your fag is wagging and spectacles are twinkling,
> when tea is brewing or the glasses tinkling,
> then of your meaning often I've an inkling,
> your virtues and your wisdom glimpse . . .

Charles Williams' writings encompassed fiction, poetry, drama, theology, church history, biography and literary criticism. Anne Ridler perhaps captured the essence of Charles Williams when she wrote: 'In Williams' universe there is a clear logic, a sense of terrible justice which is not our justice and yet is not divorced from love.' (George MacDonald similarly spoke of God's 'inexorable love'.) For Anne Ridler 'the whole man . . . was greater even than the sum of his works'. Similarly T.S. Eliot—who greatly admired Charles Williams—said, in a broadcast talk: 'It is the whole work, not any one or several masterpieces, that we have to take into account in estimating the importance of the man. I think he was a man of unusual genius, and I regard his work as important. But it has an importance of a kind not easy to explain.'

Like Tolkien and Lewis, Williams' thought and writings centred around the three themes of reason, romanticism★ and Christianity.

Like Lewis, he was an Anglican, but theologically he was

somewhere between Lewis and the Roman Catholic Tolkien. His interest in romanticism comes out, in a literary way, in his interest in and use of symbols—or 'images', as he preferred to call them. In the business of living, he was interested in the experience of romantic and other forms of love, and the theological implications of human love. As regards reason, he rejected the equation of rational abstraction with reality, and helped to introduce the writings of Søren Kierkegaard to English readers. Yet he felt passionately that the whole human personality must be ordered by reason to have integrity and spiritual health. His least satisfactory novel, *Shadows of Ecstasy* (1933), concerns a conflict between the over-intellectualised European races and the deeply emotional, intuitive approach to life of the Africans. Charles Williams constantly sought the balance between the abstract and the 'feeling' mind; between intellect and emotion; between reason and imagination.★

Charles Williams was in his early forties when his first novel, *War in Heaven*, was published in 1930. Prior to this he had brought out five minor books, four of which were verse and one of which was a play. His important work begins with the novels; it is after 1930 that his noteworthy works appear, packed into the last fifteen years of his life. During these final years twenty-eight books were published (an average of almost two a year) as well as numerous articles and reviews. The last third of these years of maturity as a thinker and writer was spent in Oxford.★ These years involved Williams' normal editorial duties with Oxford University Press, lecturing and tutorials for the university, constant meetings with The Inklings, and frequent weekends in his London home. His wife stayed behind to look after the flat when Williams was evacuated to Oxford with O.U.P.

Charles Williams was born in Islington, London, on 20th September 1886. His father was a foreign correspondence clerk in French and German to a firm of importers until his failing eyesight forced the family to move out of London to the countryside at St Albans. There they set up a shop selling artists' material, and his father contributed short stories to various periodicals. He guided his son's reading, and they went on long walks together. Charles Williams dedicated his third book of poems to 'My father and my other teachers'.

The talented boy gained a County Council scholarship to St Albans Grammar school. Here he formed a friendship that lasted many years with a George Robinson, who shared his tastes, pursuits and literary inventions. With Williams and his sister Edith, the friend sometimes acted plays to the family circle. The two friends gained places at University College, London, beginning their studies at the age of fifteen. The family unfortunately was not able to keep up paying the fees, and Charles Williams managed to get a job in a Methodist bookshop. His fortunes changed through meeting an editor from the London office of the Oxford University Press, who was looking for someone to help him with the proofs of the complete edition of Thackeray which, in 1908, was going through the press. Williams stayed on the staff until his death, creating a distinctive atmosphere affectionately remembered by those who worked with him, particularly women. He married, was considered medically unfit for the wartime army, and lost two of his closest friends in the Great War. In 1922 his only son, Michael, was born. In the autumn of that year Charles Williams began what was to become an habitual event—giving adult evening classes in literature for the London County Council to supplement the modest family income. He wrote his series of seven supernatural thrillers, including *The Place of the Lion*, for the same reason.

When Williams was evacuated with the O.U.P. to Oxford he made a vivid impact there, captured in John Wain's autobiography, *Sprightly Running*. He comments: 'He gave himself as unreservedly to Oxford as Oxford gave itself to him.' Williams' arrival in Oxford, and Lewis' friendship with him, was not perhaps entirely welcome to Tolkien, as it meant he had less of Lewis' attention. In his letters he often mentions seeing Lewis 'and Williams' rather than Lewis alone. When Williams died suddenly in 1945 however he felt deep sorrow over the loss of his friend, writing a letter to his widow.

Oxford University recognised Charles Williams in 1943 with an honorary M.A. In his Preface to *Paradise Lost*, C.S. Lewis publicly acknowledged his debt to Williams' interpretation of Milton. T.S. Eliot praised his work on Dante, as did Dorothy L. Sayers (who made a lively translation of *The Divine Comedy*).

*See also* STORY, THEOLOGY OF.

## Further reading

Alice Hadfield, *Charles Williams: An exploration of his life and work* (1983); Humphrey Carpenter, *The Inklings: C.S. Lewis, J.R.R. Tolkien, Charles Williams and their friends* (1978); Glen Cavaliero, *Charles Williams: Poet of theology* (1983); John Wain, *Sprightly Running: Part of an autobiography* (1962, 1965).

**Winterfilth**   The tenth month in the Shire* Reckoning, equivalent to October. Its name refers to the filling or completing of the days before Winter (from 'winterfylleth').

**Wiseman, Christopher**   A close friend of Tolkien's youth, and a member of the T.C.B.S.* Though he was from a Methodist family, he found a great affinity with the Roman Catholic Tolkien. According to Tolkien's biographer, Humphrey Carpenter, they shared an interest in Latin and Greek, Rugby football, and a zest for discussing anything under the sun. Wiseman was also sympathetic with Tolkien's experiments in invented language, as he was studying the hieroglyphics and language of ancient Egypt. Tolkien and Wiseman continued to meet after the latter went up to Cambridge University. He served in the Royal Navy during World War I and was the only one of Tolkien's close friends to survive it; the other T.C.B.S. members, G.B. Smith★ and R.Q. Gilson,★ perished. After the war, Wiseman eventually became head of Queen's College, a public school in Taunton, and the two men didn't meet very frequently. When they did meet, they found they had less and less in common. The gap in Tolkien's friendship was then filled by C.S. Lewis,★ whom he met in Oxford in 1926. The friendship with Wiseman was never entirely forgotten, however. There is a note of Tolkien visiting him in his retirement. Tolkien's last published letter mentions him.

**Wizards**    The most well-known of the wizards are Gandalf★ and Saruman.★ The origin of the five or so wizards was known only by a small number, such as Elrond★ and Galadriel.★ They appeared in Middle-earth★ in about the year 1000 of the Third Age.★ This was the time when the shadow and menace of Sauron★ began to reappear. They were sent as emissaries from the Valar★ to encourage the native powers of the enemies of Sauron. They were capable of error and failure, and the power of the One Ring★ affected them. The wizards were Maiar★ in human form.

The three wizards who are agents in the tales are Saruman the White, Gandalf the Grey and Radagast★ the Brown. Another two wizards are called the *Ithryn Luin*, the Blue Wizards, in *Unfinished Tales*.★ Their names were Alatar and Pallando. The Blue Wizards had the role of 'missionaries to enemy occupied lands' away from the familiar lands that are the setting of *The Lord of the Rings*. Typically, in a letter, Tolkien writes of his suspicion that the Blue Wizards failed, as Saruman did. He suspected that they were founders or beginners of secret cults and 'magic' traditions that persisted into the Fourth Age.★

Though Tolkien could find no modern word to say what Istari or wizards were, they could be described as incarnate angels* or, more strictly, messengers (of the Valar). In another place, he characterises them as guardian angels. By 'incarnate', Tolkien meant that 'they were embodied in physical bodies capable of pain, and weariness, and of afflicting the spirit with physical fear, and of being "killed", though supported by the angelic spirit they might endure long, and only show slowly the wearing of care and labour' (Letter 156).

In another letter to a publisher he explains:

> Their powers are directed primarily to the encour-agement of the enemies of evil, to cause them to use their own wits and valour, to unite and endure. They appear always as old men and sages, and though (sent by the powers of the True West) in the world they suffer themselves, their age and grey hairs increase only slowly.

Gandalf's function is particularly to watch over human affairs. By 'human', Tolkien explicitly means 'Men and hobbits' (Letter 131).

*See also* PROVIDENCE.

**Wormtongue**  In *The Lord of the Rings*,* the nickname of King Théoden's* treacherous counsellor, Gríma, who was in league with Saruman* to control Théoden, and to pass on intelligence to the wizard.*

**Woses**  At the time of the events recorded in *The Lord of the Rings*,* these were primitive Men living in Druadan Forest. They helped the Riders of Rohan* to move secretly through the forest on their way to join the forces against Sauron.*

**Wright, Joseph**  As a schoolboy Tolkien was delighted to acquire a second-hand copy of Joseph Wright's *Primer of the Gothic Language*. As a student at Oxford* Tolkien chose Comparative Philology as his special subject (*see*

PHILOLOGIST, TOLKIEN AS A), so he had the same Joseph Wright as a lecturer and tutor.

This Yorkshireman of humble origins (he started as a woollen-mill worker from the age of six) had, by a long struggle, become Professor of Comparative Philology. The struggle included teaching himself to read at the age of fifteen. Among the many languages he later studied were Sanskrit, Gothic, Russian, Old Norse and Old and Middle High German. One of his achievements was the six large volumes of his English Dialect Dictionary.

Joseph Wright communicated to Tolkien his love for philology, and was a demanding teacher.

# Y

**Yavanna**    One of the Valar★ in *The Silmarillion*,★ elder sister
of Vána★ and wife of Aulë. Her name means 'giver of
fruits'. Yavanna watched over the flora of the world, and
planted the first seeds of all plants. Her greatest work was
the creation of the Two Trees.★ Sometimes she appeared as
a tree★ reaching to the heavens.

**Years of the Trees**    In *The Silmarillion*,★ before the rising of
the sun and moon, time was measured according to the
blooming of the Two Trees★ in Valinor★ (Aman). Years
were longer than solar years.

**Yuledays**    In the Shire★ Reckoning, the first and last days of
the year, belonging to no month.

# Books by J.R.R. Tolkien

*A Middle English Vocabulary.* The Clarendon Press: Oxford, 1922. Prepared for use with Kenneth Sisam's *Fourteenth Century Verse and Prose* (The Clarendon Press: Oxford, 1921) and later published with it.

*Sir Gawain and the Green Knight.* Edited by J.R.R. Tolkien and E.V. Gordon. The Clarendon Press: Oxford, 1925 (new edition, revised by Norman Davis, 1967).

*The Hobbit, or There and Back Again.* George Allen and Unwin: London, 1937; Houghton Mifflin Company: Boston, 1938.

*Farmer Giles of Ham.* George Allen and Unwin: London, 1949; Houghton Mifflin Company: Boston, 1950.

*The Fellowship of the Ring: Being the First Part of The Lord of the Rings.* George Allen and Unwin: London, 1954; Houghton Mifflin Company: Boston, 1954.

*The Two Towers: Being the Second Part of The Lord of the Rings.* George Allen and Unwin: London, 1954; Houghton Mifflin Company: Boston, 1955.

*The Return of the King: Being the Third Part of The Lord of the Rings.* George Allen and Unwin: London, 1955; Houghton Mifflin Company: Boston, 1956.

*The Adventures of Tom Bombadil and Other Verses From The Red Book.* George Allen and Unwin: London, 1962; Houghton Mifflin Company: Boston, 1963.

*Ancrene Wisse: The English Text of the Ancrene Riwle.* Edited by J.R.R. Tolkien. Oxford University Press: London, 1962.

*Tree and Leaf.* George Allen and Unwin: London, 1964; Houghton Mifflin Company: Boston, 1965.

*The Tolkien Reader.* Ballantine Books: New York, 1966.

*Smith of Wootton Major.* George Allen and Unwin: London, 1967; Houghton Mifflin Company: Boston, 1967.

*The Road Goes Ever On: A Song Cycle.* Poems by J.R.R. Tolkien, music by Donald Swann. Houghton Mifflin Company: Boston, 1967; George Allen and Unwin: London, 1968. (Enlarged edition, 1978.)

*Sir Gawain and the Green Knight, Pearl and Sir Orfeo.* Translated by J.R.R. Tolkien; edited by Christopher Tolkien. George Allen and Unwin: London, 1975; Houghton Mifflin Company: Boston, 1975.

*The Father Christmas Letters.* Edited by Baillie Tolkien. George Allen and Unwin: London, 1976; Houghton Mifflin Company: Boston, 1976.

*The Silmarillion.* Edited by Christopher Tolkien. George Allen and Unwin: London, 1977; Houghton Mifflin Company: Boston, 1977.

*Pictures by J.R.R. Tolkien.* Edited by Christopher Tolkien. George Allen and Unwin: London, 1979; Houghton Mifflin Company: Boston, 1979.

*Unfinished Tales of Númenor and Middle-earth.* Edited by Christopher Tolkien. George Allen and Unwin: London, 1980; Houghton Mifflin Company: Boston, 1980.

*The Letters of J.R.R. Tolkien.* Edited by Humphrey Carpenter, with the assistance of Christopher Tolkien. George Allen and Unwin: London, 1981; Houghton Mifflin Company: Boston, 1981.

*The Old English Exodus.* Text, translation and commentary by J.R.R. Tolkien; edited by Joan Turville-Petre. The Clarendon Press: Oxford, 1981.

*Mr Bliss.* George Allen and Unwin: London, 1982; Houghton Mifflin Company: Boston, 1983.

*Finn and Hengest: The Fragment and the Episode.* Edited by Alan Bliss. George Allen and Unwin: London, 1982; Houghton Mifflin Company: Boston, 1983.

*The Monsters and the Critics and Other Essays.* Edited by Christopher Tolkien. George Allen and Unwin: London, 1983; Houghton Mifflin Company: Boston, 1984.

*The History of Middle-earth.* Edited by Christopher Tolkien. Published in nine volumes between 1983 and 1992. In London publication was by George Allen and Unwin, Unwin Hyman and HarperCollins. In Boston (commencing in 1984) publication was by Houghton Mifflin Company.

# Books about J.R.R. Tolkien

Allan, James (ed). *An Introduction to Elvish and to Other Tongues and Proper Names and Writing Systems of the Third Age of the Western Lands of Middle-earth as Set Forth in the Published Writings of Professor John Ronald Reuel Tolkien*. Bran's Head Books: Hayes, Middx, 1978.

Andrews, Bart with Bernie Zuber. *The Tolkien Quiz Book: 1001 Questions about Tolkien's Tales of Middle-earth and Other Fantasies*. Signet Books: New York, 1979.

Becker, Alida (ed). *The Tolkien Scrapbook*. Grosset and Dunlap: New York, 1978.

Becker, Alida (ed). *A Tolkien Treasury*. Courage Books: Philadelphia, Pennsylvania, 1989.

Blackwelder, Richard E. *Tolkien Phraseology: A Companion to a Tolkien Thesaurus*. Tolkien Archives Fund: Marquette University, 1990.

Blount, Margaret. *Animal Land: The Creatures of Children's Fiction*. Hutchinson: London, 1974; William Morrow: New York 1975.

Carpenter, Humphrey. *The Inklings: C.S. Lewis, J.R.R. Tolkien, Charles Williams and their Friends*. George Allen and Unwin: London, 1978; Houghton Mifflin: Boston, 1979.

Carpenter, Humphrey. *J.R.R. Tolkien: A Biography*. George Allen and Unwin: London, 1977; Houghton Mifflin: Boston, 1977.

Carter, Lin. *Tolkien: A Look Behind The Lord of the Rings*. Ballantine: New York, 1979.

Day, David. *A Tolkien Bestiary*. Mitchell Beazley: London, 1979; Ballantine: New York, 1979.

Elgin, Don D. *The Comedy of the Fantastic: Ecological Perspectives on the Fantasy Novel*. Greenwood, 1985.

Ellwood, Gracia Fay. *Good News from Tolkien's Middle-earth: Two Essays on the 'Applicability' of The Lord of the Rings*. William B. Eerdmans: Grand Rapids, Michigan, 1970.

Etkin, Anne (ed). *Eglerio! In Praise of Tolkien*. Quest Communications: Greencastle, Pennsylvania, 1978.

Evans, Robley. *J.R.R. Tolkien*. Crowell: New York, 1976.

*The Filmbook of J.R.R. Tolkien's 'The Lord of the Rings'*. Ballantine Books: New York, 1978.

Flieger, Verlyn. *Splintered Light: Logos and Language in Tolkien's World*. William B. Eerdmans: Grand Rapids, Michigan, 1983.

Fonstad, Karen Wynn. *The Atlas of Middle-earth*. Houghton Mifflin: Boston, 1981.

Foster, Robert. *The Complete Guide to Middle-earth: From the Hobbit to the Silmarillion*. George Allen and Unwin: London, 1978; Ballantine Books: New York, 1978.

Giddings, Robert and Holland, Elizabeth. *J.R.R. Tolkien: The Shores of Middle-earth*. Eletheia Books: Maryland.

Giddings, Robert (ed). *J.R.R. Tolkien: This Far Land*. Vision: London; Barnes and Noble: Totowas, New Jersey, 1983.

Gose, Elliot. *Mere Creatures: A Study of Modern Fantasy Tales for Children*. Toronto, 1988.

Grotta, Daniel. *The Biography of J.R.R. Tolkien: Architect of Middle-earth*. Running Press: Philadelphia, 1978.

Harvey, David. *The Song of Middle-earth: J.R.R. Tolkien's Themes, Symbols and Myths*.

Helms, Randel. *Tolkien and the Silmarils*. Houghton Mifflin: Boston, 1981.

Helms, Randel. *Tolkien's World*. Houghton Mifflin: Boston, 1974.

Hillegas, Mark R. (ed). *Shadows of Imagination: The Fantasies of C.S. Lewis, J.R.R. Tolkien and Charles Williams*. Southern Illinois University Press: Carbondale, 1969, new edition 1979.

*A Hobbit's Travels*. Running Press: Philadelphia, Pennsylvania, 1978.

*A Hobbit's Journal*. Running Press, Philadelphia, Pennsylvania, 1979.

Huttar, Charles A. (ed). *Imagination and the Spirit: Essays in Literature and the Christian Faith*. William B. Eerdmans: Grand Rapids, Michigan, 1971.

Isaacs, Neil D. and Zimbardo, Rose A. (eds). *Tolkien: New Critical Perspectives*. The University Press of Kentucky: Kentucky, 1981.

Kilby, Clyde S. *Tolkien and the Silmarillion*. Harold Shaw: Wheaton, 1976.

Kocher, Paul H. *Master of Middle-earth: The Fiction of J.R.R. Tolkien*. Houghton Mifflin: Boston, 1972. British edition: *Master of Middle-earth: The Achievement of J.R.R. Tolkien*. Thames and Hudson: London, 1972.

Kocher, Paul H. *A Reader's Guide to the Silmarillion*. Thames and Hudson: London, 1980.

Little, Edmund. *The Fantasists: Studies in J.R.R. Tolkien, Lewis Carroll, Mervyn Peake, Gogol and Kenneth Grahame*. Avebury, 1984.

Lobdell, Jared. *England and Always: Tolkien's World of the Rings*. William B. Eerdmans: Grand Rapids, Michigan, 1981.

Lobdell, Jared. *A Tolkien Compass*. Open Court Publishing: La Salle, Illinois, 1975; Ballantine: New York, 1980.

Lochhead, Marion. *Renaissance of Wonder: The Fantasy Worlds of C.S. Lewis, J.R.R. Tolkien, George MacDonald, E. Nesbit and Others*. Canongate: Edinburgh, 1973; Harper and Row: San Francisco, 1977.

Matthews, Richard. *Lightning from a Clear Sky: Tolkien, the Trilogy and the Silmarillion*. Borgo: San Bernardino, 1978.

Melmed, Susan Barbara. *John Ronald Reuel Tolkien: A Bibliography*. University of Witwatersrand Department of Bibliography, Librarianship and Typography: Johannesburg, 1972.

Miesel, Sandra. *Myth, Symbol and Religion in The Lord of the Rings*. T–K Graphics: Baltimore, 1973.

Miller, Stephen O. *Middle-earth: A World in Conflict*. T–K Graphics: Baltimore, 1975.

Montgomery, John Warwick (ed). *Myth, Allegory and Gospel: An Interpretation of J.R.R. Tolkien, C.S. Lewis, G.K. Chesterton and Charles Williams*. Bethany Fellowship: Minneapolis, 1974.

Morrison, Louise D. *J.R.R. Tolkien's The Fellowship of the Ring: A Critical Commentary*. Monarch: New York, 1976.

Morse, Robert E. *Evocation of Virgil in Tolkien's Art*. Bolchazy-Carducci Publishers: Oak Park, Illinois, 1987.

Nitzsche, Jane Chance. *Tolkien's Art: A 'Mythology for England'*. St Martin's Press: New York, 1979.

Noel, Ruth S. *The Languages of Tolkien's Middle-earth*. Houghton Mifflin: Boston, 1980.

Noel, Ruth S. *The Mythology of Middle-earth*. Houghton Mifflin: Boston, 1977; Thames and Hudson: London, 1977.

O'Neill, Timothy R. *The Individuated Hobbit: Jung, Tolkien and the Archetypes of Middle-earth*. Houghton Mifflin: Boston, 1979.

Palmer, Bruce. *Of Orc-rags, Phials and a Far Shore: Visions of Paradise in The Lord of the Rings*. T–K Graphics: Baltimore, 1976.

Petty, Anne Cotton. *One Ring to Rule Them All: Tolkien's Mythology*. University of Alabama Press, 1979.

Purtill, Richard L. *J.R.R. Tolkien: Myth, Morality and Religion*. Harper and Row: San Francisco, 1985.

Purtill, Richard L. *Lord of the Elves and Eldils: Fantasy and Philosophy in C.S. Lewis and J.R.R. Tolkien*. Zondervan: Grand Rapids, Michigan, 1974.


Ready, William. *The Tolkien Relation*. Regnery: Chicago, 1968.

Reilly, Robert J. *Romantic Religion: A Study of Barfield, Lewis, Williams and Tolkien*. University of Georgia Press: Athens, 1971.

Rogers, Deborah Webster and Rogers, Ivor A. *J.R.R. Tolkien*. Twayne Publishers: Boston, 1980.

Rossi, Lee D. *The Politics of Fantasy*. UMI Research, 1984.


Sale, Roger. *Modern Heroism: Essays on D.H. Lawrence, William Empson and J.R.R. Tolkien*. University of California Press: Berkeley and Los Angeles, 1973.

Salu, Mary and Farrell, Robert T. (eds). *J.R.R. Tolkien, Scholar and Storyteller: Essays in Memoriam*. Cornell University Press: Ithaca, 1979.

Shippey, T.A. *The Road to Middle-earth*. George Allen and Unwin: London, 1982; Houghton Mifflin: New York, 1983.

Shorto, Russell. *J.R.R. Tolkien: Man of Fantasy*. (Foreword by G.B. Tennyson.) The Kipling Press: New York, 1988.

Strachey, Barbara. *Journeys of Frodo*. Unwin Paperbacks: London, 1981.


Tolkien, Christopher. *The Silmarillion by J.R.R. Tolkien: A Brief Account of the Book and Its Making*. Houghton Mifflin: Boston, 1977.

Tolkien, John and Priscilla. *The Tolkien Family Album*. Unwin/Hyman: London, 1992.

Tyler, J.E.A. *The New Tolkien Companion*. St Martin's Press: New York, 1979.

Urang, Gunnar. *Shadows of Heaven: Religion and Fantasy in the Writing of C.S. Lewis, Charles Williams and J.R.R. Tolkien*. United Church Press: Philadelphia, 1971.

West, Richard C. *Tolkien Criticism: An Annotated Checklist*. Kent State University Press: Kent, Ohio, 1970.

Wilson, Colin. *Tree by Tolkien*. Covent Garden Press: London, 1973; Capra Press: Santa Barbara, 1974.

Yoke, Carl B. and Hassle, Donald M. (eds). *Death by Serpent*. Greenwood, 1985.

Zipes, Jack. *Breaking the Magic Spell: Radical Theories of Folk and Fairy Tales*. University of Texas Press: Austin, 1979.

# *Reference guide*

This guide provides a handy reference by grouping together the titles of some of the related articles in *The Tolkien and Middle-earth Handbook*. The sections are as follows:

1 The life of J.R.R. Tolkien
2 The works of J.R.R. Tolkien
3 The themes of J.R.R. Tolkien
4 The thought of J.R.R. Tolkien
5 *The Silmarillion*
6 *The Hobbit*
7 *The Lord of the Rings*
8 Middle-earth
    (i) General
    (ii) Beings and peoples
    (iii) Geography, places and things
    (iv) History

## 1  The life of J.R.R. Tolkien

Auden, W.H.
Barfield, Owen
Birmingham
Coghill, Nevill
d'Ardenne, Simonne
Dyson, H.V.D. 'Hugo'
Gilson, R.Q. 'Rob'
Gordon, E.V.
Havard, R.E. 'Humphrey'
Inklings, The
*The Letters of J.R.R. Tolkien*
Lewis, C.S.
MacDonald, George
Morgan, Father Francis
Oxford
Sarehole Mill
Sisam, Kenneth
Smith, G.B.

305

## 5 *The Silmarillion*

307

Hobbits
Huan
Húrin
Idril
Ilúvatar
Imrahil
Inklings, The
Isildur
Kíli
Legolas
Lúthien
Maedhros
Maglor
Maiar
Mandos
Manwë
Melian
Meriadoc ('Merry') Brandybuck
Morgoth
Nazgûl
Nienor
Níniel
Orcs
Orodreth
Oromë
Peregrin ('Pippin') Took
Radagast
Rangers of the North
Roäc
Rosie Gamgee
Saruman
Sauron
Sea-elves
Shelob
Silvan Elves

Sindar
Smaug
Stoors
Teleri
Théoden
Third House of the Edain
Thorin Oakenshield
Thorin and Company
Thorondor
Thráin II
Thranduil
Trolls
Tulkas
Tuor
Turgon
Túrin Turambar
Ulmo
Ungoliant
Vairë
Valar
Vána
Varda
Voronwë
White Council
Wizards
Woses
Yavanna

## (iii) Geography, places and things

Aglarond
Almaren
Alqualondë
Aman
Amon Obel
Amon Rûdh

## THE TOLKIEN SOCIETY

The Tolkien Society was founded in 1969 and is now a charity registered in the UK. It provides a focal point for the many people interested in the works of the late Professor J.R.R. Tolkien, who is Honorary President *in perpetuo* of the Society. His daughter Priscilla is Honorary Vice President. The Society is independent of Tolkien's publishers HarperCollins.

Its members are kept in touch by the Bulletin Amon Hen, which contains news of Society events, book reviews and short articles. The journal Mallorn contains longer articles on Tolkien's works, from many critical viewpoints; literary criticism of Tolkien and allied writers, and some poetry and stories by members in the Tolkien tradition.

The Society holds three national meetings a year: the AGM and Dinner with Guest Speaker, the Seminar and the 'Oxonmoot', an autumn weekend in Oxford which includes visits to places of interest to the Society. Local groups or 'smials' have been set up throughout the world. *For details of subscription rates or for more information about the Society or Tolkien and his works write to The Tolkien Society (CD), 12 Mortimer Court, St John's Wood, London NW8 9AB.*

*Also by Colin Duriez*

# The C. S. Lewis Handbook

A comprehensive guide to his life, thought and writings.

C. S. Lewis was one of the foremost writers and thinkers of the twentieth century. This handbook offers, for the first time, a guide to *all* his work, as well as to his friends and the main themes of his life.

It is an invaluable reference tool for anyone wanting to know about:

- The Narnia Chronicles
- The science fiction stories
- Lewis's considerable corpus of literary criticism
- His primary concerns
- His many books on theology and apologetics
- His key associates
- The debates in which he participated

Who was Prince Caspian? What were Lewis's views on pain. Who were his close friends? What did he say about the imagination? *The C. S. Lewis Handbook* is laid out in an easy-to-follow dictionary format, and includes substantial essays on the major aspects his life and thought.

'A fine companion to Lewis's work.'
　　　　　　　　　　　　　　　　　　　*– Dr Andrew Walker*
*Director, C. S. Lewis Centre*

'The book will be welcomed by a very wide readership which will find its enjoyment and understanding of Lewis enhanced by it . . . Recommended.'
　　　　　　　　　　　　　　　　　*– David Porter*
*Christian Arena*

'This systematic and distinguished compilation has been constructed by a writer who brings to his subject encyclopaedic knowledge and a passionate admiration . . . exceptionally satisfying.'
　　　　　　　　　　　　　　　　　　*Life and Work*

*£7.99 from Monarch Publications*　　　　　　　　*256 pp*

# Monarch Publications

*Books of Substance*

All Monarch books can be purchased from your local general or Christian bookshop. In case of difficulty they may be ordered from the publisher:

> Monarch Publications
> Owl Lodge
> Langton Road
> Speldhurst
> Kent
> TN3 0NP

Please enclose a cheque payable to Monarch Publications for the cover price plus: 60 pence for the first book plus 40 pence per copy for each additional book ordered to a maximum charge of £3.00 to cover postage and packing (UK and Republic of Ireland only).

Overseas customers please order from:

Christian Marketing PTY Ltd
PO Box 154
Victoria 3215
Australia

Omega Distributors Ltd
69 Great South Road
Remuera
Auckland
New Zealand

Struik Christian Books
PO Box 193
Maitland 7405
Cape Town
South Africa